Language, Gender and F

Language, Gender and Feminism presents students and researchers with key contemporary theoretical perspectives, methodologies and analytical frameworks in the field of feminist linguistic analysis.

Mills and Mullany cover a wide range of contemporary feminist theories and emphasise the importance of an interdisciplinary approach. Topics covered include: power, language and sexuality, sexism and an exploration of the differ-ence between Second and Third Wave feminist analysis.

Each chapter presents examples from research conducted in different cultural and linguistic contexts, which allows students to observe practical applications of all current theories and approaches. Oral and written language data, from a wealth of different contexts, settings and sources, is thoroughly analysed throughout. The book concludes with a discussion of how the field could advance and an overview of the various research methods, pertinent for future work in language and gender study.

Language, Gender and Feminism is an invaluable text for students new to the discipline of Language and Gender studies within English Language, Linguistics, Communication Studies and Women's Studies, as well as being an up-to-date resource for more established researchers and scholars.

Sara Mills is Research Professor in Linguistics at Sheffield Hallam University, UK.

Louise Mullany is Associate Professor of Sociolinguistics at the University of Nottingham, UK.

Language, Gender and Feminism

Theory, methodology and practice

Sara Mills and Louise Mullany

Routledge
Taylor & Francis Group

LONDON AND NEW YORK

First published 2011
by Routledge
2 Park Square, Milton Park, Abingdon, Oxon, OX14 4RN

Simultaneously published in the USA and Canada
by Routledge
711 Third Avenue, New York, NY 10017

Routledge is an imprint of the Taylor & Francis Group, an informa business

British Library Cataloguing in Publication Data
A catalogue record for this book is available from the British Library

Library of Congress Cataloging in Publication Data
Mills, Sara.
  Language, gender and feminism : theory, methodology and practice /
Sara Mills and Louise Mullany.
    p. cm.
  1. Language and languages--Gender. 2. Language and languages--
Sex differences. 3. Feminist theory. 4. Women--language. 5. Sexism
in language. 6. Sociolinguistics. I. Mullany, Louise. II. Title.
  P120.S48M556 2011   306.44--dc22
  2010049754

ISBN: 978-0-415-48595-1 (hbk)
ISBN: 978-0-415-48596-8 (pbk)
ISBN: 978-0-203-81466-6 (ebk)

Typeset in Goudy
by Bookcraft Ltd, Stroud, Gloucestershire

MIX
Paper from
responsible sources
FSC® C004839

Printed and bound in Great Britain by
CPI Antony Rowe, Chippenham, Wiltshire

To baby Abigail

Contents

Acknowledgements

We wish to express many thanks to our undergraduate and postgraduate students who have studied language and gender with us at Sheffield Hallam University and at the University of Nottingham. Many of the issues expressed in this book have been debated within the classroom and we have learnt a great deal from these discussions – particular thanks to Fiona Bousfield, Tony Fisher, Sarah Gormley and Myriam Trabelsi. We are also grateful to the following friends and colleagues for discussing various ideas with us over the years: Svenja Adolphs, Jo Angouri, Francesca Bargiela-Chiappini, Judith Baxter, Derek Bousfield, Ron Carter, Chris Christie, Jodie Clark, Jennifer Coates, Kathy Conklin, Jonathan Culpeper, Bethan Davies, Zoltan Dörnyei, Karen Grainger, Sarah Grandage, Sandra Harris, Kevin Harvey, Kate Haworth, Janet Holmes, Lucy Jones, Peter Jones, Carmen Llamas, Miriam Locher, Susan McRae, Meredith Marra, Andrew Merrison, Roshni Mooneeram, Emma Moore, Liz Morrish, Pia Pichler, Helen Sauntson, Stephanie Schnurr, Catherine Smith, Peter Stockwell, Maria Stubbe, Joan Swann and Dominic Watt.

We are very grateful to the following for providing information about language practices in a range of different countries: Fiona Bousfield, Olga Castro, Sarah Durling, Denise Elekes, Anna Esch, Therese Frey, Sarah Grandage, Naima Lamrani, Roshni Mooneeram, Yonatan Shemmer. Special thanks to Roshni Mooneeram for her feedback on earlier drafts of this material and to Sarah Grandage, for passionately discussing many of the issues that appear in this volume. Heartfelt thanks from Louise to Matthew Green for all the numerous gender conversations, unfettered support and so much more.

We would also like to thank Sophie Jaques, Louisa Semlyen and Eloise Cook at Routledge for their patience, enthusiasm and care in steering this book through to completion. Finally, we are grateful to the Terrence Higgins Trust for permission to include the poster 'I Love My Gay Son', which appears in Chapter 6.

1   Contemporary issues in language, gender and feminism

Feminism is for Everybody
hooks 1990

Introducing the field

The initial development of language and gender studies as an area of academic enquiry in its own right is generally accepted to have begun in Western cultures in the mid-1970s. There are some earlier examples, such as Otto Jespersen's (1922) consideration of 'deficiencies' in women's language, along with collections outside academia of proverbs and folk linguistic beliefs about women's talk in many different languages, including stereotypes of women being terrible gossips and talking far too much (see, for example, Sunderland 2006). However, the 1970s are viewed as the time when linguists began to explore the interplay between language and gender in a systematic way and most importantly from an explicitly *feminist* perspective.

Academic studies do not exist in a vacuum, and research questions and areas of investigation are clearly shaped by the social, political and economic issues circulating within particular societies where research is taking place. There are firm links between the formation and subsequent developments within the field of language and gender studies and developments within 'feminism' as a political movement.

During the same time period, there was also an observable 'linguistic turn' in disciplines across the social sciences, arts and humanities. It was realised that an intimate link between language and ideology existed, and that by studying language use, one could discover a great deal about the ways in which societies function and the way that individuals and groups construct identities and cultures. Social relations are mediated through language – everything we do and think, we do through language – and thus analysis of language can be seen as a clear index of the way individuals negotiate with social forces. The linguistic disciplines where language and gender studies now currently thrive (sociolinguistics, discourse analysis, conversation analysis, pragmatics and linguistic anthropology) were becoming established as legitimate linguistic sub-disciplinary areas in their own right during the 1960s and 1970s. The combination of the broader socio-political landscape in terms of gender politics and the rapid expansion of linguistic studies producing empirical investigations of real-life linguistic data resulted in the well-established field of language and gender studies that exists today.

There are many different types of 'feminism' in circulation, and researchers may conceive of 'feminism' in differing ways, depending upon their political perspective(s). Arguably, though, academic feminism as a whole, in its most general sense, can be seen as possessing two unifying factors:

1   It is a political movement which focuses on investigating gender, that is, the way that women and men come to construct themselves, their identities and their views of others as more or less feminine or masculine, straight or gay.
2   It is a movement which has the overall emancipatory aim of redressing gender inequalities (cf. Christie 2000).

However, it is important to point out right at the beginning of this volume that language and gender studies do not *have* to be feminist in orientation. Jespersen (1922) provides a good example of this. Leading language and gender researcher Deborah Cameron (2006) has pointed out that non-feminist studies will present descriptive linguistic accounts of gender and language, often detailing processes of language shift or change (for example, Labov 1972; Trudgill 1974; Milroy 1987), or present descriptions of how women and men use language in specific locations at particular points in time (Trudgill 1974; Bradley 1998; Cheshire 1998). The key difference between this knowledge-gathering research and 'feminist' research is that the latter has a *specific political purpose* by focusing on gender as a social, political and ideological category.

It should be noted that the term 'feminism' is one which has tended to be somewhat downplayed in some areas of academic research over the last 10–15 years. Whilst there was a period during the 1980s and 1990s in many parts of the Western academic world when feminism was thriving and was positively evaluated by many (Whelehan 1995), there has been a backlash against feminism within these cultures and it is now often difficult to use the term feminism easily. McRobbie (2009), for example, believes that feminism has been undermined, partly because of a backlash against feminism but also, paradoxically, precisely because it has been partly integrated into mainstream agendas: she argues pessimistically that 'for feminism to be taken into account it has to be understood as having already passed away' (McRobbie 2009: 12). We would argue that this is not necessarily the case; the fact that feminist demands are still voiced, even if they are not explicitly termed feminist, can be viewed as an indication of the way that feminism has become part of common-sense assumptions and thus part of the mainstream in many Western societies.

In other cultures, for example Japan, feminism has not had a positive evaluation at any stage and has often been opposed (Nishimura pers. com. 2009). In some Arab cultures, feminism has been seen as a Western import and has been resisted by many (see Sadiqi 2010; Sadiqi and Ennaji 2010). In developing countries, it is difficult to expound critiques of gender relations without taking on Western models, and this leads to some difficulties in adopting the term feminism. Sunderland (2009) reports that in African contexts, feminism is too frequently derided as being anti-family and anti-male, though on the positive side a journal has recently emerged entitled *Feminist Africa*. In China, Yang (2007) reports that the concept of 'women's liberation' was hugely popular during the Maoist regime, but now there is much resistance to it. There has been a return in popular culture to openly espousing essentialist biological differences and resistance to 'liberation' (though Yang is careful to point out that Maoist 'liberation' was a top-down discourse that had very little to do with really improving women's lives). At the time of writing, feminism and/or women's liberation are contested terms, which are opposed in various locations around the world. This has led some researchers and publishers in the field to be tentative about using the term feminism.

For us, we feel it is politically important to continue to use the term feminism overtly within the field of language and gender research and beyond. We do the research we do in order to change the way that women and men think about the language that they use and the way that others represent women and men in language; ultimately this has an impact on the way that women and men are treated and the way that they think about themselves. Feminism is central to these research goals. Overall, we define the specific political purpose of feminist linguistic studies as producing work which investigates the role that language plays in creating, sustaining and/or perpetuating unequal gender relations and discrimination against women and gay, lesbian and transgendered people. Our commitment to this position runs throughout the book.

Litosseliti (2006a: 21) argues that we need to recognise that campaigns around language have to be posed alongside other campaigns; it is not sufficient simply to campaign about language. Effective change has to come at both the personal and the institutional level. A focus on language has to be part of a focus on gender inequality in general, and viewed in the context of wider social and institutional change. For example, a change in the language used in rape reporting and court examination of rape victims needs to materialise within the context of legal and social changes. Such changes would involve, most notably, a more realistic correlation between crime and convictions. Changes would also involve the provision of better support for victims and the inclusion on the agenda of male rape. Empirical language analysis regarding how rapists and their victims are perceived and treated can then reflect as well as help consolidate the legal, institutional and social developments in this area. Thus, feminist linguists need to continually assess how their analysis of discrimination in language meshes with other campaigns. Research with an interdisciplinary focus, where questions of gender politics are placed at the centre of the project, can greatly aid this process and help to ensure that academic research is directly aligned with the most up-to-date political developments in the society under study.

Feminist language and gender researchers are thus advised to consider very carefully the research questions and topics that they choose to pursue. There is a primary need to embrace real-world problems and concerns regarding gender relations in the society under study. Studies should focus on challenging gender norms and exposing how power and privilege have become naturalised in the contexts where research is taking place. The overarching aim is that the research findings can go some way towards fulfilling the political goal of aiming to redress gender imbalances and move a step closer towards bringing about gender emancipation and equality. Holmes and Meyerhoff (2003a: 10) emphasise the inextricably related issue that researchers should be 'directed by the needs and interests of the communities of speakers studied', as opposed to producing research simply for the sake of 'academic appetite'. This type of research commitment has sometimes been referred to as 'advocacy research' or 'standpoint' research, defined as the principle that academic research should be 'with' and 'for' the community under study instead of simply producing work 'on' particular subjects (Cameron et al. 1992: 15). From a feminist linguistic perspective, the production of new linguistic knowledge is ideally required to sit alongside broader political principles and goals. Adopting the advocacy position may involve engaging in a careful and sometimes difficult process of negotiation with those being researched in order to decide upon investigations that could be of practical relevance to them and/or of mutual benefit to both parties. We will discuss these issues at length in Chapter 5 when we focus more specifically upon feminist linguistic research methodologies and methods.

There have been differing levels of explicitness regarding the overarching political goals of research produced in recent language and gender studies. There have also been different outcomes for feminist language and gender projects in terms of how much attention researchers pay to outlining how their findings can be utilised to contribute to fulfilling broader feminist goals in wider society and/or how they can be of benefit to those who have participated in the research project itself. Cameron (2005, 2009) posits that an observable dip in attention to social activism within recent language and gender research can be partially accounted for by broader theoretical shifts. She draws attention to a transition from the dominant focus of research which tended to ask the explicit political question 'what is to be done?', that is, how do we go about bringing social change to redress issues of gender inequality, which she aligns with modernity, to instead a postmodern focus on 'who am I?' The latter question has brought with it a significant shift to a focus on 'identity' research. This 'identity turn' has been dominant not just in language and gender studies, but also across the humanities and social sciences. It is combined with a theoretical shift to viewing identity as socially constructed. As a consequence, the focus has arguably shifted from one of collective political action towards one of individualism and a focus upon self-identification. Lazar (2009: 397) has characterised this as a shift from 'we-feminism' to 'I-feminism'. It is connected to a much broader shift in the socio-political landscape, and although significantly different in terms of political intention it can be seen as potentially related to the conditions where unhelpful notions such as post-feminism, based on an obsession with individuality and self-improvement, have emerged. This, in combination with the dominant focus on small-scale, qualitative studies in local contexts, has led Cameron (2009) to ponder the following, challenging question:

Have contemporary researchers, with their theoretical focus on agency, identity and the details of local practice, moved away from 'classical' feminist concerns about the institutionalising, especially in domains such as education, politics, work and religion, of ideologies and practices that reproduce gender inequality at the level of the whole society? (Cameron 2009: 8)

This so-called 'identity turn' and the transition from 'modern' to 'postmodern' theorisation are crucial to contemporary feminist linguistic thinking. These considerations and debates inform our thinking throughout this book. Identity research is embedded within every chapter of this publication, but identity does not constitute the whole of our focus. Some gender and language volumes published over the last 10 years or so have dedicated a specific chapter (or chapters) to identity (see, for example, Talbot 1998/2010) or whole volumes to gender and identity (see Bucholtz *et al.* 1999). In the light of the above arguments, we have chosen not to take this approach here as we believe that feminist linguistic research is most effective when questions of identity are integrated with attempts to answer the broader 'we-feminism' questions of collective political action.

Studying language, gender and feminism

Since its inception in the 1970s, the study of language and gender has grown exponentially and it now has a clearly established institutional status. For instance, there are a number of undergraduate and postgraduate courses on language and gender in universities throughout the world. The subject area of language and gender also occupies a place in some pre-university school curricula; for example, in the UK A-level system (for students aged 16–18). Feminism should be present as a fundamental component of such courses, but the level of explicitness of a feminist focus may well vary from programme to programme. Language and gender studies also has its own international, peer-reviewed journal publications, the best-known being *Gender and Language* and *Women and Language*; additionally, articles on gender and language regularly appear in a range of other, high-profile international linguistics journals. As McElhinny and Mills (2007: 4) report, these include: *Language in Society, Journal of Sociolinguistics, Pragmatics, International Journal of the Sociology of Language, Language Variation and Change, Language and Education, Applied Linguistics, Discourse & Society, Critical Discourse Studies, Language and Literature* and *Discourse Analysis On-Line*. There are active international electronic discussion and mailing lists and an international organisation, the International Gender and Language Association (IGALA), which holds a biennial conference and also has its own book prize for outstanding research in gender and language. There are also a wide range of other conferences, symposia and workshops held in various global locations. While earlier conferences tended to be hosted in the West, more recent events include a conference devoted to the study of language and gender in African contexts, held in Nigeria (April 2010), and IGALA6 held in Tokyo (September 2010).

Even the most cursory glance through an internet-based keyword search of 'language and gender' publications will reveal a range of book titles that already exist in this field. Some of the most notable of these are Coates' (1998) *Language and Gender: A Reader*, Holmes and Meyerhoff's (2003b) *Handbook of Language and Gender*, Eckert and McConnell-Ginet's (2003) *Language and Gender*, Sunderland's (2006) *Language and Gender: A Resource Book*, Litosseliti's (2006a) *Language and Gender: Theory and Practice*, Jule's (2008) *A Beginner's Guide to Language and Gender* and the second edition (2010) of Talbot's *Language and Gender: An Introduction*. Alongside these more explicitly named titles are also a number of other, specialised publications focusing on language and gender in particular settings, or on a particular theory or approach. We will draw upon the full range of these publications throughout this book.

The sheer volume of publications, in conjunction with the range of academic courses currently offered in this subject area, is reflective of this burgeoning research area. These courses are an important product of the vast amount of academic enquiry that has taken place and are a testament to those researchers who led the field in its early stages of development. At the start of the second decade of the twenty-first century, even if you are geographically remote, a basic degree of computer literacy, combined with access to an internet connection, will open up a whole range of language and gender resources and networks – a dramatically different situation from the handful of resources available to the field's earliest scholars (see Cameron 2006a for further discussion). However, it is notable that, at present, access to global English is also required in order to gain access and take advantage of these online resources.

With mention of the above language and gender book titles, it seems appropriate at this juncture to articulate exactly why we decided to write this book with this specific title at this particular moment in time.

Language, Gender and Feminism: new directions

In this volume we are aiming to present a state-of-the-art view of contemporary language and gender research specifically from a feminist standpoint. The discipline of language and gender studies is currently entering a new phase of development, and our aim here is to introduce, discuss and interrogate these new developments particularly from a theoretical and methodological perspective.

In line with the overt commitment to feminism that we have just outlined for this volume, other commentators have also called for language and gender research to rediscover its political voice and its original motivation for coming into existence in the first place, reflecting a general sense that the political meaning and overarching political goals of research may have become somewhat obscured in recent times, with issues of gender politics being pushed into the background (Holmes and Meyerhoff 2003a; Philips 2003; Cameron 2006a, 2007a, 2009; McElhinny 2007a). Phillips (2003: 266) observes a 'loss of a broader practical political perspective' within feminist linguistic investigations, and Holmes and Meyerhoff (2003a: 14) point out that there is a real and urgent need for language and gender scholars to reassert their research in a form of 'social activism'.

One way in which the discipline can attempt to achieve more social activism based on its research findings is to integrate and discuss feminism far more explicitly, ensuring that it is firmly in the foreground, so that it occupies a more overt and central role in language and gender studies, hence its inclusion as part of our book's title. While some undeniably important work has been published *describing* relationships between language and gender, we fully endorse the view that language and gender studies have an overarching responsibility 'to contribute to the wider struggle against unjust and oppressive gender relations, by revealing and challenging the ideological propositions which support and naturalize those relations' (Cameron 2007a: 16). This should be the discipline's main motivation. The practical applications in terms of addressing explicit political questions, issues and problems regarding unequal gender relations should be made transparent in the research findings. We will explore this issue in more detail in the next section of this chapter, which addresses sexual politics.

It is important to point out that language and gender research which explicitly foregrounds feminism and overtly draws upon feminist principles and politics has not necessarily been totally absent in the last decade. For instance, within studies analysing discourse in particular, some researchers have explicitly used 'feminist' as a prefix to detail more precisely the approach they have taken, ensuring that feminism is directly foregrounded in their research. To offer just some examples, Christie (2000) defined a 'feminist pragmatics', Kitzinger (2000) a 'feminist conversation analysis' and Lazar (2005b) has developed 'feminist critical discourse analysis'. Researchers have also drawn attention to a 'feminist sociolinguistics' (McElhinny 2003; Mullany 2007). It is more rare for researchers to explicitly state their feminist political position, though some do choose to do so. For example, Deborah Cameron (2006a: 7) directly identifies herself as a 'radical materialist' feminist. All of this work has shown how feminist linguistic research can play important roles in challenging gender relations by unpicking and making transparent ideological relations which may otherwise remain hidden in spoken and written language.

In addition to calls for research to become more explicitly politically motivated, researchers have also recently called for more integrated methodological approaches in language and gender studies, which has tended to be dominated for almost the last 20 years by qualitative methodologies. Some researchers have recently begun to extol the virtues of using mixed-methodological approaches, where quantitative and qualitative approaches are combined, along with a focus on selecting methodologies for practical reasons, that is, selecting a method because it is best suited to a particular research question, as opposed to a more deep-seated loyalty to a specific methodological paradigm. This has been referred to as the 'pragmatist' approach, and its advantages include improving research validity and the ability to reach wider audiences (Dörnyei 2007). We will explore all of these methodological issues at length in Chapter 5.

From our perspective, whether we are discussing particular theoretical approaches or methodological paradigms, the most important thing not to lose sight of at any stage of the research process is the need to avoid adopting entrenched positions if the discipline is to move forward. As Holmes and Meyerhoff argue, it is essential to avoid adopting 'narrow paradigms which are potentially damaging to the spirit of enquiry', as well as ensuring that there is resistance to 'pressures toward the development of restrictive and limited orthodoxy in the kinds of theoretical frameworks and research methodologies which are judged acceptable' (Holmes and Meyerhoff 2003a: 15).

While areas of tension between different paradigms can potentially be very productive sites for the development of a discipline, this will only work if researchers *do not* rigidly situate themselves in 'armed camps' (Silverman 2000: 10). It is crucial that researchers do not become dogmatic about the alleged 'superior' nature of their chosen paradigms and, instead, remain open-minded about the potential benefits of different theories and methodologies.

Before moving on to consider the 'political' nature of research in more detail, it is also important to highlight that although the current state of the field of language and gender studies is undeniably shaped by the historical development of the discipline, our aim in this book is not to provide a general chronological overview of language and gender research, which has tended to become a commonplace structural feature of many language and gender publications. There are other volumes which have done this comprehensively already and the field is not in need of another volume which repeats what has been very successfully articulated many times before (see, for example, Coates 2004; Sunderland 2006; Talbot 1998/2010).

This particular narrative trajectory is also very much focused on the way the field of language and gender developed within English-speaking communities, predominantly in the UK and North America, and it thus has a tendency to underplay work in this field that has taken place in other countries. In contrast, the three volumes of work by Hellinger and Bußmann (2001, 2002, 2003) present a very different narrative trajectory, and theirs is a perspective which has a focus on a whole range of different global languages. They analyse how gender is played out in 30 languages and in this way reveal the way that not all languages handle gender in the way that English does, and that feminism has developed in different ways in these different contexts. For example, Hachimi (2001) examines the way that the languages used in Morocco are gendered; she shows that few women read and write Standard Arabic or Educated Moroccan Arabic, instead speaking Moroccan dialect or Berber, and some women choose to speak French because of its prestige and the fact that it indexes modernity. Others writers in the Hellinger and Bußmann collection, such as Tobin (2001), describe the way that gender works in languages, such as Hebrew, which do not mark pronouns for gender but which nevertheless 'require gender categorisation on all levels of language at all times' (Tobin 2001: 192). Turkish also does not mark gender in pronouns, as Braun (2001) notes, since the affix 'o' refers to she, he or it; yet gender marking is still an essential element in the language. In each different language and each different culture, there will be a wide variety of ways in which gender manifests itself in language and language constructs gender, and feminist analysis will tailor itself to the particular circumstance.

Another alternative perspective and one that offers a further example of a different research trajectory that has lacked attention in mainstream feminist linguistics is the plethora of research that has been conducted on language and gender in Chinese contexts. These works have been published both in Chinese and in English. In 1997, Majorie Chen began to compile an online bibliography of language and gender research. She sets out her rationale for doing this by commenting that 'scholars studying gender issues were generally quite unaware of what has been written to date on Chinese, with the result that publications typically contain little to no references to Chinese' (Chan 2010). She goes on to observe that this situation has shown some improvement over time, partly as a consequence of more research being published in English and appearing in major linguistics journals, which favour English as the language of publication. Some examples of this research include Fan's (1996) work on language, gender and Chinese culture, Hong's (1997) work on gender in Chinese request patterns, Liming's (1998) work on Chinese women's language characters and Wong's (2008) work on the politics of labelling amongst gay men in Hong Kong.

Other examples of alternative foci include studies of remote geographical locations and minority languages including Keenan's (1974) work on language, gender and the family in a Malagasy-speaking village in Madagascar, Brown's (1980) work on the dialect of Tzeltal, in a study of language, gender and polite-ness in a Tenejapa community in Mexico, Nwoye's (1998) study of language and gender in relation to the language of Igbo spoken in Nigeria and Keating's (1998) work on gender and status in Pophepi in Micronesia in the Pacific. We will refer to examples from these alternative trajectories at relevant stages in this volume.

By side-stepping the traditional 'chronological' narrative, we hope that we will make this book more accessible to those who have different trajectories for the development of language and gender studies in their own country. At the same time, we are by no means claiming that our book will be completely comprehen-sive, or that all languages in the world will be included or that all countries where feminist language and gender research has ever been conducted will be refer-enced here. Such an extensive encyclopaedic endeavour would take many years to complete and is well beyond the aims that we have for this single publication.

Instead we aim to focus on how contemporary feminist issues in language and gender research have emerged, and consider how students, researchers and scholars can help to move the discipline forward. Inevitably, this will involve reference and consideration of the findings of Western studies; that is, after all, our area of expertise. But it is a Western perspective informed by an awareness of its place within an international and increasingly global context. Our perspec-tive will also involve some reference to seminal studies and the range of different theories and methodologies which have emerged since the field's inception – it is essential to look at a field's historical development in order to understand the current context of the discipline – but this will not include a blow-by-blow account of the various historical transitions and it should be in full knowledge that the historical positioning of the discipline contains a distinctly Western bias.

Sexual politics

The inclusion of 'feminism' in our book's title does not mean that all of the work contained within this volume will necessarily be feminist in nature. On the contrary, it is important to look across the wider field of 'sexual politics', characterised by Cameron (2006: 3) as 'contending forces that are active around gender relations'. Feminism is thus located within this overarching arena of sexual politics, alongside a range of other movements and organisations, such as the movement for lesbian, gay and transgender rights. From this broader perspective, feminism in all of its different forms can be viewed as one part of a much larger political landscape. All discursive and political campaigning elements concerned with gender can be seen to constitute sexual politics (see Chapter 2 for a fuller discussion of sexual politics). In addition to pro-feminist groups, this also includes, at the other end of the spectrum, male supremacist and male-rights groups such as the UK group Fathers4Justice and other anti-feminist groups, such as anti-abortion campaigners, commercial organisations that are part of the sex industry and certain religious organisations (see Cameron 2006a).

Cameron (2006a: 3) goes on to point out that 'language enters into sexual politics in two main ways. On the one hand, language is the medium in which many conflicts about the nature and proper relationship of men and women are played out; on the other, it is potentially a focus for conflict in its own right.' It is only by looking across the much broader political landscape that we will be able to form a more comprehensive picture of the complex interplay between language, gender and feminism in contemporary societies.

Feminism has been involved in a struggle to establish itself as a legitimate political movement since its inception (Whelehan 1995). It has met with resistance in many shapes and forms throughout its difficult and often turbulent history. In this initial chapter we will draw attention to evidence which we believe clearly proves that gender equalities still have not been achieved, either in countries in the developing world or in Westernised countries where feminism and women's movements have a longer history (see the section on 'Critical self-reflexivity', below, pp. 19–21). Despite the undeniable advances and achievements of feminism as a political movement in many countries, we believe that there is still a real and urgent need for feminism. Feminist linguistics has an important part to play in this process.

Post-feminism

It could be somewhat tempting to dismiss or give short shrift to terms such as 'post-feminism' currently circulating in popular culture and the mass media. 'Post-feminism' can be defined as the passing of or the alleged end of feminism, since it is argued that it is no longer needed.[1] However, no matter how tempting it is to dismiss such a term, as we have argued above, the broader political landscape, including sites of resistance, of which 'post-feminism' is a prime example, needs to be analysed and critiqued. As Lazar (2005a: 17) highlights, post-feminism is a 'global neo-liberal discourse' that is dominant and pervasive in late modern capitalist societies. It is only by engaging and critiquing terms such as 'post-feminism' that it will be possible to engage with the field of sexual politics as a whole, as well as to make it possible to establish a legitimate public voice, so that academic scholars are not accused of being 'disconnected' from those individuals and groups that they are aiming to work alongside in wider society.

Although 'feminism' is still a term that has political currency and resonance in language and gender studies and in many other humanities and social sciences disciplines, there is an undeniable resistance and range of negative connotations attached to the term and its collocates in popular culture. It is only by investigating terms such as 'post-feminism' that we will be able to engage properly in these debates. As radical feminist Deborah Cameron (2006: 8) points out, although we are now living in a 'post-feminist' age, there is still a substantial amount of politically significant work on language and sexual politics that needs to be done. Cameron goes on to point out that one particular arena where such research needs to take place is the examining and contesting of the myths surrounding and perpetuated by 'post-feminism' itself. Lazar (2005a: 17) also makes this point, arguing that there is a pressing need to produce a critique of post-feminism as 'it lulls one into thinking that struggles over social transformation of the gender order have become defunct in the present time'. Lazar's (2005b) collection goes some way towards this. We will come back to the importance of this work in Chapter 4, when considering 'feminist critical discourse analysis'.

Interestingly, Lazar (2005a) also mentions that a handful of researchers who define themselves as 'feminists' have simultaneously embraced some aspects of post-feminism. She draws attention to Natasha Walter (1999) as one example of a self-proclaimed feminist who argues in favour of a form of 'power feminism', defined as when certain commodities can be seen to give women a sense of empowerment. However, 11 years later, Walter (2010) has just released a brand-new publication where she admits that she was far too optimistic in her 1999 book. In contrast, the sub-title of her new book is *The Return of Sexism*. We will pick up on this issue again in Chapter 2, where we consider that a feminist resurgence may well be emerging.

Researchers in other academic disciplines have produced thought-provoking critiques of the phenomenon of 'post-feminism'. Feminist linguistics can benefit a great deal by taking an interdisciplinary approach and utilising work which has been published in other areas, including communication studies, media studies and cultural studies (some of the most notable of these are McRobbie 2007, 2009; Tasker and Negra 2007; Negra 2009). Language and gender researchers very frequently draw upon a range of spoken and written texts from the mass media and popular culture, and the recent theoretical critiques of post-feminism by academics working in these other disciplinary fields can bring a great deal of contemporary theoretical insight to the linguistic study of gender (cf. Lazar 2009).

Post-feminism works to nullify critique of gender and treats 'women' as a homogeneous mass, making any political struggles on the basis of gender and class, and/or ethnicity, age, sexuality difficult. As McRobbie (2004: 260) argues, 'the new female subject is, despite her freedom, called upon to be silent, to withhold critique, to count as a modern sophisticated girl, or indeed withholding this critique is a condition of her freedom'. Lazar (2009), in her work on the de-politicising effects of the global beauty industry, also observes a move to a state of withholding critique, which has been brought about by post-feminism. Through her thorough linguistic analyses of advertising discourse, she characterises this development as resulting in a 'culture of non-critique'. Furthermore, Tasker and Negra (2009) make the following point:

> Postfeminist culture's centralization of an affluent elite certainly entails an emphatic individualism, but this formulation tends to confuse self-interest with individuality and elevates consumption as a strategy for healing those dissatisfactions that might alternatively be understood in terms of social ills and discontents. (Tasker and Negra 2007: 2)

The culture of post-feminism can therefore be seen as playing an important role in maintaining the status quo, keeping women focusing upon themselves as individuals, working to foreground the importance of individual consumption over everything else (cf. hooks 1990). The beauty industry and its constant focus on the need for self-improvement is a good example of this global strategy, which can be examined linguistically through the study of advertising language (Lazar 2006, 2009; Mooneeram and Mullany 2011). The preoccupation with individualism and the maintenance of individualism through consumerist culture, with individuals striving to become part of an 'affluent elite', works to keep broader, collective political issues obscured, making any focus on the wider social ills and discontent surrounding gender relations far less likely to come to the fore.

If we look at the developing world and take China as an example (Yang 2007a, 2007b; Zhang 2007), there are some interesting similarities between current perceptions of a decline of/lack of need for feminism in wider society. Although these similarities have resulted from different historical and political backgrounds, there are some parallels that can be drawn. In a contemporary Chinese context, Zhang (2007: 413) observes that 'the advent of the market economy and a sweeping consumer revolution have led to the decline of state feminism and a return to delineating (hetero)sexuality and gender differences'. Although the historical conditions of political development are very different, there are similarities between current popular perceptions of feminism losing force in China and current popular perceptions of feminism losing force in Western countries and a number of other locations. Yang's (2007a, 2007b) work presents clear evidence of an increased emphasis on biologically essentialist positions, and these can be seen as feeding into the production of post-feminist discourses, which often have essentialised differences at their heart. These similarities can be seen as partly related to the spread of the neo-liberal global market economy in China (Yang 2007a, 2007b). This signals the importance of producing language and gender research on globalisation, including gendered consumerist cultures. We will return to the issue of globalisation in the section on 'Globalisation and multilingualism' below, pp. 18–19.

The burgeoning self-help industry which exists in many different societies worldwide is another good example of consumerist culture centred around the individual. Any social problems are conceptualised as the individual simply needing to learn to change or accept, which they can do if they consume the information given in self-help materials, masking societal power and working to prevent manifestations of disgruntlement with sexual politics on a broader social scale. A significant number of self-help volumes currently adorn the shelves of bookstores in many different societies around the world, in addition to the many related websites (for example, www.marsandvenus.com). These claim to focus upon language and aim to solve gender-based communication problems between individuals, usually in intimate heterosexual relationships. These publications often inform readers, that is women, the targeted consumers of these publications, that by simply learning to change their individual speech styles and accepting differences between women's and men's language as the result of inherent 'biological' differences between them, which are completely beyond their control, harmony will result. Such advice is often explained by rather trite analogies which do nothing more than reinforce biological determinism, such as 'Men are from Mars, Women are from Venus' (Gray 1992, 2002).

These popular-culture publications are completely devoid of any linguistic knowledge of how language is actually used by speakers in naturally occurring settings, let alone any considerations of societal power, ideology or the crucial role played by context and socio-cultural norms in governing gendered linguistic behaviour. Cameron's (2007b) *The Myth of Mars and Venus* provides a superb critique of these publications. Cameron succeeds in providing a thorough critique based on a substantial range of empirical linguistic evidence.

In summary, 'post-feminism' currently has had something of a stronghold in discussions of sexual politics around the world. However, we aim to show that feminism is not dead and gone – the need for feminist study is still very much alive. Despite the early gains that were made by feminist movements, emancipation and/or equality still has not been achieved, and language and gender studies have an important role to play in the future of this movement.[2]

Feminist models

Historically, a range of different models of 'feminism' have emerged from across various disciplines in the humanities and social sciences. Some of the most significant of these 'feminisms' include: 'liberal' feminism, 'French' feminism, 'materialist' feminism, 'Marxist' feminism, 'socialist' feminism, 'radical' feminism, 'postcolonial' feminism and so on (see Whelehan 1995; McElhinny 2007a). On rare occasions, feminist linguists may explicitly state their particular political stance in their work – we have already referred to the example of Cameron (2006a) identifying herself as a 'radical' feminist. Jule (2008: 9) observes that language and gender studies often seem to connect most often with liberal feminism, which she defines as producing commentary on 'society's view of women as indicative of society's patriarchal attitudes and values, particularly regarding laws and human rights'.

The liberal feminist stance seems to be the one which is assumed within Western feminist thinking and thus many feminist linguists' work takes the view that feminism is concerned with equality of opportunity and reform. In other contexts, the aim of feminist campaigns is not to be seen as the equals of men, but for women's emancipation in terms of difference of identity and treatment in law to be significantly improved. An excellent example of this is Sadiqi's (2010) report on women's rights in North Africa.

However, the majority of feminist linguistic researchers do not tend to overtly define or align themselves with a specific feminist model, liberal or otherwise. There has also been some debate, in recent years, regarding the nature of 'patriarchy', that is, a social system which operates in the interests and benefit of men rather than women. It is questionable whether 'patriarchy' is still the most effective term to use to talk about or conceptualise the exercise of societal power (Mills 1995; Walsh 2001). The difficulty with using a term such as 'patriarchy' is that it assumes a certain stability to patriarchy itself, thus making it more difficult to challenge and transform. The use of the term also assumes that a culture is patriarchal throughout, making it seem as if women are completely powerless. In more recent work, feminists have tried to develop ways of examining cultures so that these studies can pinpoint areas of discrimination, whilst at the same time highlighting the strategies that women have used to resist that discrimination.

McElhinny (2007a) observes that language and gender studies have tended to stay rather disengaged from the wider social-theoretical debates about feminism which have taken place in other humanities and social science disciplines. Instead of being most influenced by debates on, for example, the role of housework and domestic labour, as focused upon by Marxist feminists and other feminist groups (for example, Rowbotham 1973; Oakley 1975), language and gender studies instead have been influenced by a more generic categorisation system which uses a metaphor of different feminist 'waves'. This overarching 'waves' model has had more of an impact upon the framing and articulation of language and gender studies than any other particular 'feminist' paradigm.

The 'waves' model can provide useful reference points for exploring the different nuances of the feminist movement in relation to language and gender studies. Currently there are three different feminist 'waves' which have been categorised. 'First Wave' feminism is most commonly associated with the suffragette movement in the late nineteenth and early twentieth century in the UK and the United States. Some researchers go back further to Mary Wollstonecraft, especially the publication of her hugely influential *Vindication of the Rights of Woman* in 1792, and cite her as the founder of modern feminism (Walter 2010).[3] However, from a specifically linguistic perspective, the 'waves' that are of most interest are the 'Second Wave' and 'Third Wave', as these correlate most closely with the initial development and then the rapid expansion of feminist linguistic studies.

The differences between the Second and Third Wave approaches are sometimes alternatively referred to as the distinction between modern and postmodern approaches respectively (Swann 2002; Cameron 2005). We will focus in detail upon the differences between Second and Third Wave feminism, especially from a linguistic perspective, in Chapter 3, but we will briefly introduce both of these concepts here, as they play an influential role in characterising contemporary issues in the field.

Second Wave feminism developed in the 1970s. It presupposes that there are differences between women and men and it takes the notion of difference as a starting point for research. Feminist linguistic research thus started to produce empirical evidence of differences between women's and men's language use, alongside explanations as to why these differences had been found. 'Women' and 'men' were therefore treated as two homogeneous groups. Freed (2003: 703) argues that 'the fundamental problem with describing human beings in terms of difference is that the concept invariably leads to a ranking or privileging of one group over another'. It also leads to 'women' and 'men' being treated as two unified groups, with no room for diversity amongst them.

However, as the population as a whole differentiates between women and men as two homogeneous categories in terms of how it treats members of societies, then as academics we need to be fully aware of this and take this into account when conducting linguistic analyses. That is to say, we should not accept the division between men and women uncritically, and should not build research projects whose aim is exclusively to show that women speak differently from men. Rather, we should recognise that men and women are treated differently within society. Our research should focus on investigating the difference, if any, that gender makes to language use, and not assume that it necessarily makes a difference.

Furthermore, the overwhelming focus of Second Wave research tends to be on white, middle-class, heterosexual women in Western contexts. In contrast, Third Wave feminism argues for the analysis of diversity in terms of gender identities, looking for a range of different identity positions including differences *amongst* groups of women and *amongst* groups of men. Third Wave studies have also attempted to diversify the field beyond looking at the language of white, middle-class, straight Western women. At the time of writing, researchers are still seeking to expand the discipline by producing research that is much more diverse in its focus (see Bucholtz 2004; McElhinny 2007b; Pichler and Eppler 2009; Mullany 2010a).

In Third Wave feminism, there has also been an increasing emphasis on examining gender alongside all other relevant social identity variables which may have been 'backgrounded' in much earlier Second Wave work. There have been moves to examine a range of different social-class groupings, instead of just focusing on the middle classes (see, for example, Pichler 2009); there have also been moves to foreground studies examining gender and ethnicities much more (see Morgan 2004, 2007; Troutman 2006). Since the late 1990s, studies of language and sexualities alongside gender have emerged, focusing on both sexual orientation and the erotic (see Livia and Hall 1997b; Cameron and Kulick 2003).

Studies on more marginal or 'queer' identities have become more prominent as a part of this focus on sexualities (Jones 2009, forthcoming). There is now also far more of a focus on empirical analysis of men's language as well as women's language than there was in the field's earlier stages of development. This research does not assume that a separate men's language exists; rather, the focus falls upon the way that the language men use in particular contexts is associated with particular qualities or values. This research also examines the way that the very notion of men's speech is constituted (see Johnson and Meinhof 1997; Coates 2003). Other developing research areas include focusing on gender and religious identity (see the work of Jule 2005, 2007; Jule and Pedersen 2006; Murphy 2010a).

This diversification of the field has gone some way towards addressing another important concern that researchers have had, namely that gender was being foregrounded/prioritised over all other social identity variables (Swann 2002). Looking at the diversity of gender identities emerging within and alongside a range of other complex social identity variables including race, ethnicities, sexualities, social class, education and age has resulted in more nuanced studies emerging. Such studies have been approached in a variety of different ways depending upon researchers' backgrounds and favoured theories and methodologies. We will discuss these issues in depth throughout the book.

An examination of gender inequalities and public settings has also been dominant in recent years and this focus has figured heavily in Third Wave feminist approaches. In earlier research there was frequently a tendency to analyse informal conversation (Zimmerman and West 1975; Fishman 1980; Coates 1989); although informal conversation continues to be an interesting arena to analyse, it now seems that there has been an observable move to analyse gendered identities in institutions and also to analyse the variety of speech styles available to men and women in different institutional contexts, for example, in the workplace environment (Thornborrow 2002; Holmes 2006; Mullany 2007; Schnurr 2009; Baxter and Wallace 2009; Baxter 2010).

Cameron (2009) argues that one of the problems feminists have had to face, since the 1970s, is that removing institutional barriers to women's participation in certain activities and increasing access to public, institutional settings and resources has not automatically produced equality. Old divisions and patterns of behaviour can persist within institutions long after the original structural biases have disappeared. A number of unanswered questions and problems relating to gender relations in institutional settings remain and these can be fruitfully explored from a linguistic point of view. Many Third Wave feminists thus continue to focus on institutional settings to investigate gender relations and the broader issues of language and sexual politics within institutions (see, for example, Baxter 2006c, 2010; Mullany forthcoming).

Caveats

Overall, Third Wave feminism is generally deemed to be the most representative of current work in the field of language and gender studies. However, there are certain caveats to focalising feminist linguistic theory using the terminology of the waves model (or the alternatively named 'modern' to 'postmodern' model) that need to be taken into consideration before we move on.

The first caveat is that the waves model can be viewed as representing the socio-historical developments in Western societies and therefore the ordered progression it signifies may not be as applicable in other contexts that fall outside of the dominant Western perspective. However, much of the terminology and many of the conceptual frameworks associated with Second Wave and Third Wave feminist theory have been drawn upon fairly extensively by feminist linguistic researchers in a range of different global locations. For example, in Lazar's (2009) work in Singapore she argues that, although the terminology of the waves model represents the tradition of Western development, the tenets of Second and Third Wave feminism will be recognisable to a Singaporean audience. Although we must not lose sight of the fact that the model generally represents Western socio-historical transitions, arguably a consequence of it tracking the chronological development of the discipline of language and gender studies which emerged from Western academic contexts, many of the theoretical concepts that are of the most use in exploring research questions in the world can be fruitfully explored by adapting concepts from the Third Wave and sometimes the Second Wave category.

The next caveat relates directly to the notion of linearity itself. The linearity implied by the terminological distinctions that are used, with either the waves metaphor or with the addition of the prefix 'post' to 'modern', is problematic. Generally speaking, Third Wave feminists have been critical of Second Wave analysis because of its 'essentialist' focus on comparing male and female speech. But sometimes this split between Second and Third Wave feminism is the result of a reductive view of Second Wave feminism. In order to produce sophisticated, complex analysis, it is tempting to caricature the work to which one is reacting. However, it is vital for us to recognise the debt which we owe to Second Wave feminism and to recognise the complexity of many of the positions which were developed within this framework.

Some researchers may identify themselves with Third Wave feminism more, but elements of Second Wave feminism may still be clearly observable in their work. Thus, rather than seeing Second and Third Wave feminist linguistics as chronological, they can be seen as approaches which may be more or less appropriate depending on the socio-cultural context and exactly what the researcher is analysing. For example, in the case of sexism, for certain types of sexism, where a stereotypical view of women or men is being referred to, a Second Wave feminist approach may be far more applicable. In other cases, where the sexism is peculiar to a particular context and can only be inferred, a Third Wave approach is preferable (see Mills 2008 and Chapter 7, below).

In summary, Second Wave feminism did not suddenly end and then Third Wave feminism begin, nor did postmodernist feminism suddenly supersede modernist feminism. There are many points of crossover between them, and it is not uncommon to see elements of Second and Third Wave feminism co-occurring. The Second and Third Wave approaches or the modern and postmodern approaches are therefore 'better seen as representing tendencies in feminist thought which have historically overlapped and coexisted' (Cameron 2005: 483). The models are not and should not be seen as separate, discrete or strictly linear categories. Indeed, Cameron (2009) argues that transitions in movements in feminist linguistics may not be as different as first thought. She points out that we need to be sure that we do not 'overstate the extent of shifts which have taken place' and it is essential to 'consider those shifts which have occurred in relation to the wider intellectual and social and political context' (2009: 4). The implied linearity of the waves or modern to postmodern model has been enough for some researchers outside linguistics to argue against their use (see McRobbie 2009), but the models have undeniably played a prominent role in recent contextualisations of feminist linguistics as a political movement (see Baxter 2003, 2006c; Mills 2003a), if approached with the above caveats clearly in mind. We will explore the differences, similarities and subtle nuances between Second and Third Wave feminism further in Chapter 3 when theorising gender.

Globalisation and multilingualism

As we mentioned earlier, research on monolingual white women from English-speaking Western cultures, in particular, has tended to dominate language and gender research. While there is still a need for such research, it is also crucially important to diversify the field as much as possible and examine the experiences of others within this increasingly globalised world. Most recently studies have been produced which look at language and gender in a range of different global contexts and in multilingual environments (for example, Lazar 2005b; McElhinny 2007b). The interplay between language and gender needs to examine gender alongside other crucial social identity variables in a range of different international contexts if gender relations and gender inequalities are to be properly addressed in a much more inclusive sense.

The essays in McElhinny's (2007b) publication include ground-breaking language and gender research examining the interplay between gender and language in a range of globalised settings including China, Tonga, Vietnam, Nigeria, India, Japan, the Philippines and Catalonia. As part of this collection, Besnier (2009: 425) outlines the importance of contemporary studies investigating the impact of globalisation, arguing that it 'offers local lives both new opportunities and constraints. Global forces may provide new forms of imagined experience, through television soap operas, the Internet, and white-collar work … at the same time, globalization has all-too-well documented nefarious effects, a simple example of which is the economic enslavement of people to menial and unstable work.' This includes domestic work taken on by migrants and also low-paid employment in call centres. It is most frequently women who end up occupying most of this type of employment in many different parts of the world.

Besnier's (2007, 2009) work focuses upon how globalisation is affecting gendered self-presentation in Tonga. He looks at the public arena of the marketplace, where goods are being sold from a wider global world, and also examines code-switching from Tongan to English in the context of a transgendered beauty pageant (Besnier 2007). Gaudio's (2007) work looks at the emergence of new public spheres and how this has affected gender and language use in Nigeria. Pujolar (2007) focuses on migration through a language and gender lens, examining how immigrants in Catalonia, Spain, face struggles surrounding gender, ethnicity and social class in language classes where they are attempting to learn Catalan. Yang's (2007b) work in China examines the positioning of women and gendered discourses in relation to the emergent neo-liberal global market economy. Research on non-white, non-middle-class groups within Westernised countries has also emerged, for example Trechter's (1999) work on native American languages, including a focus on speakers of Lakhota, Ahlers' (2008) work on language revitalisation amongst Californian Indian tribal groups, including the minority languages Elem Pomo and Luiseño, Pichler's (2009) investigations of the talk of British Bangladeshi girls in London's East End and Miskimmin's (2007) work on the language used in Head Start educational programmes aimed at aboriginal families in Toronto, Canada.

Transitions in approaches to language and gender studies are heavily interwoven with the socio-political landscape where research takes place. Current areas of exploration for language and gender studies on the contemporary subject of globalisation highlighted by McElhinny (2007) could include a newer focus upon debates regarding the values of affirmative action and emergent issues such as transnational domestic labour migrants, gender segregation of the workplace and the rise of the service economy and feminisation of its work practices. Cameron (2000, 2003, 2006a) has examined this feminisation of work practices in her research on women in call centres and the types of language skills which are considered to be stereotypically feminine. Other debates from which language and gender is also largely absent include considering how feminists can become active in debates about colonialism and imperialism and in discussions of gender and sexual identities in global locations.

Critical self-reflexivity

Lazar (2005a) points out that it is essential for feminist linguistic research to be self-reflexive, that is, to reflect upon one's own academic practices. In this book we have attempted to cover a wide and varied range of issues regarding contemporary feminist issues relating to language and gender. We may agree with some positions more than others and this will be evident in our writing. Our own biases as language and gender researchers will inevitably be present at various stages in this book, and it would be disingenuous of us to suggest that we are offering a purely descriptive or 'neutral' account of the field. As previously stated, we do not believe that the primary aim of language and gender studies should be to describe, but that it should be designed to produce suggestions for action to bring about social change on the basis of thorough linguistic analysis. That said, we have tried to leave space for you as the reader to make up your own mind about the interplay between language, gender and feminism and the various theoretical and methodological approaches on offer.

It is also important to highlight again at this stage that our research expertise is in Western cultures. Lazar (2005a) considers the issue of the dominance of white Western scholars, like ourselves, and who has the right to speak on behalf of or for which group. Drawing on the work of van Dijk (1994), Lazar (2005a: 18) observes that, when researching a community outside one's own, researchers need to be very careful that they do not end up producing a form of academic ethnocentrism, 'based upon seldom questioned feelings of scholarly and cultural superiority'. She argues that studies may become problematic if researchers investigate research sites of which they are not a member where they are not doing so in collaboration with members of that community. In such situations, if the expertise comes from the traditionally dominant group, then such studies run the risk of reproducing a position of external superiority. Researchers from the West (or the North) need to ensure that they do not re-enact 'historical imperialism in academic neo-imperialist terms' (Lazar 2005a: 18).

Sunderland (2009) addresses this issue in recent work that she has been conducting on language and gender in African contexts. She states that although her work potentially runs the risk of being perceived as a form of neo-colonialism, she avoids this by being part of a network of African gender and language researchers. She also argues that, by being an outsider, she has the advantage of being an 'ethnographer' who can offer an 'outsider perspective' (Sunderland 2009: 129; the ethnographic approach to data collection is fully introduced and discussed in Chapter 5). She also makes the point that because Africa is now 'global', along with the rest of the world, arguably we are all integrated into a global scholarly network.

However, there is also a need for researchers to ensure that they do not engage in what Lazar terms 'marked inclusion', whereby instead of being viewed as part of the mainstream, non-Western geographical locations are seen as 'other' and somewhat 'marked', and discussion of them remains tokenistic. In this book we have tried our best to ensure that we have not tokenistically included non-Western studies in a paternalistic way. What we have tried to do is to consider the position of Western women and men alongside women and men from other cultures and cultural groups. In some ways, by placing Western women in a global context, it makes it easier to analyse the specificity of Western women and men's linguistic behaviour, which then makes it difficult to make generalisations about women and men as a whole. We can thus see that the way Western women and men behave and are treated is only one way among many, and it is certainly not necessarily better than other ways.

Indeed, through researching language and gender studies in other cultures, we can begin to see that, for example, for many Muslim women, the sexualisation of Western women is seen not as sexual liberation and something to be emulated, but as an enslavement; and that the veiling and confinement of women in certain cultures has a wide range of interpretations and functions, none of which has to do with being governed by men (see Lewis and Mills 2003). Western feminists need to ensure that their views of women in other cultures are not based on stereotypes, but are based instead on empirical research and consultation with those women themselves.

Fifteen years ago, feminist theorist Imelda Whelehan (1995) observed how some feminist researchers were beginning to respond to the need to redress the balance of the overwhelming dominance of feminism's focus on the politics of white middle-class women, with broader considerations of how race and social class also play crucial, interconnected roles in how femininity gets imbued with social meaning. As part of this commentary, she drew attention to a crucial argument that bell hooks (1989) makes in terms of who should be 'allowed' to talk/represent/analyse social groups to which they themselves do not belong. In particular, this argument was made in reference to some white feminists who had refused to speak on behalf of black women, as they did not see it as their place to do so. hooks argues that, no matter how well-meaning this principle may be, it can be very damaging; she makes the point that such refusals to speak on behalf of black women serve only to reinforce the dichotomy between black and white female experiences, which, in turn, can serve to reinforce racist perspectives: it takes 'the burden of accountability away from white women and places it solely onto women of colour' (hooks 1989: 47).

We endorse hooks' position and believe that it should be the responsibility of everyone within a research field to address problems of bias that exist within any given research field. We need to set analysis of the language of one's own group alongside that of a group to which one does not belong. In this way, it is possible to make comparisons between the language use of particular groups, rather than assuming that it is possible to describe the language of groups in isolation. This point is relevant not just to race but also to social stratification and a whole host of other social identity variables. Of course, this is far from an unproblematic process and one that, at the very least, requires a significant amount of researcher reflexivity and a carefully chosen methodological process. However, to deny researchers the opportunity to study groups other than the ones to which they themselves belong can be limiting and ultimately result in disciplines being stifled and/or dominated by a focus on the same types of individuals from similar backgrounds – within academia, most likely the dominant group of white middle classes.

As already observed, within language and gender studies there has been an undeniable focus on white middle-class women, reflecting a dominance observed by Whelehan (1995) in feminist studies more generally. If engaging in research outside one's own group, then it is important to take the above points into account when deciding upon research questions, who you should work with, designing research methodologies and when selecting appropriate theoretical frameworks.

The title of bell hooks' 1990 publication, quoted at the beginning of this chapter, is intended to act as a continuous theme throughout the book, a constant reminder that feminism as a political movement should be relevant to everybody – not just white middle-class women in Western societies.

Structure of the book

We have structured this book so that we begin by providing an overview of contemporary debates about language, gender and feminism, so that the current socio-political state of feminism as a political movement is clearly understood in relation to language and gender studies. In Chapter 2, we continue this focus by examining why feminism is still required, including presentation of evidence of a recent resurgence in feminism.

In Chapter 3, we examine the various theoretical approaches there have been to theorising gender. As a key part of this we focus in more detail upon gender theorisation within Second Wave and Third Wave feminism and on how different types of femininities and masculinities are encoded linguistically. We then move in Chapter 4 to detail the various feminist linguistic approaches which have been drawn on in the study of language and gender. Here we give details of approaches such as feminist sociolinguistics, feminist discourse analysis and feminist pragmatics. We have set these particular approaches out in this way so that readers can see clearly that there is not simply one way of approaching analysis from a feminist perspective.

In Chapter 5, we examine the methodological approaches which feminist linguists have adopted within language and gender studies. Here, we discuss quantitative and qualitative approaches and we describe the ways in which analysts in recent years have begun to use mixed-methodological approaches and employ multiple research methods. We examine particular research methods such as ethnography, interviews, focus groups, questionnaires and transcription. Collectively, Chapters 1–5 should be seen as providing the reader with a theoretical and methodological overview of feminist linguistic study.

In the next two chapters, we examine two particular areas of analysis within contemporary feminist linguistic studies, where we show theory and methodology in action: the analysis of sexualities in Chapter 6 and the analysis of sexism in Chapter 7. Throughout these two chapters we give examples of feminist analysis of language and gender which apply relevant elements of theoretical and methodological knowledge that are presented earlier in the book. In the final chapter, Chapter 8, we examine problems and issues within current research and then go on to point to the different directions in which the field of feminist language and gender studies could progress in future. Our discussions in this book illustrate the richness of research within feminist language and gender studies and they demonstrate that feminist analysis has moved away from simply comparing the way men speak to the way women speak towards a more complex conceptualisation of gender, as it is worked out within particular contexts.

2 Why we still need feminism

Contemporary issues in sexual politics

In this chapter, we present a range of evidence as to why feminism is still needed, particularly within the context of language and gender research. It is important that we are clear about the link between feminism as an analysis of social inequality and the type of analysis which feminism leads to in language and gender research. All of the social, political and economic problems associated with gender relations that are highlighted here need to be explored from a range of different perspectives and disciplines across academia, including linguistics. By producing analyses of a range of different types of spoken and written language which are associated with and are a part of these problems, feminist linguists can play a part, alongside other disciplines, in the overarching feminist goal of researching gender relations with the aim of bringing about gender equality and emancipation via social change. As Talbot (1998/2010: 118) points out, 'looking at language critically is a way of denaturalising it'.

The centenary of International Women's Day was commemorated on 8 March 2009.[1] To mark this occasion the UK-based University and College Union (UCU) compiled a range of global facts and figures to demonstrate how much more still needs to be achieved by feminism. The following list presents a clear set of reasons why the need for feminist research is still far from over. Despite the current salience of terms such as 'post-feminism', there is an urgent need for feminist research to be undertaken within and across the world to investigate a range of social, economic and political problems based on or as the result of gender relations:

Highly unlikely they surveyed enough businesses.

- women make up 33 per cent of managerial and administrative posts in the developed world. In Africa, Asia and the Pacific the figure is even lower – 15 per cent and 13 per cent respectively;
- two-thirds of illiterate adults in the world are women;
- the majority of the 1.3 billion people in the world living in poverty are women;
- a major cause of death for women between 15 and 44 is male violence. Fifty per cent of murdered women are killed by their current or former partners;
- 1,500 women a day die unnecessarily of childbirth or causes related to pregnancy;

who deems it unnecessary? Why?

- 19 million abortions take place in unsafe conditions killing 68,000 women a year. Approximately 40 per cent of these are performed on young women between 16 and 24;
- only 6 of the 194 presidents are women. In 2007 only 19 per cent of countries achieved the recognised benchmark of 30 per cent parliamentary representation (Bennett 2009).

Amnesty International's *Amnesty Magazine* (2008) recently examined the United Nations' Universal Declaration of Human Rights on the Declaration's sixtieth anniversary, specifically from the perspective of women's rights. Some of the Declaration's Articles directly intersect with the above problems. Despite the Universal Declaration stating that everyone is entitled to 'a standard of living and health care adequate for their health and well-being, especially mothers and children' (Article 25), 'the right to education, including free and compulsory primary education' (Article 36) and the right to 'life, liberty and security of the person' (Article 3), the evidence in the above list from the UCU demonstrates that these declarations are clearly not being met. Article 7, 'All are equal before the law and are entitled without any discrimination to equal protection before the law', does not protect women from violence; in countries such as Sierra Leone, women are viewed as minors in the eyes of the law, to be represented only by a husband, father or brother.

Article 16 states that 'Men and women of full age have the right to marry and find a family, with free and full consent, and equal rights during and after marriage' is also broken in a range of locations by forced and under-age marriages. However, in Morocco, in 2004, a new law was passed which gave women the right to divorce their husbands, brought restrictions on polygamy and changed the minimum age for marriage from 15 to 18 (Sadiqi 2010). Thus, there are positive changes in certain countries which will lead to further changes as women begin to influence legislature more.

People trafficking is very closely related to poverty, violating Article 4 of the Declaration, that 'no-one shall be held in slavery or servitude'. *Amnesty Magazine* (2008) reports that trafficking, especially sex trafficking, affects women and girls far more than men and boys. Recent estimates show that people are trafficked from at least 127 countries to 137 potential destinations (United Nations, cited in *Amnesty Magazine* 2008).

Article 23 states that 'Everyone has the right to work, to free choice of employment, to fair and equal pay and to form and join trade unions.' *Amnesty Magazine* (2008: 15) documents that two-thirds of all employed women in South Asia work without pay, usually in a family business or on a farm; job advertisements in Ukraine regularly specify that a man is required for appointment; in parts of central America companies routinely demand that female job applicants have a pregnancy test. Article 23 is also not met by the well-documented pay gap that still exists between women and men for doing exactly the same job in many countries (Baynard 2010). 'The pay gap between men and women in Europe has barely changed for the better in 15 years', argues Ian Traynor (2010) in the UK-based broadsheet newspaper the *Guardian*. Inequalities in European pay range from 5 per cent in Italy to 30 per cent in Estonia. In the UK women are paid 79 per cent of male rates, according to a survey of women's pay in the EU by Eurobarometer. In the US, women now constitute half of the workforce, and in four out of ten US families, women are now the primary breadwinner, according to a report by the Center for American Progress published in 2009 (cited in O'Hara 2010); however O'Hara argues that dated attitudes to family-friendly working hold many women back, because the workplace is still designed to serve the needs of single male breadwinners in relation to leave-time, promotion, hours and benefits (O'Hara 2010: 1).

Additionally, the lack of progress made by women across the world in terms of breaking through the 'glass ceiling', the metaphorical barrier preventing women from entering into the higher echelons of power in the workplace, has resulted in it recently being rebranded as a 'concrete' ceiling (Johnson 2006; Wahlin 2007; Mullany 2010b). In the UK in particular, the Equality and Human Rights Commission (2008) projects that it will take another 73 years for women to be equally represented in the boardroom of the FTSE 100 companies.[2] The statistics show that women from ethnic minorities are more discriminated against. Only 11 per cent of directorship posts in FTSE 100 companies are occupied by women, but less than 1 per cent of posts (0.7 per cent) are held by women from ethnic minority groups.

The role of feminist linguistics

So, we have outlined a whole range of significant socio-political problems thus far in the chapter, but what can feminist linguistics do in order to help investigate these problems? This could include, but is not necessarily limited to, producing critical analyses of the way that language enforces or naturalises divisions within the workplace; the way that public speaking is viewed as 'masculine' (Mills 2006); how the oversexualisation of public culture, observable through analysing media and advertising language, can influence gendered expectations of women, men and heterosexuality (Cameron 2009; Lazar 2009); the way that competence and believability are associated with certain forms of 'masculine' speech in environments such as courtrooms (O'Barr and Atkins 1980); the way that male parliamentarians do not observe the speaking rules in the British Parliaments (Shaw 2002); the way that boys in classrooms can claim teachers' talking time through their more boisterous talk (Sunderland 2000; Baxter 2003) and need to be controlled; the way that mothers may defer to the authority of fathers in relation to children in their talk (Tannen *et al.* 2007), the way that those accused of rape may justify their actions through the language they use in court and be believed by the judge and jury (Ehrlich 2003), to mention but a few examples.

Language is used as tool to constrain, coerce and represent women and men in oppressive ways, and producing linguistic analysis within socio-cultural contexts can reveal some of the mechanisms of how this takes place. A whole range of different studies are drawn upon in the remainder of this book to illustrate the value of producing feminist linguistic analysis in order to help provide a way forward for a whole host of significant gender-based social and political problems regarding language and communication. By drawing attention to the way that language works to 'normalise' unequal gender roles, we, as feminists, can bring about consciousness-raising in relation to the way gender may operate in society as a whole.

To focus on more specific, recent examples that have come to light whilst we have been writing this book, in August 2009, in Afghanistan a written bill focusing on the rights of husbands in marriage had its wording changed by government officials and was passed by 'official' publication in the country's gazette. The changes in wording mean that a husband legally now has permission to starve his wife if she refuses to have sex with him at least once every four days. Women's groups in Afghanistan have argued that the new wording violates the country's constitution, which is supposed to include a commitment to the principle of equality. Additionally, as part of the new bill, women have no custody rights for any of their children – fathers and grandfathers are given exclusive custody. Women also have to gain the permission of their husbands if they want to enter the workplace. The bill was rewritten and passed by President Karzai just days before the August 2009 presidential election and resulted in a publicly risky demonstration by hundreds of women, which is alleged to have been organised by the underground political organisation called the Revolutionary Association of the Women of Afghanistan (Boone 2010). Boone also reports that the women protesters who were brave enough to take to the streets were faced with an angry counter-demonstration (Boone 2010). Political commentators argued that President Karzai was using the bill as a vote-winning strategy, as he needed the support of fundamentalists within Afghanistan. Whilst women have had the right to vote in Afghanistan since 2004, the turnout at the 2009 election was low, hampered by violence and threats of violence. As one news agency reports:

> Despite a tendency to blame violence against women on the Taliban, the July report says women in public life have also been targeted by 'local traditional and religious power holders, their own families and communities and, in some instances, by government officials'. (Mojumdar 2009)

A comparative written-text analysis of these political documents before and after these changes were made, and/or analyses of media representations of all of these events, including representations of sexual politics throughout the presidential election process, or interviews with voters or protesters, could provide interesting linguistic insights. This latter suggestion of protester interviews poses a range of ethical questions as well as questions surrounding access to data. Boone (2010) reports that the Revolutionary Association of Women in Afghanistan operates as a splinter cell group, akin to a terrorist organisation, with members being unaware of others' identities in case they get caught by the country's intelligence service. Research access to such informants would thus be impossible. We will come back to the issue of research access in Chapter 5, when thinking about methodologies and study design.

Under Iranian law, women can still be stoned to death for adultery, whereas the punishment for adultery by males is rarely administered. Men are also allowed to have several wives. A recent international campaign (2010) has been mounted to prevent the stoning for adultery of an Iranian woman, Sakineh Ashtiani Mohammedi; she was initially sentenced to stoning, but this punishment has at present been commuted to execution by other means. Fathers in Iran can also marry off their young daughters to older men without their consent. Women are banned from occupying certain positions of power and thus having a voice in the public sphere. They cannot become judges, regardless of their qualifications. In Saudi Arabia women still do not have the right to vote, the only country in the world that does not allow this. Women are also not allowed to drive. If a woman is in the company of a man who is not a close relation, then she risks being arrested for prostitution. Again, a feminist linguistic analysis can highlight how language is normalising such unequal gender roles. As we have highlighted in Chapter 1, the production of language analysis is just one part of a much larger feminist political process, but raising awareness of inequality and the need for emancipation through language use is one stage in attempting to change gender practices within a particular society.

Shirin Ebadi, lawyer, Nobel prize winner and campaigner for women's rights in Iran, has recently drawn parallels with First Wave feminism in Britain as an 'inspiration' for current Iranian activists who are fighting for women's rights and who are frequently being imprisoned, often in solitary confinement. She argues:

> The suffragettes and their momentous struggle for women's rights in Britain have been an inspiration for women around the world. This month is exactly 80 years since their campaign led to the bill for women's emancipation being presented at the Palace of Westminster. I know that women in modern Britain do not live in a discrimination-free utopia. But the law at least, is mostly on their side. (Ebadi 2008: 39)

By quoting Ebadi here, we are certainly not arguing that Britain has all of the answers for the rest of the world, nor that it is a model that should be held up for other societies to follow. We are not engaging in any form of neo-imperialism, nor are we arguing that women in other cultures should be seen as being on a level where First Wave feminism is needed, whereas women in the West are located at the level of Third Wave feminism. There are still a whole range of gender issues, combined with discrimination on the basis of social class, race, ethnicity, age, sexuality, religion and so forth that need to be resolved in the UK. To cite just a few examples, there are still numerous examples of so-called 'honour killings' (a problematic term which we as gender and language theorists need to contest), where female family members are killed for allegedly bringing the 'reputation' of the family into 'disrepute'; one in four women in the UK will experience violence at the hands of a current or former partner and currently two women a week are killed by a current or former partner; 2,000 women a week will be raped each year (Banyard 2010: 106–7); every year 30,000 women in the UK are sacked for being pregnant (Banyard 2010: 75). Rather, this comment by Ebadi is included here as it, first, shows an awareness of the 'waves' model outside of academia and, second, demonstrates how different generations of women who have engaged in collective action can provide inspiration for one another in dispersed locations in different historical times and spaces.

The longevity of feminism and the different stages that feminism has gone through in different locations throughout the world can be seen as key strengths. Feminists can draw upon a whole range of different political experiences, as an aid to one another. Sharing such information has been made easier and quicker by the Internet. If the Universal Declaration of Human Rights is perceived to be a benchmark for acceptable gender practices globally, then regardless of what countries we as researchers come from, we will share this benchmark for acceptable practices and have something approaching a shared outlook on what gender emancipation should look like.

A feminist resurgence?

From the perspective of communication studies, McRobbie (2009) views post-feminism in Western cultures as 'a situation which is marked by a new kind of anti-feminist sentiment which is different from the backlash against the seeming gains made by feminist activities in an earlier period, i.e. the 1970s and 1980s'. She argues that, in the UK, 'elements of feminism have been taken into account, and have been absolutely incorporated into political and institutional life' (2009: 10). One would think that this is a very positive state of affairs, as it seems to suggest that feminism has been taken on board. However, instead, McRobbie argues that the collectivist ideals of feminism have been transformed into an individualistic discourse and the vocabulary of feminism has been taken over by what McRobbie terms 'faux feminism' (2009: 1), resulting only in a very watered down, de-politicised version of feminism.

McRobbie maps out a set of possible positions for young women: post-feminist masquerade (where feminist ideals are aimed for, but within an individualistic frame), the figure of the working girl (financially independent); the phallic girl (the ladette), and the global girl. All of these roles offer young women the possibility of freedom and change, but only if they do not adopt the discourse of feminism. McRobbie is able to analyse the way that popular culture and government institutions in the UK offer these roles to young women. Thus, we can see the way that the campaigns for sexual equality of the 1960s and 1970s have led to women being 'liberated' sexually, but this so-called liberation seems to be working very much in men's interests, for example through pole dancing and lap dancing (though see below for evidence of resistance to this). From her perspective, she argues that young women are presented with a situation which tells them that they are equal, that they can choose their future, 'yet which also suggests that this equality has been mysteriously arrived at, without requiring adjustment or dramatic change on the part of patriarchal authority' (2009: 105). Thus she argues that the history of feminist campaigns is erased.

In a recent article in the *Guardian*, Raven (2010) argues that some women turned their backs on feminism in the 1990s. She draws attention to the fact that women themselves campaigned to have control over their sexuality and reproductive rights, but, like McRobbie (2009), she also notes that the growing sexualisation of Western women means that sexuality is determined by male sexual interests. For example, she describes the outrage which many felt when the UK 'celebrity' Katie Price (famous first and foremost for nothing more than being a topless model) brought her young daughter named Princess to a photo shoot wearing heavy make-up and false eyelashes. Raven notes that in a recent study of 1,000 British girls, 60 per cent said that they wanted to be glamour models and 25 per cent said that they would consider becoming lap dancers. She argues that 'We are culpable. Thinking women have turned their backs on feminism. This might not have been a disaster if we had remained neutral. But we too have found the governing philosophy of [Katie Price] compelling' (Raven 2010: 2).

Raven argues that women turned their backs on feminism because they saw it as unglamorous and inhibiting, and some of them rejected feminism, because they thought that the revolution had achieved its goals, as Walter had stated in her earlier book *The New Feminism* in 1999: 'As women break down every corridor of power in Britain, we can see that we are in the final stretch of a long feminist revolution that is taking women from the outside of society to the inside, from silence to speech, from impotence to strength.' However, instead of seeing the 'revolution' through its alleged 'final stretch', Western women have shied away from feminism and it became a negatively evaluated word, something whose value you would have to argue for. The Western oversexualisation of women has advanced so much that according to a UK Home Office report, during the 1990s the number of men paying for sex doubled, with an estimated 80,000 women involved in prostitution and 921 brothels in London alone. Raven comments: 'The [sex] industry's efforts to make it seem like a normal leisure pursuit rather than a form of abuse appears to be paying off' (Raven 2010: 4). She adds:

> The free-thinking, life-loving desiring person described in Greer's *The Female Eunuch* now seems a historical figure. In her place we have Madonna-ised woman grinding out routines in front of a mirror, with her eyes asking 'am I hot?' Her ambitions have been curtailed, just like Friedan's housewife. How very far this creature is from the feminist ideal. (Raven 2010: 4)

Despite the dominance of 'post-feminism' as a global, neo-liberal discourse, as discussed in Chapter 1, and the pessimism of McRobbie and Raven's comments above, it is notable and indeed somewhat promising that there has recently been clear evidence of a 'backlash' against post-feminism itself in very recent popular-culture publications which, we argue, signals the potential emergence of a feminist resurgence in popular culture and the mass media in the West. We mentioned in Chapter 1 that Walter (2010) has rethought her 1999 position of embracing post-feminist ideas and as a key part of this she decries the return of sexism in her new book *Living Dolls: The Return of Sexism*. A growing number of other, similar publications specifically targeted at mainstream, popular-culture audiences have very recently emerged. All of these are specifically designed to put feminism firmly back on the map and many are written by and targeted at the young women whom McRobbie portrayed as being trapped within a post-feminist discourse with only a limited number of subject positions available. There is clear resistance emerging. It is important for academic feminist linguistic research to be fully cognisant of these developments so that it can attempt to intersect with these studies and thus directly engage with these issues currently being debated within popular-culture audiences, as Cameron's (2007b) *The Myth of Mars and Venus* has succeeded in doing.

From this more optimistic perspective, it is possible that there may be something of a feminist resurgence over the next few years as women in many different parts of the world appear to have started to grow tired of the one-dimensional, objectified manner in which they are encouraged to behave to show that they are allegedly 'empowered'. Globalised consumerist culture offers reductive and objectifying perceptions of idealised femininity and 'womanhood'. The objectifying portrayal of women consistently viewed as little more than commodities defined by their bodies has inspired writers to take action and bring feminism back to the fore. Another key theme that these writers have attempted to unpick is the rise of biological determinism as a way to 'justify' dominant femininities or other traditionalist positions that negate or ignore many of the gains of the feminist movement.

Some of the most notable of the popular-culture publications which reject 'post-feminism' in favour of a feminist resurgence include Levy's (2005) *Female Chauvinist Pigs: Women and the Rise of Raunch Culture*, Faludi's (2008) *The Terror Dream* and Valenti's (2007) *Full Frontal Feminism: A Young Woman's Guide to Why Feminism Matters*, Walter's (2010) aforementioned book, Banyard's (2010) *The Equality Illusion: The Truth about Men and Women Today* and Redfern and Aune's (2010) *Reclaiming the F Word*.

Although these authors are not linguistics researchers, language issues are frequently touched upon, and all of these publications can be seen as having implications for feminist language and gender research. Film studies academics Tasker and Negra (2009: 3) refer to the development of books such as Levy's (2005) as marking 'a new space of convergence between journalism, popular fiction and academic analysis'. This fusion has the potential to become powerful in future and this focus on popular culture by academics should be warmly welcomed.

Whilst it is notable that many of the books listed above have tended to emerge from within dominant Western cultures, many of the issues that are raised in these publications will be relevant to various other locations, particularly though not exclusively to cultures where a neo-liberal discourse of post-feminism dominates (see, for example, Yang (2007a, 2007b) for a discussion of this discourse in relation to China). Additionally, many of these publications explicitly focus on a more global perspective in addition to focusing on examples from within their own cultures. For instance, as UK-based authors Redfern and Aune (2010: x) point out, 'in an increasingly global society, feminism transcends national boundaries, so we'll ... showcase examples of feminist activism beyond the UK'. Another 2010 publication dedicated to global gender politics which deserves special mention is Kristof and Wudunn's *Half the Sky: How to Change the World*. This volume focuses in particular upon African and Asian countries and sets out a range of examples of twenty-first-century feminist issues and human rights violations including sex trafficking and prostitution, 'honour' killings, physical, sexual and emotional violence, female infanticide, genital cutting and maternal mortality. Women's stories of abuse, neglect and exploitation, gathered by the authors in their roles as political journalists, are told from a plethora of countries including Cambodia, Rwanda, Congo, Iraq, India, Afghanistan, Pakistan, Malaysia, Thailand and China. This volume aims to operate as a rallying cry for all readers to take action to begin to redress such human rights abuses, and there are a series of suggestions for immediate practical action for people worldwide (see Kristof and Wudunn 2010: 279–84).

Coming back to the other titles, Levy (2005) focuses on producing a critique of 'raunch' culture, a culture, that is, where women are expected to behave in openly sexualised ways, and she examines how this sexual behaviour accords with dominant male fantasies of women's behaviour, for example women watching strip shows, watching pornographic movies, engaging in pole dancing and so on. She asks, 'how is resurrecting every stereotype of female sexuality that feminism endeavoured to banish *good* for women?' (2005: 4). Walter (2010) also focuses on this oversexualisation of women in Western cultures and characterises it as part of a return to sexism which needs to be addressed by engaging in direct political action.

One example of such political action which is currently operating is the OBJECT movement based in the UK which targets the mainstreaming of pornography and women's objectification. It is currently the UK's leading organisation campaigning against the culture of sexual objectification. This movement started in response to the large number of lap-dancing clubs that were opening up in city centres. OBJECT has been a very successful political movement so far and has succeeded in getting the UK government to change the law which previously allowed lap-dancing clubs the same planning permission as coffee shops or karaoke bars. One of OBJECT's latest campaigns, reported in the *Guardian* on 15 October 2010, is 'Feminist Fridays', where members target large stores who have refused to move pornographic 'lads' magazines' to the top shelves. OBJECT's political campaigning has resulted in a code of practice being drawn up by the government, recommending top-shelf location for all such magazines so that they are not seen by children. However, this code of conduct is currently voluntary. Feminist activists are entering stores not abiding by the code and covering the front page of those magazines still at eye level with messages on brown-paper bags directly addressing the potential buyer. This includes the following linguistic manifestations: commands: 'Love women hate sexism'; exclamatories: 'Women are human too!!!'; combined statements and commands: 'Women are not objects don't buy this', 'This magazine dehumanizes women don't buy it'; and questions: 'Why isn't this on the top shelf?' (Basu 2010: 1).

Valènti (2007) adopts the overt political aim of encouraging her target audience of young women (roughly aimed at women under 30) to openly call themselves feminists. Valenti's book can be seen as a reaction against the rise of post-feminist discourses and the growth of the 'new right' in the US in particular. Valenti (2007) observes that, within politics, the mass media and conservative organisations in particular, there is currently a persistent trend to attempt to convince the world that feminism is dead, as it is no longer needed. She goes on to argue her position that the 'obsession with feminism's demise is laughable' and illustrates this by drawing on numerous sources from the mainstream US media sources to illustrate how 'feminism is the media's favourite punch bag' (2007: 11) for both national and international political issues:

> The horrors that feminism is supposedly responsible for range from silly contradictions to plainly ludicrous examples. In recent articles, feminism has been blamed for promoting promiscuity; promoting men-hating; the torture at Abu Ghraib; ruining 'the family'; the feminization of men; the 'failures' of Amnesty International … [as well as] an increase in the number of women criminals. (Valenti 2007: 11–12)

Valenti informs her readership that many of them will hold feminist principles but they may well feel reticent to use the word 'feminist' in a self-referential manner because of fear of negative evaluation, a consequence of the pejorative associations that the term 'feminism' and the identity label 'feminist' currently have in mainstream societies. However, she poses the following set of challenging questions to her readers:

> Do you think it's fair that a guy will make more money doing the same job as you? Does it piss you off and scare you when you find out about your friends getting raped? Do you ever feel like shit about your body? Do you ever feel like something is wrong with you because you don't fit into this bizarre ideal of what girls are supposed to look like? Well, my friend, I hate to break it to you but you're a hardcore feminist. I swear. (Valenti 2007: 6)

There are a number of linguistic techniques that Valenti can be observed using in order to engage directly with her audience in a dialogic manner. One of Valenti's techniques which breaks down traditional language and gender stereotypes is the frequent use of expletives throughout her volume. Although stereotypically associated with 'masculine' language (see Chapter 3), Valenti's use of expletives arguably provides an overt way of breaking the stereotype of 'little ladies' (Lakoff 1975) or 'good girls' (Bucholtz 1999a) who do not swear, overtly breaking a persistent, deeply ingrained stereotypical expectation of gendered language in Western cultural practice.

Another of Valenti's (2008) publications, *He's a Stud, She's a Slut and 49 Other Double Standards Every Woman Should Know*, addresses a topic that has previously been closely examined by feminist linguists. Her listings are highly reminiscent of 1980s, Second Wave feminist linguistic studies which examined sexist uses of language (for example, Kramerae and Treichler 1985; Cameron 1985). This 2008 work illustrates, in lay terms, how semantic asymmetries, semantic non-equivalence and other broader issues of gendered discourses within sexual politics, which were a major concern in the 1980s, are still issues where gender inequalities can be clearly seen. Once again, this work uses a similarly informal, colloquial style to directly engage with her audience. Some of her entries include:

He's a politician, she's a fashion plate.
He's angry, she's PMSing.
He's the boss, she's a bitch.
He's dating a younger woman, she's a cougar.
He walks freely, she gets harassed. (Valenti 2008: 54–122)

As a key part of all of her 50 entries, Valenti has a section at the end of each one dedicated to giving explicit, practical suggestions about what the reader should do if they come across such double standards. In reference to the first example in the above list, the 'politician' versus the 'fashion plate', Valenti suggests the following as a course for feminist political action if readers encounter women politicians being focalised through their appearance as opposed to their political skill. The important role played by language can be clearly seen in her advice here:

> When you see a biased article, write a letter to the editor! Send it around to your friends with a note about how gross and sexist it is. When you hear friends talk about political candidates and someone makes a comment about a woman's appearance – speak out! Don't let it go unnoticed. And take the bull by the horns: Look into organisations that promote women's leader- ship and political participation. Encourage your friends to run for office. And wear whatever you damn well please. (Valenti 2008: 57)

Faludi (2008) clearly articulates how, in times of political and social change, traditional gender roles get reinvoked and feminism gets pushed into the back- ground. In *The Terror Dream*, Faludi observes the following media reactions immediately after 9/11:

> Within days of the attack, a number of media venues sounded the death knell of feminism. In light of national tragedy, the women's moment had proved itself, as we were variously informed, 'parochial', 'frivolous' and 'an unaffordable luxury' that had now 'met its Waterloo'. The terrorist assault had levied 'a blow to feminism' or, as a headline on the op-ed page of the *Houston Chronicle* pithily put it, 'No place for Feminist victims in Post 9-11 America'. (Faludi 2008: 21)

Faludi then goes on to articulate how essential feminism is in such political climates. She observes that directly after 9/11, women on US broadcasting networks started to physically disappear – their contributions (both oral and in print) vanished from the media in general. The same finding in the UK written media was also discussed by linguist Litosseliti (2006b) in the days after the attack. She argues that dichotomous gender ideologies of women being 'emotional' in contrast with men being 'objective' result in women being assigned to 'soft' news (such as domestic stories and features) and this ensures that women continue to be associated more with private instead of public spheres. We will come back to this significant issue again in Chapter 3, when discussing femininities and masculinities alongside the notion of feminine and masculine 'social spaces' (Freed 1996).

Although not a linguist by profession, Faludi (2008) makes some very interesting and pertinent observations about language use. She draws attention to politicians strategically referring to nations via the metaphor of 'girls' needing to be rescued, which she insightfully terms 'sex-coded rescue language' (2008: 45). Faludi (2008) observes how the 'nation as girl' metaphor and a focus on women's rights in Afghanistan and Iraq were only highlighted when the US government was attempting to justify war. When the US invaded Afghanistan and Iraq, President Bush focused on the need to 'liberate' Afghan women from their veils, and pictures of veiled women featured heavily in reports on the early stages before the invasion; however, once the invasion had been launched, any focus on women's rights disappeared. As soon as dictators had been overthrown, an interest in gender politics was lost.

Further evidence of a feminist resurgence can be seen in the revival of certain political events which were firmly associated with the Second Wave movement. For instance, in the UK, it is notable that political marches termed Reclaim the Night, where women take to the streets to protest about safety issues after dark in response to sexual assaults, have started to run again. From 2004 these have been reinstated and take place every year in London, as well as in a number of other British cities including Sheffield, Edinburgh and Cardiff. In Ipswich (a town in the east of England), a Reclaim the Night march took place in 2007 in direct protest at the murder by a serial killer of a number of women working as prostitutes. Walter (2010) lists the resurgence of the Reclaim the Night movement as clear evidence that feminist action is on the rise again in the UK.[3]

It is undeniable that early work on language, gender and feminism has achieved much, and the growth of the academic field of feminist linguistics is evidence of its early successes. However, there is still much work to be done, and the aim of this chapter has been to present you with a snapshot of the current state of the field and the crucial wider political backdrop where feminist linguistic research is currently taking place, as well as to present ideas, suggestions and hopefully inspiration as to where research needs to take place in the future. In the remainder of the book we will detail a full range of different linguistic theories and methodologies which can be used to successfully conduct feminist linguistic studies in a variety of different spheres.

Men in/and feminism

In the 1970s and 1980s there was a great deal of discussion about the role of men in feminism in the Western world. Whelehan (1995) argues that, at the height of the Second Wave, women wanted a movement that was independent of men to explore political ground that had been denied to them for so many years. They also wanted a space where men would not dominate the proceedings.[4] Therefore, the term 'feminist' was seen as reserved for women only. The 'separatist' view, as it became known, was, and still is, a source of controversy, revolving especially around the complex question of how feminist change can be brought about without consciousness-raising for men changing men's lives as well as women's.

During the 1970s, pro-feminist men's movements began to emerge which engaged in such consciousness-raising activities. In the UK, such movements were heavily interwoven with socialism and focused on how a critique of patriarchy and the sexual division of labour should also revolve around a critique of capitalism and the social class system. However, Whelehan (1995: 180) draws attention to a double bind faced by heterosexual men, in that just by acknowledging collusion as an oppressor does not stop the oppression or men's individual privilege. She goes on to point out that the emergence of the gay liberation movement was seen as key to commencing a convincing challenge to heterosexist constructions of masculinity, but this in itself draws attention to the problem of heterosexual men who need to find a way of defining themselves 'without seeming to be parasitic upon gay politics or feminism, and thereby find a role that is peculiar to [themselves]' (1995: 181). Seidler (1991) has pointed out that the crucial problem of pro-feminist men's reactions to feminism is one of feeling guilty, which in turn leads to inertia.

Within academia, in the 1980s women set up many consciousness-raising and research groups, which were often seen to be at the cutting edge of political and cultural theory. At that particular moment in time, Second Wave feminism was positively viewed by many within academic institutions and male academics could arguably gain kudos through reading feminist work and engaging with it. Many male academics wanted to join women's groups and to write and teach about feminist theory (see Cameron 2006a). During this time, male academics questioned women's right to own feminism exclusively and many men got involved in debates regarding feminist theory and political labelling. Some male academics called themselves 'feminist', and this led to the coining of the differential and rather awkward terms 'male feminist' and 'female feminist' (see Boone 1990). As Whelehan (1995: 187) points out, so-called 'male feminists' were not satisfied with the terms 'pro-feminist' or 'anti-patriarchal', but as a consequence of their coining they were guilty of constructing 'artificial boundaries around feminism which are counter-productive' to the broader goals of feminism as a political movement. As the status of feminism has changed so much, it is now quite rare for men within academia to choose to position themselves explicitly within feminist theory. However, the influence of these discussions is still felt very strongly in the questioning and critique of gender relations and the representation of gender in many different academic subjects.

While the interest of male academics writing about 'feminism' has become much less popular in the Third Wave movement, and despite populist claims of a 'post-feminist' world, pro-feminist male consciousness-raising groups are still very much in existence. A pro-feminist international organisation known as the White Ribbon Campaign has its own 'International Day for the Eradication of Violence against Women' when white ribbons are worn. It was originally set up by men and targeted specifically at other men in Canada in 1991, following the murder of 14 women engineering students at a university college in Montreal by a male anti-feminist. This movement and the international day are now recognised and actively supported in over 55 countries on every continent. Some countries have a policy of male-only membership, other countries have both men and women as members and white ribbon bearers.

The development of online communities via the Internet has resulted in a recent growth spurt in such organisations. For example, the London Pro-Feminist Men's Group was set up recently with the following aims:

> We're a group of men meeting in London every 2 weeks. The aims of our meetings are:
>
> * to support each other in our personal struggles as men, including our efforts to rid ourselves of sexist behaviour
> * to discuss issues around gender politics generally
> * to plan what kind of action we can take as pro-feminists.
>
> LPFMG, 5 May 2010

Interestingly, and perhaps unsurprisingly, the debate around labelling which preoccupied activists and academic researchers during the Second Wave is still a topic for discussion and debate. A recent example can be seen from the London Pro-Feminist Men's Group's presence on the social networking site Facebook. One potential member questioned the list owner, via electronic communication, as to why the group called themselves the 'London *Pro-Feminist* Men's Group' and not the 'London *Feminist* Men's Group'. The list owner gave the following response on behalf of the founding members:

> London Profeminist Hi! As you may already know there are many and different opinions on the issue of this distinction. If we wanted to give a reason for our choice, we would say that the LPMG chooses to identify itself as 'pro-feminist' instead of 'feminist' cause 'we don't need and we don't want to steal the word from the feminist movement'. This is the opinion of many feminists also and we respect that. Of course, the feminist (or anti-sexist, anti-patriarchist) struggle aims to liberate men also from patriarchy and this is very much where our words and actions tend to contribute. However, it is always good to remind people that the structural inequalities and hierarchies still exist and that being a man in a patriarchal society is in no way the same with being a woman (most of all, in terms of experiences). Men can empathize with let's say the victims of patriarchy, however we should not ever forget that this empathy is a choice (while oppression isn't).
>
> From LPFMG, 23 March 2010

Turning now to slightly different identity labels, in Western cultures, the 'new man', identified as the caring, feminist-orientated man who shares household work and childcare responsibilities with women, was an identity position which has been much derided by the mainstream media. Many commentators in magazines and newspapers reviled the new man as the 'toxic waste of feminism' (Goodwin, cited in Gill 2007: 210). The new man identity has also been referred to by the rather derogatory acronym 'SNAG', standing for Sensitive New Age Guy (see Talbot 1998/2010). The 'new man' was followed almost immediately by the 'new lad', the reinvention of the stereotypical values of the 'macho' man, that is, football-loving, sexist views of women, with perhaps slightly less of the physical prowess and violence of the traditional 'macho' man.

Many of the feminist books published in the last two years take the position that without trying to change men and break down stereotypes and ideologies of masculinities as well as femininities, then Third Wave feminism, or 'reclaimed' feminism (Redfern and Aune 2010), as a political cause, will not succeed in achieving its aims. The involvement of men is seen to be crucial. Banyard (2010) makes a series of compelling arguments for the importance of involving men far more directly in feminist research and political action. This can bring us back once again to hook's assertion that 'feminism is for everybody', and this should be entirely inclusive of men. Banyard (2010) draws attention to illustrative examples of men throughout history, including John Stuart Mill in the UK in the nineteenth century, who dedicated a significant proportion of his political career to feminist campaigning and women's suffrage in particular. She also cites a number of contemporary examples of men who have helped the women's rights movement and the feminist cause. In the Arab world, the early feminists were largely male and men are still involved in the Arab feminist movement (Badran and Cooke 1990).

Banyard also draws attention to the importance of acknowledging the plurality of masculinities and to an academic study by Chambers *et al.* (2004) which documents the significant number of boys in schools who are subjected to homophobic bullying through the use of verbal terms of abuse, including 'gay' being used as a pejorative term. They argue that such bullying has a great deal in common with sexism, and that such constructions of masculinities take place within the 'heterosexual matrix'. Another recent example of political intervention, which on this occasion attempts to deal with the problem of such verbal homophobic bullying, has taken place in a school in London, UK, where a teacher brought in lessons specifically on the topic of how gay men were persecuted through history, including Oscar Wilde and Andy Warhol. They claim this has been successful in 'more or less eliminating homophobic bullying over the last past five years' and these teachers are currently working on sharing this interventionist tactic with numerous other schools (Shepherd and Learner 2010; see also Chapter 6).

Banyard focuses on profiling current activist Jeremy Coutinho, chair of OBJECT, the activist organisation highlighted above (see p. 31). He argues that feminism became an acute issue for men during the 1990s in the UK when lap-dancing clubs started to open up at a rapid rate and magazine culture began to be filled by pornography. He is very clear that such blatant sexism in everyday life is an issue for men just as much as it is for women. Banyard (2010: 229) points out that 'to bring about gender equality one major change we need to make is to redefine what it means to be a man'. She also cites the work of John Anderson, who currently works with young people in London. She reports the view that he expressed to her in an interview regarding the fundamental role that feminism can have in improving the lives of boys and men. He states the following:

I see a lot of young men frustrated by the gender stereotype they are confined to follow. I think feminism offers men the opportunity to fulfil their potential and interests, not those imposed on them. In starkest terms, I think feminism is the solution to countering the machismo culture which is so prevalent in young people in London, and is, I think, one of the main factors behind the terrifying levels of knife crime which kills mostly young men. (Banyard 2010: 234)

In summarising her position that men's involvement is essential to current battles and any future successes of feminism, Banyard makes the following argument:

Feminism helps men. Gender inequality forces them into a mould of dominance, aggression and control ... it is crucial that men get active in feminist campaigns and that gender equality initiatives specifically target men. The very future of feminism depends upon it. (Baynard 2010: 234)

Although she draws upon primarily UK-based examples, the principles behind Banyard's work and the range of different perspectives she offers can arguably be applied to a number of different cultural settings worldwide.

In terms of the crucial issue of redressing the sexual division of labour within the home and childcare imbalances, Redfern and Aune (2010: 134) point out clearly that men whom they term 'feminist dads' are working with mothers to change attitudes and everyday practices. They draw attention to emerging online networks including the blog entitled 'Feminist Dad' and also refer to how 'feminist-minded men' are being welcomed on feminist parenting forums, such as 'Mothers for Women's Lib'. They refer to how men provide childcare at the annual Feminism in London conference in the UK. They draw attention to a series of online blog comments made in 2009 by Hugo Schwyzer, an American academic and writer, as further evidence that feminist fathers are key to changing attitudes to childcare in heterosexual families as well as policies:[5]

Here's what I can say about being a feminist father at this point: men can parent small infants very well, thank you, if they're willing to overcome the programming that says women 'mother' while men 'babysit'. Men can feel an intense bond with a baby and a fierce sense of protectiveness; men can change diapers and wipe up endless amounts of spit-up ... raising babies is not just a women's responsibility. Testosterone is no barrier to tenderness. (Schwyzer, cited in Redfern and Aune 2010: 135)

Thus, despite the discursive pressures examined in work by Sunderland (2006) which shows that men in childcare and parenting magazines are represented as incompetent, some fathers in Britain are taking a much greater role in childcare and are openly adopting a feminist agenda. This now seems to be a good example of where feminist protests about men's involvement in childcare have been mainstreamed and now form the basis of common-sense assumptions.

Beyond equal opportunities

At the start of the second decade of the twenty-first century feminism is clearly not the same as it was in the 1960s, or the 1980s, or ten years ago for that matter, at the turn of the millennium. It is clear that it is more integrated into the expectations of women than it ever was before, but it is also clear that it is not something which many women openly admit to believing in. Feminism also seems to have broadened its horizons from a focus on equal opportunities for women to a recognition that perhaps this is only one stage in an overall strategy. If we argue for equal treatment for women, then what often happens is that women are treated as if they were men. For example, within certain workplaces, it may be difficult for women to mention childcare responsibilities, as this seems to be drawing attention to their difference as women (see Mullany 2007).

One rather telling example of this is taken from a report on equal opportunities within the British prison and police service which found that there was institutional sexism, broadcast in the UK on BBC Radio 4's programme *Woman's Hour*, 13 May 2009; when pressed in a radio interview to give an example of this sexism, the report writer stated that all of the uniforms in the police and prison service were modelled on the male body and women were not given uniforms which were fitted to the female shape. This is an apt example and also an overarching metaphor for the way that equal opportunities have operated at least within Western contexts. Women are allowed to work but they do so only by masquerading as men and by erasing the elements which make them different as women, and that makes them what Eckert (1998) has referred to as 'interlopers' (see also Lakoff 2003; Mullany 2007). This focus on difference does not reduce women's difference to the biological or sexual. However, when women find it necessary to almost deny the demands of responsibilities for children when they take a job, it is clear that equal opportunities as a feminist strategy is not sufficient.

It is also clear that simply focusing on choice is not sufficient. 'A woman's right to choose' whether and when to have children was an important campaign in late twentieth-century Britain but, as Gill (2007) has shown, if the key issues on which we are deciding to exercise our choice are the choice to stay at home and look after children, the choice to take our husband's name and the choice to have an extravagant white wedding in Western cultures, then the notion of choice needs to be scrutinised.

We will explore the significant issue of equal opportunities and going beyond equal opportunities in the remaining chapters of the book, where an agenda for the future of language, gender and feminism will emerge.

3 Theorising gender

An important stage in emancipation is identifying mechanisms of oppression. Before change can even be wanted, what appear to be natural aspects of the everyday lives of women and men have to be exposed as culturally produced and as disadvantageous to women (and ultimately, because of this, some men would say to themselves as well). This means beginning with an understanding of how gender is socially constructed.

Talbot 1998/2010: 117

Feminism, gender and language studies

As we established in Chapter 2, feminism as a political movement, attitudes towards feminism and feminists themselves have changed a great deal in recent years, not only in terms of academic perspectives on the roles of women and men, but also in terms of the way that feminism is viewed within popular culture as a whole. In this chapter, we will provide a detailed theoretical focus on feminism and its interplay with language, building upon the foundational concepts that were introduced in Chapter 1. We will relate the discussion of feminist theory to examples of spoken and written language analysis, including a number of case-study illustrations from particular feminist linguistic studies. It is worth noting that the linguistic researchers to whom we refer may not have explicitly or overtly named themselves as feminist scholars, but we have interpreted their work as feminist in nature, based upon the definition given at the beginning of this volume: a study that has emancipatory aims.

In Chapter 1, we introduced the 'waves' model and stressed the Second and Third Waves in particular, which correlate with the start and subsequent development of feminist language and gender studies. We favour the 'waves' terminology for consistency over the alternatively named 'modern' to 'postmodern' models of feminism. We decided upon this set of terms as we believe that the waves model carries fewer theoretical preconceptions than other choices.[1] Furthermore, the waves metaphor is far more effective in conceptualising the Second and Third Wave as movements which run into one another – these are movements without firm or linear boundaries.

The following bullet-point list presents a very useful summary of the key differences in approaches to language and gender from a Second Wave to Third Wave approach. This will act as an overarching reference point for the theoretical issues surrounding the theorisation of gender that will be focused upon in this chapter (see also Baxter, 2006a):

- Gender has progressed from being conceptualised as something that individuals have, an essential quality acquired through the socialisation process, to something that individuals do/actively perform. From the specific perspective of language, gender is co-constructed *within* interactions.

- Sex and gender were distinguished as biological versus socially constructed categories respectively in earlier approaches, with sex providing a basis for gender. However, now the distinction between sex and gender has been questioned: sex has been seen as constructed and always viewed through a gendered lens (Bem 1993; Hall and Livia 1997b).

- Assumptions that gender pre-exists the interactions and affects the way that the interaction develops are replaced with the view that participants in conversation bring about their gendered identity, thus seeing gendering as a process of emergence, and one that is not completed.

- Presupposing that gender differences exist is replaced by an emphasis on diversity – a range of pluralised gender identities are analysed; similarities between women and men and differences amongst groups of women and amongst groups of men are seen as equally important.

- 'Big' stories about gender are replaced by 'local' explanations, which fits in with wider postmodernist-influenced theoretical positions that 'big stories are bad, little stories are good' (Potter 1996: 23). Researchers have looked 'locally' at how gender is discursively constructed through language in specific 'communities of practice' (Eckert and McConnell-Ginet 1992; see Chapter 4).

- A mainstream focus on men and women as generic categories is expanded to include a turn towards focusing on non-mainstream identities, sexual identities and a focus on heteronormativity as an ideological construct.[2]

- Gender and power: the notion of patriarchy and the assumption that 'women' (as a homogeneous group) are oppressed by 'men' (as a homogeneous group) is supplemented by a focus on the notion of power as fluid and enacted within discourse. Thus, it is possible to focus on the way wider power differences affect women, as well as the way particular power dynamics are acted out in interactions. There is a simultaneous emphasis on the plurality of femininities and masculinities and an emphasis on female agency and discourses of resistance, leading to a much more nuanced view of gender and power.

- Gender and social structuration: Third Wave research emphasises the importance of examining broader social practices and examining gender and power from a macro perspective. Language should be seen as being produced within an ideological system that regulates the norms and conventions for 'appropriate' gendered behaviour. This point is heavily interrelated with a 'discourse turn': a focus upon examining interactions/texts in their much broader social and societal context.

In this chapter, we first define gender and then go on to give detailed illustrations of Second and Third Wave feminist linguistic analyses, and in the process give examples of issues where there are different perspectives from these two waves of feminist research. We examine Second and Third wave perspectives on identity categories, the construction of meaning and variables including power, race, social stratification and sexuality. Finally, we examine gender stereotyping .

Defining gender

As demonstrated above, in recent years, gender has begun to be theorised in more productive ways. Researchers have moved away from a reliance on binary oppositions and global statements about the behaviour of all men and all women, to more detailed and mitigated statements about certain groups of women or men in particular circumstances, who reaffirm, negotiate with and challenge the parameters of permissible or socially sanctioned behaviour (Coates and Cameron 1989; Bergvall *et al.* 1996; Johnson and Meinhof 1997). Rather than seeing gender as a possession or set of behaviours which is imposed upon the individual by society, as many essentialist theorists have previously done (see Butler 1990; Fuss 1989, for a critical overview), many feminists have now moved to a position where they view gender as something which is enacted or performed, and thus as a potential site of struggle over perceived restrictions in roles (Crawford 1995).

Many Third Wave feminist linguists draw upon/adapt the work of Judith Butler, particularly her notion of performativity (Butler 1990, 1993, 1997, 2004). Gender within this type of analysis is viewed as a verb, something that you 'do' in interaction, rather than something which you possess (Crawford 1995). Butler draws on the notion of performativity from speech-act theorists who are concerned with what you do with language (for example, promising, threatening, and so on), but Butler is not simply concerned with this type of performativity and its effects. She brings to this notion of linguistic performativity an Althusserian focus on how the individual is constituted in particular ways by the use of certain styles of language (Althusser 1984). Thus, gender is not a given, but rather a process which one constantly has to perform: gender is a 'doing, an incessant activity performed' (Butler 2004: 1). Gender is constructed through the repetition of gendered acts and varies according to context. Furthermore, Butler points out that our gender identities are not created in isolation by us as individuals. It is important to realise that 'one does not "do" one's gender alone. One is always "doing" with or for another' (Butler 2004: 1). Althusser's work (1984) here is important. Butler draws on the notion of interpellation or 'hailing' to describe the process whereby we as individuals come to be called upon to recognise ourselves as particular types of individuals with particular values, viewpoints and needs/desires.

For example, if, as a woman, you adopt a particular 'girly' tone of voice and accompany this with non-assertive behaviour, simpering and giggling, then you are likely to be constituted by others in the contexts in which you use these styles as (within the work environment) non-competent and (within relationships) as submissive.[3] This type of hegemonic 'feminine' behaviour will also have an impact on how you view yourself and what you think it is possible for you to do.

However, that is not to say that you will consistently use this style in all contexts, or that interpretations of this style by others are universal. Interpretations and evaluations of gender performativity are context- and culture-dependent.

In many readings of Butler's work, gender is seen as almost like a costume that one puts on – the individual chooses what sort of identity they would like to have and simply performs that role.[4] However, social groups constrain individual perceptions of the possibilities available to individuals. Gender is constructed or takes shape over time, *within* interactions, as Holmes and Meyerhoff (2003a: 9) state: 'a gendered dimension to interactions emerges rather than being assumed at the outset'. Whilst it is clear that individuals are sexed as males and females, and that this plays a role in the way that they conceive of themselves, it is largely through interaction that one begins to sense what sort of girl or boy or man or woman it is possible to be and how feminine or masculine it is possible to be within a particular context. It is largely an individual's weighing up of what they think the context will approve of or favour that leads to individuals performing particular types of gender identities. That is not to say that women and men are necessarily such well-behaved subjects, since it is clear that very often individuals will react against the stereotypical expectations of the group, but nevertheless the expectations of others and group expectations are an important part of constructing yourself as a gendered individual.

Therefore, it is clear that institutional and contextual constraints determine the type and form of identity and linguistic routines which an individual considers possible within an interaction. Some theorists have criticised Butler for placing too much emphasis on individual agency to the neglect of powerful societal forces governing our gendered linguistic behaviour (Walsh 2001). However, Butler (1990: 33) has always acknowledged that a 'rigid regulatory frame' is in operation which regulates our behaviour within particular societies and that, if you step outside the boundaries of acceptable interactional patterns, you may be subject to negative evaluation. Nevertheless, as McElhinny (2003) points out, Butler's 'rigid regulatory frame' has been critiqued for being too abstract. It is therefore important to emphasise that the stress on performativity does not suggest for Butler that one can just be anything that one decides to be:

> If I were to argue that genders are performative, that could mean that I thought that one woke in the morning, perused the closet ... donned that gender for the day and then restored the garment to its place at night. Such a wilful and instrumental subject, one who decides *on* its gender, is clearly not its gender from the start and fails to realise that its existence is already decided *by* gender. (Butler 1993: x)

In her later work, Butler further illustrates what she meant by the 'rigid regulatory frame' in response to earlier criticisms. She explicitly articulates that 'persons are regulated by gender ... this sort of regulation operates as a condition of cultural intelligibility for any person. To veer from the gender norm is to produce the aberrant example that regulatory powers (medical, psychiatric, legal to name a few) may quickly exploit to shore up the rationale for their own continuing regulatory zeal' (Butler 2004: 52).

For Butler, gender pre-exists the individual and is negotiated by them in their performance of their identities. This performativity is a constant process rather than something which is ever achieved: 'that this reiteration is necessary is a sign that materialisation is never quite complete, that bodies never quite comply with the norms by which their materialisation is impelled' (Butler 1993: 2). Thus, although the individual is not in control of the production of its gender identity, but rather negotiates with the styles of language available within a particular society and context, there is the possibility of some measure of resistance and hence the possibility of change.

Eckert and McConnell-Ginet (2003), drawing on Butler's work, define gender in the following, useful way:

> Gender is not a part of one's essence, what one is, but an achievement, what one does. Gender is a set of practices through which people construct and claim identities, not simply a system of categorising people. And gender practices are not only about establishing identities but also about managing social relations. (Eckert and McConnell-Ginet 2003: 305)

This more relational view of gender is important, as the gender identity that we construct plays a role in the relations we have with others; it affects those relations. Furthermore, Butler goes on to state that 'in saying that gender is performance we are not saying that it is not real. We are saying, rather, that this personal reality comes not from within, but from our participation in the global performance that is the social order' (Butler 1993: 321). The importance of paying attention to the overarching processes of social structuration that are present in all of our interactions is emphasised here in reference to 'global' performance.

Wodak (1997) also questions the notion of gender, arguing that we should not see it as a separate entity from the wider society. She argues for viewing the relation between gender and society as a dialectical one:

> By only changing the organisational systems, no changes in gender roles will be achieved, and vice versa; by changing gender roles, no significant change of the structures would be achieved. The processes would have to be seen in a dialectical way: both would change each other and would have to be changed themselves (attitudes towards women and men, as well as organisational structures). (Wodak 1997: 108)

Thus, if we see changes in gender roles affecting structures and vice versa, we must see gender as infused with and influenced by the wider society rather than as a variable which needs to be considered in isolation.[5]

This important questioning of the notion of gender does not mean that the category of gender is empty and that there is no such thing as gender difference. For as Freed (1996) argues, despite the fact that the category 'woman' is not one which is homogeneous, that does not prevent people classifying you as a woman and making judgements about you on the basis of that classification (Freed 1996). McElhinny (2003: 24) argues that a Third Wave feminist analysis would 'investigate how categories such as "woman" are created and which political interests the creation and perpetuation of certain identities and distinctions serves'. What has to be reconsidered is the simple binary division between female and male, and also the way that gender operates at the level of a system which has been institutionalised. This system operates in stereotypes and assumptions which have a material impact on groups as well as individuals in terms of what is thought to be appropriate behaviour, as we will show towards the end of this chapter.

The local focus of Third Wave feminism is one of its benefits, but it does make it somewhat difficult to discuss the impact of the values and pressures of the wider society; talking about society above the level of individual communities is more difficult, and it is clear that the wider society as a whole needs to be discussed in terms of the impact it has on practices within communities of practice (McElhinny 2003). Third Wave feminist linguistics tries to maintain a balance between a focus on the local and an awareness of the negotiations at the local level with structures which are largely imposed. Bucholtz (1999a) characterises the theorisation of gender within Third Wave feminism in the following summary:

> [L]anguage users' identities are not essential to their natures but are produced through contingent social interactions; ... those identities are inflected by ideologies of gender and other social constructs; ... speakers, writers and signers respond to these ideologies through practices that sometimes challenge and sometimes reproduce dominant beliefs; and ... as new social resources become available, language users enact and produce new identities, themselves temporary and historical, that assign new meanings to gender. (Bucholtz 1999a: 20)

However, perhaps this quotation draws our attention to the difficulties encountered by Third Wave feminist linguistics, since it does not seem possible to maintain both a focus on contingent social interactions and wider societal notions such as ideologies of gender without some fundamental rethinking of our models of language and gender. Perhaps what needs to be borne in mind when comparing these two different types of feminist linguistic analysis is that they should not be polarised and set in opposition to one another. As Holmes and Meyerhoff (2003a: 15) state, 'It may be useful if those working in language and gender research resolved to avoid using terms such as "essentialist" to dismiss research which focuses on the big picture, research which attempts to identify regularities and makes generalisations about global patterns observable in the relationship between language and gender.'

It is clear that feminist research needs to be able to make generalisations about gender and language. But the generalisations that we make need to be qualified, so that we can recognise that all women and all men do not behave in homogeneous ways. Any move away from 'local' research further towards 'global' generalisation has rather significant methodological implications, and we will discuss these more fully in Chapter 5.

Theorising gender and language through Second and Third Waves

As highlighted in Chapter 1, despite its many achievements, Second Wave campaigning was largely focused on the needs of heterosexual white middle-class women. Second Wave issues of gender relations, including access to contraception and abortion, greater access to work in the public sphere and equal opportunities legislation, are in the process of being achieved by feminist activists in many countries in the world, as Kristof and Wudunn (2010) demonstrate in their inspiring book *Half the Sky: How to Change the World.* This publication details the way that feminist activists have challenged the constraints imposed upon women in the developing world, particularly within African and Asian contexts.

Much of the politicisation process in Western cultures was achieved through the sharing with other women of the 'stories' of the oppression which each one had suffered, and this is a similar strategy to that used by Kristof and Wudunn, who have collected various narratives of women and issues of gender politics in their work as journalists. This strategy can be very effective and works well as a form of consciousness-raising and the development of a strong sense of collective experience. Skeggs (2004: 58) argues that this focus on what she terms 'wounded attachment' 'is premised on the belief that the experience of pain, hurt and oppression provides greater epistemological authority to speak'. In contexts where the theorisation of Third Wave feminism has become dominant, there has been something of a rejection of this 'wounded attachment' focus of the Second Wave by feminist linguists – rather than assuming that oppression leads, for example, to men and women speaking in different ways in the West, with men being direct and forceful, and women being hesitant, polite and apologetic, a Third Wave feminist linguistics questions whether all women and all men within particular cultures speak in the same way.

Second Wave feminism often focused on the level of gender and the individual and arguably did not deal sufficiently with the relation between gender, the individual and the social; thus Scott argues that 'we need to deal with the individual subject as well as social organisation and to articulate the nature of their inter-relationships, for both are crucial to understanding how gender works, how change occurs' (Scott, cited in McElhinny 2007a: 2). The early linguistic work which stemmed from Second Wave feminism tended to focus mostly on the stereotypical speech of middle-class women and made generalisations about women's language on the basis of anecdotal evidence (Lakoff 1975; Spender 1980). Thus, women were assumed to be oppressed in similar ways by men and by a patriarchal social system; research drew attention to the way in which women's use of language exhibited powerlessness and weakness.

Lakoff and Spender both characterised women's speech as hesitant, deferent and polite and suggested that elements such as tag-questions (elements such as 'don't you'? and 'isn't it'? added at the end of the statement) and back-channel behaviour (supportive sounds by the listener such as 'mmm', 'yeah' and 'hmmhmm') were more likely to be found in the speech of women than of men, and that men interrupted women more than vice versa. Deborah Tannen (1991) later challenged this work by suggesting that women's and men's speech were characterised by a difference in style rather than a difference in power and that misunderstandings occurred between men and women because women try to establish empathy or rapport in speech, whilst men try to establish a place for themselves within a hierarchy. Lakoff, Spender and Tannen's Second Wave research assumed that women's and men's language is necessarily different, even though they often disagreed as to the cause of that difference. This focus on global gender differences has been critiqued by a number of feminist linguists who have suggested that what is needed is a form of analysis which is less focused on the individual woman or man and the society as a whole, and more focused on the way that context and the individual mutually shape the way that interaction takes place (Troemel-Ploetz 1998; Bergvall *et al.* 1996).

What has brought about this change in feminism is often called the 'discourse turn', that is, as Eckert and McConnell-Ginet (2003: 4) put it, the move away from 'correlations between linguistic units and social categories of speakers to analysis of the gendered significance of ongoing discourse'. Rather than focusing on words in isolation, instead there is a move to analyse those words in relation to context and the wider community of practice or society. Eckert and McConnell-Ginet go on to say that this discourse turn 'need not mean that we ignore linguistic units like speech sounds or words, but it does require that such units be considered in relation to the functions they serve in particular situated uses and it also requires that the units themselves not be taken as fixed and immutable' (2003: 4). Thus, tag-questions within Third Wave feminist linguistics would not be assumed to have only one function within an interaction, and stress would be laid on the multiple possible interpretations that there might be of particular uses of tag-questions, both for the speaker and the hearer/s (Cameron *et al.* 1989).

Second Wave feminist linguistics was concerned with analysing the inherent meanings of words and often made statements about the abstract meanings of words, constructing dictionaries of sexist language and advising on the avoidance of certain words (Miller and Swift 1982/1989; Kramarae and Treichler 1985). For example, 'gossip' was classified by Second Wave feminist linguists as a term which was used about women's speech in a pejorative way. Thus, if someone described a group of women talking as 'gossiping', it might be considered that the speaker was trying to portray their talk as trivial or malicious. There was also a tendency to assume that certain words or ways of speaking were simply more powerful than others; thus, interrupting was seen as a powerful strategy, and hesitating was seen to be a powerless strategy. In this early theorising it was assumed that the form of an utterance had a clear correlation with the function that it performed. Thus interruption was seen to have only one function and that was to exert power over others. Hesitation was interpreted as displaying submissiveness.

After Cameron *et al.*'s (1989) work on the multifunctionality of tag-questions and Toolan's (1996) important work on the difficulty of assigning clear functions to specific formal linguistic features, the notion that there was a clear link to be made between power and, for example, talking time was made more problematic (see Thornborrow 2002 for further discussion). Instead, whilst it is clear that an individual who interrupts frequently throughout a business meeting may be attempting to claim power for themselves, it is probably the case that someone who interrupts frequently will be viewed negatively by others. It has been shown that those in positions of power often do not have to interrupt others, as their interlocutors will allow them more verbal 'space'; it is those who are trying to claim power who interrupt more (Diamond 1996; Manke 1997). This is not to say that interruption has no relation to power relations, but rather that the relation between power (function) and interruption (form) are very complex and need to be assessed within each context.

Third Wave feminist linguistics focuses on the way that words are made to mean in specific ways and function to achieve certain purposes in particular contexts (Christie 2000). Thus, rather than discussing oppressive global social structures such as patriarchy, Third Wave feminists analyse the way that gender and conflict are managed by women at a local level (Cameron 1998a); more recently this has been with an acknowledgement of the need for an analysis that simultaneously engages in global issues of gender politics in the society under study and the broader question of political action (Baxter 2006c; Cameron 2006a, 2009). Thus, for example, whilst a Second Wave analysis might focus on the use of the generic pronoun 'he' to refer to both men and women, or the derogatory terms used to describe women such as 'bitch' or 'slag', a Third Wave feminist analysis might focus on the way that within a particular context, a certain hesitation and ironic intonation might be considered to be sexist when articulating the word 'chairperson' to describe a female chair.

A further example of the difference of approach to gender in Second and Third Wave feminism is that some Third Wave feminists have called for a reinterpretation of Islamic teachings on women. Rather than simply rejecting Islamic teachings, scholars such as Amina Wadud have shown that many teachings are based on mistranslations or misinterpretation of words with complex meanings. Rather than dismissing the Koran as anti-women, a Third Wave approach would take particular passages and tease more productive meanings out of them. For example, verse 4:34 of the Koran is usually translated as 'As for those from who ye fear rebellion, admonish them and banish them to beds apart and beat them.' Wadud instead argues that a new translation might focus on other meanings of the word here translated as 'beat' so that a more complex interpretation of the passage might read: 'As for women you feel are averse, talk to them persuasively; then leave them alone in bed (without molesting them) and go to bed with them (when they are willing)' (Wadud, cited in Kristof and Wudunn 2010: 169). This more nuanced way of bringing to the surface potential meanings within sometimes recalcitrant texts may lead to more positive teachings on women coming to the fore.

Another illustration might be the debate within feminist circles about the term to use for certain ritual practices in relation to female genitals. Second Wave Western feminist theorists in the 1980s attacked the cutting out of the clitoris and labia (excision) and the sewing up of the vagina (infibulation) of young girls in Somalia, Senegal, Yemen and other African countries (for an account, see Hirsi Ali 2007). They characterised this ritual practice as barbaric, as it is performed without anaesthetic and with only rudimentary knives or scissors. This practice was called female circumcision by supporters of the practice as it seemed to show that it was part of a woman's coming of age, just as male circumcision is. Some 130 million women have undergone this ritual (Kristof and Wudunn 2010). Western feminists argued that it should be termed Female Genital Mutilation (FGM) to show that it was not on a par with male circumcision, but involved an attempt to suppress female sexual desire (see Lewis and Mills 2003). However, many African feminists resented these Western interventions and argued that women who had not been cut would not be able to marry, because they would not be seen as clean. As Kristof and Wudunn (2010) have shown it is only recently with the move to identify this practice using the more neutral term 'genital cutting' that the practice is starting to be combated by African women themselves.[6] It is only by the very tactical naming of practices and embedding resistance within the communities themselves that they can be challenged.

However, whilst this local focus helps women to describe practices which discriminate against them, Third Wave feminists have thus far found it somewhat difficult to refer effectively to global, structural and systematic forms of discrimination, despite a commitment to exploring gender and social structuration. However, this is precisely what needs to be developed in as systematic a way as possible, if the discipline is to move forward. Kristof and Wudunn (2010) have shown that it is only by focusing on a local problem within a particular context that feminist activity can be effective. As Cameron argues (2006a: 3): 'looking locally at the relationship between language and gender in specific cases needs to be combined with "thinking globally" about the workings of gender as an overarching system of social organisation'. Gender will not be the same system throughout the world, but it is important that we fuse elements of the generalisations made at the global level from Second Wave feminism with the Third Wave feminist concern with local instantiation of gender differentiation.

Third Wave feminism is arguably less focused on the speech of individual speakers, but, rather, analyses the way that practices are gendered, and this provides good illustrations of how considering social structuration can be effective. For example, Third Wave feminist linguists analyse the way that particular institutions develop practices which are themselves gendered. Using the community of practice (CoP) framework,[7] Holmes and Stubbe (2003) assert that CoPs within workplaces can be interpreted as gendered, leading to particular feminine or masculine speech styles being the norm in particular contexts, depending upon the particular workplace's culture. They assert that, in certain workplaces which they term 'feminine', there is a greater informality, a greater 'leakage' of the home into the workplace and more small talk permitted. In 'masculine' workplaces, there is a higher level of formality and less small talk is permitted. In these differently gendered work environments, women and men may adjust their linguistic behaviour towards the norm, so that women working in an IT company that has a more traditionally masculine speech style may tend to use more masculine language, and men working in a more traditionally feminine workplace, such as nursing, may tend to use more feminine language, though on other occasions women and men may well resist the norms for particular workplaces and establish speech styles of their own (see Holmes and Schnurr 2006).

There is a focus within this type of Third Wave theorising on the complex negotiations undertaken by women and men with gendered domains (those sets of linguistic routines or contexts which appear to be gendered) and gendered stereotypes of what it is assumed that women and men can do (that is, women should be co-operative, men should be competitive). In this way, Third Wave feminist analysis makes it possible to analyse women's and men's language, without assuming that all women are powerless. Thus, Third Wave feminist linguistics examines, for example, the language of women who adopt primarily masculine forms of speaking in the public sphere. However, rather than just focusing on the individual, this form of analysis also examines the role of context and broader social forces on the individual, in that these ways of speaking may be judged by others in wider society as incompetent, aggressive, unprofessional and unfeminine.[8]

Third Wave feminist linguistics is therefore concerned with moving the analysis of gender and language away from the individual alone towards an analysis of the individual in relation to social groups who judge their linguistic behaviour and also in relation to hypothesised gendered stereotypes and analysing the way individuals react to norms which are assumed to be in place within institutions which are gendered in some way.

When theorising gender, Third Wave feminist linguistics does not assume that women are a homogeneous grouping and in fact stresses the diversity of women's speech. For example, Eckert (2000) analyses the differences between the language use of different groups of girls in a high school in America, drawing on the categories and groupings that they themselves use, such as 'jocks' and 'burnouts' (see Chapter 5 for further discussion). Henley (1995) and Bucholtz (1996) analyse the way that black American women's speech does not necessarily accord with the type of speech patterns described by Lakoff and Spender, since there are different linguistic resources available, signalling potentially different affiliations.

The essays in Coates and Cameron (1989) and in Bergvall *et al.*'s (1996) volume, as well as more recent collections including Bucholtz *et al.* (1999), Bucholtz (2004), McElhinny (2007b) and Pichler and Eppler (2009), all stress the way in which women's language differs according to context and other factors such as social stratification, ethnicity and regional and/or national affiliations. Even the notion of the status of the variable itself has been questioned. For example, Bucholtz (1999a: 8) has argued that, in Second Wave feminism, 'locally defined groupings based on ongoing activities and concerns were rarely given scholarly attention; if they were, members were assigned to large-scale categories of gender, race, ethnicity and class'. Thus, these large-scale categories are now questioned, so that rather than gender being seen as a stable unified variable, to be considered in addition to race or class, gender is now considered as a variable constrained and constituted by them and in turn defining them in the context of local conditions.

Gendered identity categories

Whereas Second Wave feminist analysis focused on 'women' as an identity category and tried to describe the way that identity was constituted for particular women, Third Wave feminism has turned away from these more established identity categories to an analysis which focuses on 'a whole set of identity features (being a manager, someone's mother, a sensible person)' which might be potentially relevant (Swann 2002: 49). Furthermore, identities are now seen as plural and potentially conflicting, even within a specific individual, in a particular interaction.

The importance of masculinity and femininity as two sides of the same coin can be clearly seen in our discussion of gendered identity categories that takes place below. However, for a long time studies of women's speech styles predominated during the Second Wave. As part of the Third Wave, studies focused solely on masculinities emerged. Although a focus on women's gendered identities through speech styles during the Second Wave was seen as logical in terms of pushing the feminist agenda and redressing the balance, feminist linguistic researchers including Johnson (1997) drew attention to the fact that, although masculinity is often commented on, there is a lack of empirical linguistic study on masculinities. Studies have thus grown since the late 1990s. Coates (2003: 54) argues that it is important to analyse masculine identity construction alongside femininity; she states that 'masculinity is meaningful only when it is understood in relation to femininity'. Masculinity has often been posited as the direct opposite of femininity. As Mills (2003a: 188) points out, one of the defining features of masculinity is seen to be aggression, which is often considered to be a biological part of being male (caused by testosterone), rather than a set of characteristics which are acquired in a complex negotiation between the individual and what they hypothesise to be the values of their communities of practice and the wider society. Masculinity is often described in terms of battle and warfare.

Cameron (2009: 12) observes that over the last 20 years both popular discourses and expert discourses have talked about masculinity being 'in crisis', and during the same period there has been the development of the masculine identity categories of the 'metrosexual' in Western societies and 'the lad' in Britain. This so-called 'crisis' in masculinity has often been attributed to social changes in employment patterns and women's increasing involvement in the public sphere, together with the impact of feminism. However, Whelehan (2000: 61) also argues the following: 'While it is true that the new lads are assuredly the product of identity crises, it is not just generated by feminism, but also by gay liberation and anti-racist movements, which act as a reminder of what mainstream male culture, such as big budget competitive sport, regularly excludes.'

Cameron (2009) points out that this has encouraged gender and language researchers to focus explicitly on the performance of masculinities in talk in order to give 'a more nuanced account of how contemporary men understand themselves as gendered beings' (2009: 12). For example, Preece (2009) looks at a group of 'lads' from different ethnic and social backgrounds, categorised as 'non-traditional' occupants of university places. She explores how they construct themselves in a higher education setting in the UK. She found that this group performed hegemonic masculinity in response to the relative lack of status that they experienced in a non-traditional social space thanks to their family backgrounds. She concludes that, although 'laddish' behaviour is seen as a barrier to learning in schools and in higher education, this issue is under-explored. She concludes that it is possible that non-elite, 'widening participation' students from underprivileged backgrounds may still be subject to negative evaluation for 'laddish' behaviour, whereas elite students may be better able to get away with 'laddishness' as they already have so much cultural capital within the higher education arena.

As another illustration, in Benwell's (2005) focus-group study on contemporary masculinities in relation to 'lads' magazines' (see also Chapter 5), she was interested in investigating the reception of these magazines by real male readers. In the two groups of young men that were interviewed she found contradictions between openly expressed negative reactions/dismissals of the magazines and the expression of far more positive attitudes by exactly the same informants, who also appeared to be 'both entertained and highly invested in defending the magazines from implicit charges of sexism or homophobia' (Benwell 2005: 167). Some of the 'lads' also echoed the opinions of the magazine editors who have been critiqued for being lowbrow, trashy and immature by other areas of the media. Her conclusions demonstrate that, even when male readers openly reject the magazines, there is an 'adoption and ventriloquization of discourse' which works to reveal to the analyst 'a more complex, ambivalent and "performative" alignment to the values of "laddish" masculinity than is proclaimed "on the record"', during the actual talk elicited (Benwell 2005: 168).

From within language and sexuality research, Queen has shown that lesbian speech is often produced in a parodic, ironic playing with hypothesised stereotypes of 'straight' feminine speech and masculine speech (Queen 1997). Halberstam (1998), in her analysis of masculine women, has tried to prise apart the relation between masculinity and men and has shown that, rather than stereotypes being fixed and either accepted or rejected by individuals, they are played with, parodied and used for particular strategic ends, and in the process of being changed and ironised by individuals, they are inevitably globally changed (see Chapter 6).

Third Wave feminist linguistics does not tend to make global statements about men's identities or women's identities through their language use but rather focuses on a more *punctual* analysis, that is one which can analyse the way that one's gendered identity varies from context to context. However, Swann has argued that this contextual focus in relation to variables has almost invalidated the notion of the variable; she argues, 'if gender identity is something that is done in context, this begs the question of how an analyst is able to interpret any utterance in terms of masculinity (or working-class, white, heterosexual masculinity). How does an analyst assess whether a speaker is doing gender, or another aspect of identity?' (Swann 2002: 48).

What Swann goes on to argue is that, rather than seeing Third Wave (or as she favours, 'post-modern') feminism as a simple reaction to Second Wave feminist linguistics, we need instead to see the way in which Third Wave feminism depends on earlier feminism; the contextualised studies are interesting 'partly because they qualify, or complexify, or introduce counter-examples' (Swann 2002: 60). Thus, the localised studies of gender should be seen against the background of the earlier global (and problematised) claims of Second Wave feminism, which they can perhaps help to modify and temper.

In order to integrate the Second Wave findings with Third Wave approaches, some researchers argue that you can use the findings of the older studies as useful starting points for research (Holmes 2000; Holmes and Stubbe 2003; Holmes 2006; Mullany 2007; Schnurr 2009). Arguably, these earlier findings provide a window onto the deeply entrenched stereotypical norms of women's and men's speech styles. We are following Mills (2003a: 184) here in defining a stereotype as being based upon 'a feature or set of behaviours which may have occurred within that community, but the stereotype is one noticeable form of behaviour which is afforded prototypical status'. These stereotypes play powerful roles in assessments of our fellow interactants' linguistic behaviour: 'stereotypes of gender, developed in interaction between the individual and the society as a whole, and within specific communities of practice, inform individual choice of linguistic style, strategy, and content, either in terms of reaffirming or challenging those stereotypes in relation to someone's assumptions about one's own gendered identity' (Mills 2003a: 190).

The speech patterns from the older studies can be viewed as reflecting societal expectations and norms of appropriate gendered behaviour. If speakers fail to stay within the boundaries of gendered speech norms, Butler's (1990: 33) 'rigid regulatory frame', then they may well be subject to negative evaluation or abuse. Table 3.1 brings together the findings of a whole range of studies on language and gender research from the 1970s, 1980s and early 1990s. It has been used frequently in contemporary Third Wave research as a starting point to see deeply entrenched societal stereotypes and norms in action. So if, for example, a woman is direct, competitive and assertive, she may well be subject to negative evaluation for being overly aggressive, bossy, bolshy and unfeminine (see Lakoff 2003; Mullany 2007; Baxter 2010). This approach, where the blending together of Second and Third Wave approaches can be clearly seen, tends to be favoured by researchers working in the fields of sociolinguistics and linguistic anthropology in particular. The different types of linguistic perspectives on assessing the interplay between language and gender and how this relates to feminism will be fully explored in Chapter 4, where we detail the various approaches that can be taken when conducting empirical research on gender and language from a feminist perspective.

Table 3.1 Widely cited features of 'feminine' and 'masculine' interactional style

Feminine	Masculine
indirect	direct
conciliatory	confrontational
facilitative	competitive
collaborative	autonomous
minor contribution (in public)	dominates (public) talking time
supportive feedback	aggressive interruptions
person-/process-oriented	task-/outcome-oriented
affectively oriented	referentially oriented

Source: Holmes and Stubbe 2003: 574.

In addition to gendered speech styles, because of associations between women and men and particular contexts, activities within those contexts are considered to be themselves feminine or masculine, and this gendered nature of the contexts and the activities can make it difficult for men to perform in those contexts seen to be feminine and for women to perform in contexts seen as masculine. Philips (2003: 258) argues that 'in activities conceptualised as public ideologically, men are talking and women aren't'.

To illustrate, Holmes (2006: 13) has discussed gendered speech styles as part of a more overarching notion of 'gendered behaviours', which she identifies as 'the ways in which people exploit gendered resources'. These resources are accumulated over time but are subject to constant change. She notes that 'the culture of a workplace is constantly being instantiated in ongoing talk and action; it develops and is gradually modified by large and small acts in regular social interaction within ongoing exchanges. Larger patterns are established through the accumulation of repeated individual instances, and each instance gains its significance against the backdrop of the established norms' (2006: 15). For Holmes, this does not mean that we conform our speech to norms which are set in stone, but that 'an utterance may be interpreted as significantly "gendered" in one context but as unmarked in another' (2006: 17).

Holmes goes on to note how in the workplace assertiveness and effective leadership are often associated with masculinity; however, this leads to a problem, as if you call assertiveness masculine, women have to go against their gender in order to be assertive. She argues that 'forms such as [imperatives] index masculine rather than feminine styles of leadership largely because they are forms which are commonly used by more powerful to less powerful people' (Holmes 2006: 38). However, imperatives are not always associated with assertiveness (for example, 'have a cake'). She argues that, 'more feminine ways of interacting at work, although often paid lip service, and apparently valued when men adopt them as aspects of their management style, are often regarded negatively when used by women in many organisations' (2006: 66). Because women use strategies which are seen as masculine they 'de-gender them and recategorise them as neutral tools of leadership discourse, rather than exclusively male discursive resources' (2006: 211).

Mullany (2007) has shown that when women business managers are assertive in their language use within certain professional workplaces by being direct and unmitigated in their speech styles, their behaviour is judged to be threatening and unfeminine by both male and female colleagues. This is arguably why some women, as Crawford has shown, rather than being assertive, decide to temper their speech by using politeness strategically:

> '[U]nassertive' speech, rather than being a (female) deficiency in social skills, may reflect a sensitivity to the social impact of one's behaviour. Tentative and indirect speech may be a pragmatic choice for women. It is more persuasive, at least when the recipient is male, less likely to lead to negative attributions about personality traits and likeability, and less likely to provoke verbal attack. (Crawford 1995: 68)

Thus, rather than asserting that women are more polite or indirect than men, Third Wave feminist linguists argue that women engage in a complex process whereby they assess others' stereotypical beliefs about gender and then tactically adopt strategies which will be most likely to achieve their ends; and some of those strategies may well be ones stereotypically associated with feminine language.

McElhinny (1998) has analysed the language of women police officers in Pittsburgh and found that they feel obliged to adopt particular masculine ways of speaking simply to appear to be doing their job in a professional way. They adopt what she calls 'an economy of affect' because disinterestedness is demanded of police officers by the public, since it signifies authoritativeness and impartiality. McElhinny argues that:

> Women who move into powerful and masculine institutions sometimes adopt the interactional behaviour characteristic of these institutions, which might disappoint some feminists. But it seems clear that who we think can do certain jobs changes more rapidly than expectations about how these jobs should be done. The process by which women enter a masculine workplace necessarily includes some adoption as well as adaptation of institutional norms. (McElhinny 1998: 322)

Walsh (2001) examined the language of women working within masculinist or male-dominated environments, for example women priests, MPs and environmental campaigners. She has found that women within institutions are often viewed very negatively and if they use direct, confrontational language they are often criticised (Walsh 2001). Shaw (2002) has also analysed the language use of women MPs and has shown that whilst women are very able to adopt the type of aggressive formalised parliamentary debating techniques which have been developed by male MPs, they may be judged differently from men when they do so. She has also shown that women MPs tend to adhere to the speaking rules very strictly, observing parliamentary forms of address, protocol and etiquette, whereas the male MPs often manage to achieve certain advantages for themselves by breaching the rules.

In Mills' (2006) work on performance anxiety, she demonstrated that female academics tended to admit to suffering more performance anxiety than male academics when giving conference papers, because public speaking is for many seen as 'masculine' behaviour. Since performance anxiety is largely brought about because of feelings of inadequacy in relation to perceptions of what is expected within a particular role, and all of the women interviewed were competent academics, the gendering of public speaking as masculine arguably played a role in these women's perceptions of the level of fit between themselves and their role. Thus, the gendering of the context as a whole is seen to play a major role in the way that individuals style their speech and view themselves in relation to their work environments. Mills (2006: 78) states that 'what seems to play a major role in the variation in gender performance is the degree to which hypothesised stereotypes of gendered behaviour within particular gendered contexts lead to assumptions about our own position within the academic community and within the public sphere'. (See also Sznycer's (2010) work on the speech of assertive female tennis players.)

Baxter argues that:

> [T]he female tendency to censure their own sex for 'standing out' is one potential reason why women sometimes find it hard to adopt authoritative or leadership positions in later life. This is not viewed as a deficiency in the female character, or even as an effect of complex male/female sociali-sation into different subcultures. Rather socio-cultural and educational discourses combine to position females in such a way that they are less likely to adopt authoritative positions as speakers than males. (Baxter 2006b: 176)

If there are discourses which suggest to girls that they should be co-operative and friendly perhaps it is true that girls must 'be taught how to deconstruct the gendered power relationships assumed within many social and educational discourses. In short, girls will need to learn *how* to talk their way to the top' (Baxter 2006b: 176).

Thus, all of these studies suggest that women, when entering primarily mascu-line environments, adopt the language styles prevalent in those institutions, and those styles themselves are both an indicator of masculinity and also of profes-sionalism. McElhinny (1998: 332) states that 'masculinity is not referentially (or directly) marked by behaviours and attitudes but is indexically linked to them (in mediated non-exclusive probabilistic ways)'.

Freed (1996), in her analysis of the language styles of intimate conversa-tion, suggests that masculinity and femininity should be seen as characteristic of the context or situation, rather than an attribute of individuals. She argues that intimate self-disclosing conversation is associated with stereotypical femi-ninity and therefore when males engage in such intimate conversations, they may tend to display the same 'feminine' speech styles as women.[9] Thus, these Third Wave feminist analyses are interested in analysing the way that masculinity and femininity can be seen to exist at an institutional level, linked in some ways to particular institutional contexts rather than simply at the level of the individual. They can be associated stereotypically with attributes such as professionalism and competence.

Furthermore, we should see women's adoption of masculine dominant forms as strategic and perhaps argue that women's adoption of positions of institu-tional status may result in the use of language styles which are characterised by a different approach to 'doing power'. Thus, as Diamond has argued in her analysis of group dynamics in a group of psychotherapists, in certain contexts, those in positions of institutional authority in fact do not use direct commands and assert-iveness, preferring to use indirectness (Diamond 1996).[10] Third Wave feminist linguistics forces us to reconsider the way that we think that power is exercised through language.

Power

Since the inception of the research field of language and gender studies, a great deal of attention has been paid to the crucial role that power relations play within feminist language and gender investigations. Indeed, theorising power is an essential part of the discipline. Second Wave feminists tended to see power as something which was restrictive and which was imposed on individuals. In recent years, however, many feminist researchers from across a variety of disciplines have drawn upon the influential work of social theorist Michel Foucault (1972, 1981) in attempting to describe exactly how power relations work and how they can be conceptualised. Most Third Wave feminist linguists have been heavily influenced by Foucault's theorisation of power and have embraced certain tenets of his work. From a Foucauldian-influenced perspective, researchers including Thornborrow (2002), Baxter (2003), Mills (2003a) and Mullany (2007) have utilised the metaphor of describing power as a 'net' or a 'web', rather than as a possession that an individual speaker may have. Power, from this perspective, is something that is fluid and needs to be enacted within interaction; it is not simply something that one person 'possesses' in relation to another. Power should instead be seen as enacted and contested in every interaction. It becomes a much more mundane, material and everyday element. Foucault's analysis is essentially a bottom-up approach; that is, examining the way that power differences manifest themselves in everyday experience, rather than examining the abstract and intangible way that power relations are imposed from above.

As a consequence of this conceptualisation of power, there is now a focus upon the local management of power relations, the way that individuals negotiate with the status which they and others have been allotted or which they have managed to achieve, and which within particular contexts they can contest or affirm, through their use of language and through their behaviour. Many feminist theorists draw a distinction between a 'fixed' institutional status, that is, the status that you are allocated through your position within an institution, often represented by a particular title, such as an official, formal job title (such as professor, chief executive officer, sales and marketing manager, etc.), and 'local' status, that is, the position that you manage to negotiate because of your verbal skill, confidence, concern for others, 'niceness' and so on. Whilst these two elements are clearly interconnected, it is now often the local, enacted status which is focused on by Third Wave feminist theorists in general (Manke 1997; Diamond 1996) and linguistics researchers in particular (for example, Baxter 2003, 2010; Mills 2003a; Mullany 2007, 2008).

However, this move away from the analysis of a fixed institutional rank to that of local status, whilst important in challenging the characterisation of women as powerless speakers, means that feminists no longer concern themselves so much with the way that institutional rank and gender relate, and the way that the basis on which local rank is negotiated may be heavily determined by stereotypes of gender and gendered practices. This means that the analysis of the speech of men and women in positions of authority may be in danger of focusing only upon the way that their speech is negotiated at the local level and will not consider the way that particular styles are authorised with reference to factors outside the local context.

Cameron (1998a) argues that a more useful approach to the analysis of power and gender is to focus less on unchanging, unequal relations between men and women but rather on the resources available to speakers in particular positions to draw upon strategically. This approach has the following advantages:

> [It] treats the structural fact of gender hierarchy not as something that must *inevitably* show up in surface features of discourse, but as something that participants in any particular conversation may, or may not, treat as relevant to the interpretation of utterances. Furthermore, it insists that where assumptions about gender and power are relevant, they take a form that is context-specific and connected to local forms of social relations: however well founded they may be in structural political terms, global assumptions of male dominance and female subordination are too vague to generate specific inferences in particular contexts, and thus are insufficient for the purposes of discourse analysis. (Cameron 1998a: 452)

Whilst it is important not to overgeneralise about men and women, as we have stressed at various points, when we focus on the particular ways that men and woman interact, we must nevertheless see that those structural inequalities, and the stereotypes that we hypothesise on the basis of our knowledge of these inequalities, do play a role in the way that the interaction takes shape.

Because of the change in focus in relation to power, there has been a move away from the analysis of subordinated women. Bucholtz argues that in the past 'much of the scholarship in language and gender has been what might be called "good-girl research" – studies of "good" (that is normatively female – white straight middle-class) women being "good" (that is normatively feminine)' (Bucholtz 1999a: 13). Now rather than analysing women's indirectness or lack of assertiveness, many linguists focus on strong women speakers and women's resistance to masculine forms of speech, such as interruption or aggressiveness (Mills 1999; Sznycer 2010).

Where many earlier studies falter in the analysis of the relationship between language, power and gender is in the assumption that there is a simple relation between them. Although it may be possible to make generalisations about the types of language which will be produced when there are differences of power and status, there is clearly no simple link between, for example, interruption and power difference (Thornborrow 2002). Many Second Wave theorists assume that because males generally have more status within a particular community that they will necessarily interrupt more, because interruption is the prerogative of the powerful. Whilst there is a stereotypical element of truth in this assertion, the results of the research are far more complex and often go against this hypothesis, both that there is a clear correlation between power and interruption and, following on from that, that males interrupt females more frequently (Chan 1992). However, if males in a particular interaction do interrupt female interactants more, or vice versa, then that may well be significant in gender terms within that interaction.

Eckert and McConnell-Ginet (2003) focus upon the way that we come to understand our position in the pecking order in a group through the way that our contributions to the ongoing talk are responded to. They state:

> A person's contribution to an ongoing discussion is determined not simply by the utterance the person produces, but by the ways in which that utterance is received and interpreted by others in the conversation. Beyond that conversation, the force of an utterance depends on what people do with it in subsequent interactions. Is it quoted? Is it ignored or disparaged? How is it interpreted? The force of an utterance is not manifest in the utterance itself, but in its fate once it is launched into the discourse / once it begins its 'discursive life'. (Eckert and McConnell-Ginet 2003: 92)

This view of power is quite different from the early feminist analysis of oppression, which is more commonly referred to as the power/dominance approach (see Coates 1998; Talbot 1998/2010; Sunderland 2006). Analyses of interruptions were the focus of much attention in Western gender and language research in the 1970s and 1980s (for example, Zimmerman and West 1975; Fishman 1980; Tannen 1984, 1989). Eckert and McConnell-Ginet (2003) point out that, although interruptions can often seem as if they are a powerful conversational strategy, in reality, they may not be very effective:

> People who interrupt constantly ... may not necessarily become powerful, but they render (at least temporarily) powerless those they interrupt. The raw display of power in interruption, though, is a very immediate form of domination and as such is easily recognised. And with recognition comes a loss of that very power. The person with the greatest power is the person who does not 'have to' interrupt the person to whom others ceded the floor willingly, and interruption can suggest not so much dominance itself but a need to establish dominance. (Eckert and McConnell-Ginet 2003: 114)

Early work by Lakoff (1975), Zimmerman and West (1975) and Spender (1980) on interruptions was very important in establishing a link between styles of talk which were seen to be stereotypically masculine and dominant, but what Eckert and McConnell-Ginet (2003) have subsequently shown is that simply using language styles which aspire to power is not enough to be powerful. Instead they have argued that we need to be very careful when we seem to be analysing gender-polarised behaviour. They make the following, crucial argument:

> It may well be that women in many communities are constrained to cloak competition in the guise of co-operation whereas men are often under pressure to present their search for intimate connections in the form of independent self aggrandisement. Thus surface style may indeed often look gender polarised ... But the deeper substance of people's aims and motives cannot be read off so easily, nor is it likely that aims and motives will prove neatly dichotomised. (Eckert and McConnell-Ginet 2003: 127)

Lakoff (2003: 162) has shown how a concern with power is important in femi-nist lingusitics from a lexical perspective, since she has found that 'English has many words describing women who are interested in power, presupposing the inappropriateness of that attitude'. She focuses on terms such as 'henpecked' and 'pussy whipped', where the woman in question is seen to be attempting to exert power over men when in a position of powerlessness. She notes that in discus-sions of women aiming for public office, these notions of the inappropriateness of women in power often surface, resulting in women being termed 'ambitious', which has negative connotations. Her analysis of the response to Hillary Rodham Clinton's campaign for the Senate and for the presidency is striking in that her gender was constantly foregrounded (see also Romaniuk 2009 for discussion of Rodham Clinton's campaign for the US presidency).

Tannen (2003: 179) argues that 'gender identity is negotiated along the dual, paradoxical related dimensions of power and connection', and nowhere can this be more clearly seen than in the analysis of family relations. In the West, there is an assumption that, within the family, relations need to be very close and egal-itarian; however, Chinese and Japanese families are generally far more clearly hierarchical (for example on the basis of age) but they are also extremely close. Within Western thinking, hierarchical relations cannot be intimate. However, in Japan 'power is understood to result from an individual's place in a network of alliances' (Tannen 2003: 182).

In Ochs and Taylor's (1992) study of the role of American fathers in the family, they showed that the mothers in their studies who had primary care of the children often got the children to report to their father about their day when the father returned home from work. This reporting positioned the father as in some senses the arbiter of this information. Tannen (2003) gives an example of a woman who tells her husband about a problem at work, expecting to receive some sympathy but her husband thinks that she is asking for advice. She suggests that 'these clashing rituals result in mothers finding themselves one down in the family hierarchy without knowing how they got there' (2003: 187). However, instructive though this example is of the way hierarchies can become established in families, we need to be very wary about making generalisations about family life on the basis of a few anecdotes. There are a whole range of inter-, cross- and intra-cultural family issues in other settings and global locations that also need to be explored.

What arguably makes this analysis by Tannen perceptive, however, is her awareness of the fact that 'what has been accurately identified as a matter of negotiating power is also simultaneously and inextricably a matter of negoti-ating connection' (Tannen 2003: 187). She analyses several family exchanges between mothers, fathers and children and notes that even when 'both mother and father espouse an ideology of equal co-parenting and wage earning, in their ways of speaking, the mothers position themselves as primary childcare providers and their husbands as breadwinners' (Tannen 2003: 200). Thus the analysis of linguistic choices in parenting discourse is of crucial importance for women and men and the perpetuation of traditional sex-roles in all cultures.

Goodwin (2006: 230) analyses the way that girls handle conflict in play and asserts that it is important that we focus on aggression in girls and women: 'conflict is negatively valued and it is often viewed by feminist researchers as an alternative to the cooperative interaction which is argued to typify female interaction'. Goodwin (2003: 243) argues that 'conflict is as omnipresent in the interaction of females as in that of males'. Thus, when we analyse the way that power is enacted within conversation we need to be acutely aware of our preconceptions about women and men.

Language, gender and social identities

It is now commonly agreed within a Third Wave approach that it is essential to consider the relationship between sexuality, gender and language in order for feminist language and gender research to be comprehensive (Cameron and Kulick 2003; Sauntson 2008). Cameron (2009) rightly points out that viewing gender and sexuality as interdependent is not in itself something new, but since the 1970s there have been social and political developments across societies which have resulted in the study of language, gender and sexuality rapidly increasing. This increase has been particularly rapid since the late 1990s. There are two societal developments in particular to which Cameron draws our attention as accelerating this focus. The first is the 'oversexualisation' of public culture discussed in Chapter 2 and the second is a shift in social attitudes towards newer understandings of sexuality, especially that being/identifying as gay, lesbian, bisexual, transgendered or heterosexual is a key part of one's identity (Baker 2008a).

Language and sexuality provides researchers with a very broad area of theorisation and analysis. It is not just a question of who one chooses to have sex with. There has been some debate amongst researchers as to exactly what should be studied. Cameron and Kulick (2003: xviii) argue that it is important not to focus solely on questions of identity when discussing sexuality. We will explore these debates and issues fully in Chapter 6, where we focus on the broader field of sexuality as a burgeoning area of current study.

As highlighted in Chapter 1, there has been little direct consideration of the importance of race and social stratification as factors which interact and intersect with gender, a result of the focus in mainstream Western feminist theory until relatively recently on the behaviour of white middle-class women's values and needs; this has resulted in the relegation of other groups of women to the status of minority groups (Kristof and Wudunn 2010; Lewis and Mills 2003; Sandoval 1991; Mohanty 1984; Minh-ha 1989; Frankenberg 1993; Afshar and Maynard 1994). Within feminist theory in general, there has been a shift in focus, from assuming that race necessarily makes a difference to language production and interpretation, to working with the idea that race can, but may not, make a difference.

Race and ethnicity are no longer discussed in the rather 'blanket' way that they were in the past; first, because there are innumerable differences in the cultural groups which are labelled as racially similar, and second, because of the challenging of the stability of the term 'race' itself, since this seems to be embedded in a nineteenth-century 'scientific' racist ideology (Jarrett-Macaulay 1996). What feminist theory is now focused on is the specificity (and perhaps also the instability) of difference, and challenging the notion that perceived difference will necessarily be the result of racial difference alone. Thus, analysis of the language of particular groups of women in particular locations is undertaken, rather than analyses of black women or white women as homogeneous groups (Edwards 1989; Bucholtz 1996; Nichols 1998). In this way, we can analyse the intersection of factors such as social mobility and employment patterns with factors such as race, as Nichols has in her analysis of the very heterogeneous speech patterns of black women in coastal South Carolina, where she found elements of both conservative and innovative usage (Nichols 1998). However, race and ethnicity are still significantly under-researched areas in feminist linguistics (see Morgan 2004, 2007 for an excellent assessment of this continuing lack of coverage).

Furthermore, feminist theory is now focused as much on the specificity of heterosexuality, middle-classness and whiteness, and the privileges which go along with these positions, as it is on the specificity of blackness, working-classness and lesbianism, so that the term 'race' is no longer used solely to refer to the analysis of black women, but is used to analyse women in relation to racial (and other) differences (Frankenberg 1993; Wilkinson and Kitzinger 1991; Maynard and Purvis 1995). Furthermore, alongside studies which analyse the privileges of white middle-class women and the problematic generalisations that have been made from their linguistic behaviour to women as a whole, there has developed a concern, particularly important in the context of this study, to also analyse the way that the speech patterns stereotypically associated with white middle-class women's speech are very often stigmatised and subject to mockery.

Social stratification is an important variable which should be considered in relation to gender. It is not an easy variable to analyse, since it is often very difficult to assign women and men to a class position (see Coates and Cameron 1989; Talbot 1998/2010). Class is a variable which has a particular set of meanings and connotations in a UK context. Discussion of social differences in other contexts such as the caste system in India may be referred to more broadly as social stratification. Furthermore, within the UK, women's relation to their assigned class position can vary greatly. For example, some working-class women choose to aspire to middle-class values and reject working-class values and culture, whilst others reject and ridicule middle-class values (Skeggs 2004). Discussions of class are further complicated because there seems to be a tendency to assume that in certain Western societies middle class = feminine and working class = masculine, thus making analysis of speech difficult without drawing on or being influenced by these stereotypes (Mills 2003a).

Many of the analyses of women's language have focused on middle-class norms, and the speech of groups of working-class women has only come to the fore through the analysis of dialect and accent. The generalising of stereotypes of middle-class white women's speech to other groups has been challenged (Coates and Cameron 1989; Talbot 1998/2010). Indeed, the specificity of middle-class white women's experience has begun to be analysed more in recent years (Vicinus 1980).

Skeggs, in her 1997 analysis of British working-class white women, has argued that assessment by others (real and imagined) is a very important factor in the constitution of their class positions. The assessment as 'common' and 'respectable' is one which weighs on a wide range of behaviours from child-rearing, drinking, sexual behaviour, physical appearance and weight, alongside linguistic behaviour, such as swearing and verbosity. Assessments of respectable behaviour have the effect of separating the person from the 'rough' working-class and moving them into a position of alignment with the lower middle class, whereas assessments as 'common' align the person with lower-working-class positions, which for women are intensely problematic, especially in relation to particular types of femininity and sexuality. Issues of language are crucial in the daily representation of oneself as classed, raced and gendered: Skeggs (1997: 6) argues that 'to be working-classed ... generates a constant fear of never having "got it right"'.

To be judged to be a working-class woman by middle-class people is always not simply to be classified into a class position but also to be categorised as inadequate and inferior:

> [I]n relation to language and this sense of 'proper', 'lady-like' usage, this is of importance, as working-class women may feel that in order to aspire to respectability, they need to use particular types of language, formalised polite-ness being one of the strategies available. ... However, other working-class women will refuse to appropriate these middle-class norms to make them their own – *not* being middle-class is certainly valued in many working-class social groups. (Skeggs 1997: 11)

Tyler (2008: 20) argues that 'social class virtually disappeared as a central site of analysis within cultural and media studies in the late 1980s, a disappearance that was mirrored by a similar retreat from class within wider social and political discourse'. Discussing class has thus become more difficult in Britain in recent years; yet many people in Britain side-step the use of the term 'class' by refer-ring to working-class people (and others) as 'chavs'.[11] This term is a much more emotionally charged word than 'working class'. Tyler's article is entitled 'Chav mum, chav scum' and analyses the vilification of the figure of the poor white working-class young mothers in contemporary Britain through the use of the term 'chav'. In her analysis, she explores the way that the 'chav mum' is 'produced through disgust reactions [towards] ... an intensely affective figure that embodies historically familiar and contemporary anxieties about sexuality, reproduction, fertility and "racial mixing"' (Tyler 2008: 18).

In critical representations of working-class women, the focus is on their supposed lack of taste in clothing, their excessive spending on vulgar jewellery and branded sports clothes and the number of teenage pregnancies. The figure of the female 'chav' is epitomised in the British comedy television series *Little Britain*, where the character Vicky Pollard, played by a male, Matt Lucas, is mercilessly undermined. In each of the comedy sketches she produces nonsensical responses to serious questions from authority figures. In one sketch detailed by Tyler, Pollard is represented going to a doctor's appointment where she is found to be pregnant:

> DOCTOR: OK Vicky, you can put your clothes back on. Well, after having a good look at you it's pretty obvious to me what the diagnosis is.

VICKY: I got the lurgy. Yeah, I know because there was this 'cause I was down the arcade and Kelly flobbed on Destiny and a bit of it landed in my hair because Kelly hates Destiny because Destiny told Warren that Kelly pads her bra.[12]

Tyler (2008: 25) comments that 'this scene invites the viewer to take up the subject position of the exasperated middle-class professional as they gaze at Vicky, the incurably sub-literate, sexually promiscuous, pregnant teenage chavette'. In the series, Vicky is represented as having 13 children, all by different fathers, and in one publicity still she is shown with a multiple pushchair with six white and mixed-race children. This figure of Vicky Pollard has become a shorthand in discussions of class for everything which is considered to be wrong with the working class. It is interesting that it is the language which she uses which is so central to the mocking of this figure.

Thus, the use of certain forms of language, such as directness, loudness and swearing, associated by the middle classes with impoliteness, may well be part of a strategy to mark oneself off from those middle-class norms of feminine behaviour and to affiliate oneself with working-class values. Therefore, rather than considering working-class women to be a homogeneous group, we should see that constructing one's gendered, raced and classed identity involves taking a stand on language. This may indeed not be a consistent stand in one's own language repertoire.

Summary

The overall focus of this chapter has been upon the theorisation of gender and how this relates to the analysis of language, framed through an examination of the ways in which Second and Third Wave feminism tend to differ in their approaches to the conceptualising of gender and language. We have examined the importance of gendered identity categories and the far-reaching effects that gendered stereotypes can play in our assessments and evaluations of one another as gendered beings. The latter part of the chapter has focused upon key theoretical concepts in defining what the focus of a gender analysis of language should consist of by discussing power, sexuality, race, ethnicity and social stratification. In the next chapter, we build upon the concepts outlined here by moving on to discuss the linguistic approaches which have been drawn upon by feminists in their analysis of language data.

4   Feminist linguistic approaches

Key issues

In this chapter, we survey a number of theoretical approaches which feminist linguists have drawn upon and developed for the analysis of the interplay between gender and language. However, before we begin, we must first carefully consider exactly what it is that feminist linguists are theorising and how this relates to the feminist theorisations of gender in the waves models, particularly the social construction of gender within the Third Wave, which we have thoroughly discussed in the previous chapter. We agree with the sentiment expressed in Cameron's (2006a) statement regarding theory and critique:

> I would not define research as 'feminist' primarily on the grounds that it adopts a 'constructionist' view of gender in which the categories 'men' and 'women' are treated as unstable, variable and thus non natural. I do not disagree with this view of gender, but proclaiming it ... is neither a defining feature of a feminist approach nor the most important task for feminist scholarship. For me what defines feminism is not its theory of gender but its critique of gender *relations*. (Cameron 2006a: 2, emphasis in original)

Thus, for us, feminist theorising in general, and when applied to linguistics in particular, is theorising which enables a change to be brought about within relations between men and women, or which brings about a change in conceptualisation, that is, it raises consciousness and thus accords with the overarching feminist goal of emancipation.

We have divided the main feminist linguistic approaches into separate sections, but this needs to be seen as simply a useful heuristic device. Most feminist theorists do not draw on one approach only; instead, they take elements from different approaches and theories as best befits their research questions. Often it can be difficult to see where the boundary of one discipline ends and the other begins, as linguistic sub-disciplines frequently blend into one another. Thus, when reading this chapter, it will be useful to recognise that most theorists do not tend to make use of these approaches exclusively. Furthermore, in order for feminist linguistics to be innovative and move forward, it is worth considering Baxter's (2003: 3) observation that simply adopting a single pre-existing model wholesale may result in 'an unquestioning and over-respectful adherence' to 'certain revered experts'.

However, it is also important to realise that some approaches are more compatible than others and that some approaches are more open to integration with some perspectives than others. For the integration of approaches to be conducted effectively, researcher reflexivity is required; this will be discussed in detail in Chapter 5 (see also Sunderland and Litosseliti 2008). The epistemological background of certain disciplines may prevent a fusion of certain approaches. There have been fairly vociferous debates between proponents of different linguistic approaches which have spilled over into the field of language and gender, most notably, debates between conversation analysis (CA) and critical discourse analysis (CDA); in addition to focusing on the range of approaches that can be taken by feminist linguists, we will also consider debates between different paradigms in this chapter. Coming back to a point we made in Chapter 1, from our perspective, the most important principle in contemporary approaches to feminist language and gender research is for investigators to avoid situating themselves in 'armed camps' (Silverman 2000: 10), which runs the danger of researchers taking the focus away from the crucial social and political questions which need to be investigated from a linguistic perspective and, instead, spending too much time battling with feminist linguists from other paradigms about whose paradigm is best.

The approaches that we discuss here are as follows: sociolinguistics and linguistic anthropology, discourse analysis, critical discourse analysis, conversation analysis, feminist post-structuralist discourse analysis and pragmatics. We are assuming a basic working knowledge of these linguistic sub-disciplines, though brief definitions are given to clarify exactly how we are defining these frameworks. There are also a handful of other approaches which we have not discussed here which have been of use to gender and language theorists. For instance, some researchers have drawn upon approaches including discursive psychology (Wetherall and Edley 1999; Edley and Wetherall 2008; Kamada 2008), stylistics (Mills 1995; Livia 2003; Page 2005) and psychoanalysis (see Cameron 1992) to analyse language and gender from a feminist perspective. Those approaches that we have selected in this chapter are those that we perceive to have the most significance for contemporary research, though of course others may disagree. The theoretical concepts introduced in the previous chapter are drawn upon to varying degrees by the approaches outlined here. There are common questions that all of these approaches to language and gender address to varying degrees of explicitness:

- How salient is gender?
- When should gender be analysed?
- When is gender significant?
- How does the language used signal something about gender relations?
- What would a more progressive use of language look like?
- When is feminism significant?
- What is the role of the analyst in producing linguistic analysis?
- What role should participants play in the analysis?

These theoretical issues impact upon the methodological choices that researchers make and Chapter 5, on methods and methodologies, should therefore be seen as a continuation of the issues discussed here.

Feminist sociolinguistics

Defined in the broadest sense as the study of the interplay between language and society, many different areas of sociolinguistics have been studied by feminist linguists. On occasions, gender and language researchers have categorised linguistic anthropology alongside sociolinguistics, as there are often significant points of crossover between the two disciplines. For example, McElhinny (2003) outlined future development where she placed the two sub-disciplines together – the difference between the two disciplines can be seen as one based upon different geographical traditions. What is termed linguistic anthropology in the US may be categorised as sociolinguistics in UK-based and European traditions, although there are methodological differences between the two positions, especially regarding ethnography, which we will detail in the next section (see Duranti 1997 for further discussion of this disciplinary distinction).

Language variation and change

Historically, one of the most significant areas of sociolinguistic study is the investigation of language variation and change (LVC), where researchers describe and assess different language varieties and examine how language use changes over time. Much of this variationist research tends to focus on phonological, lexical and/or grammatical levels of language use.

Many feminist sociolinguists have called for changes in approach from the dominant early Western sociolinguistic findings in the area of LVC studies (Coates and Cameron 1989; Cameron 1996; McElhinny 2003; Romaine 2003; Meyerhoff 2007; Talbot 1998/2010). Early sociolinguistic researchers, including Labov (1966, 1972) and Trudgill (1974), studied phonological variables in New York and Norwich (England) respectively. They generalised that females across different social-class groupings were more status conscious than males thanks to their increased use of linguistic features closer to the standard variety, as they became more conscious of their language use. Social-class categories were the foundation of these studies, and they then integrated a focus not on gender but on sex, as an *a priori* category pre-existing recorded interaction. In light of the Third Wave feminist commitment to studying gender as a socially constructed phenomenon as opposed to speaker sex, as we have seen in Chapter 3, feminist sociolinguists called for a move away from analysing sex categories, which imply that biology determines speech styles, as well as for an end to simply searching for differences in female and male speech.

Additionally, there have been many findings outside the Western world that provide clear exceptions to Labov's and Trudgill's generalisations about women's speech. Meyerhoff (2007: 218) points out that 'over and over, studies of synchronic variation in Arabic seemed to be showing men using more of the overtly prestigious variants associated with Classical Arabic and women using more variants associated with the local colloquial variety of Arabic'. Walters (1991) has also shown that where there is a foreign language introduced by colonialism in an Arab country, such as in North Africa, where French is widely spoken, young women tend to speak French rather than Classical Arabic as for many it signifies modernity. Eckert and McConnell-Ginet (2003) remark on this sort of choice of variety as playing a role in what they term the 'linguistic marketplace': that is, different varieties hold different types of symbolic capital within particular communities.[1] Bakir (1986) discovered that women in Iraq use far more of the variants associated with the local Iraqi variants whereas men were far more likely to use Classical Arabic more frequently in both phonological and grammatical variants. In Cairo, Haeri (1994) found that women were bringing in non-standard sound changes in Cairene Arabic. This finding was consistent across different groups split by educational levels, defined on a continuum from having no education to those who studied beyond college level. These findings in Arabic clearly undermine the dominant Western finding that women will use standard varieties more than men.

Romaine (2003: 109) contests the view that by analysing language variation we are simply tracing a reflection of the social order. She points out that 'the standard sociolinguistic account of the relationship between language and society often seems to suggest ... that language reflects already existing social identities rather than constructs them'. Language and gender researchers working in the area of language variation have shown how individuals make agentive choices amongst the varieties available to them, and are well aware of the associated values attached to language varieties. For example, Gal's (1998) study of women in a Hungarian village near the Austrian border shows how women's choice of German (rather than Hungarian) indicates that they are attempting to distance themselves from peasant life and choosing within the linguistic marketplace varieties which associate them with different values and opportunities.

James (1996) makes a convincing argument that any further attempts to find global patterning of female linguistic use and the most prestigious/standard variety is futile, as there is too much variation both within and across different speech communities. The linguistic realisation of particular speech styles is more complex and dependent upon a number of factors, not just upon the sex of the speaker. This does not mean that the pattern of women using more prestigious varieties will not be found, but, instead, where such a pattern is discovered, a more complex explanation is required to explain fully the intricacies of this particular linguistic situation. James argues that some factors will have more salience in some communities, cultures and contexts than in others and therefore a more meticulous analysis of particular groups is required.

Kielkiewicz-Janowiak and Pawelcyk (2009) build upon James' perspective in their recent fieldwork conducted in Poland. They examine two generations of women and men classified within a 20-plus or 45-plus age group. Using interviews and questionnaires they found that within a contemporary Polish context, following a time of significant socio-political transition, there is a specific cultural concern with standardness and the linguistic appropriateness of Polish with all speakers. This is identified as the 'Polish cult of the norm' (2009: 470). These cultural norms and expectations become combined with what they term a 'Polish mother' ideology, glorified by the Catholic church as a woman who is both patriotic and caring/nurturing. This ideology results in the norms of linguistic appropriateness being ascribed to the role of women – it is seen as women's responsibility to both spread and cultivate the prescribed standard variants. Women are therefore allocated the role of 'educators' and 'language guardians' (2009: 462). Standard varieties within Poland are thus firmly encoded with femininity. Both generations of women are aware of this, though Kielkiewicz-Janowiak and Pawelcyk report that the women of the younger generation are more likely to show an awareness of language variation and more of an acceptance of variants that are not prescribed by the standard norm than the women of the older generation.

Romaine (2003: 100) points out that within variationist research the concept of social class has been fundamental, with gender differentiation being 'derivative' of social class. This is problematic, first as it pushes gender into the background and second because of the masculine bias contained within early Western social stratification research, whereby women were classified only according to their husband's occupation or, if unmarried, their father's (Labov 1972; Trudgill 1974). Romaine (2003) points out that this problem of defining and categorising via social class still persists, with women and men continuing to have unequal relations with one another within societal class structures. For instance, in many countries there is still a higher concentration of women in lower-paid occupations than men (Romaine 2003; Cameron 2006a). A potential way forward suggested by Romaine (2003: 115) is for sociolinguistic research to undergo 're-examination from a new, non-class-based standpoint'. Romaine thus argues that social class should not be the fundamental starting point of variationist sociolinguistic studies, thus signifying a clear departure from classic variationist research. However, as we highlight at various points in the book, class and social stratification as a whole are still influential factors for feminist linguists in certain societies; exactly how class and social stratification are conceptualised and assessed has consistently been a matter for much debate (see Skeggs 2004; Kerswill 2007) and will continue to be so. Perhaps the most important aspect from a feminist linguistic point of view is that a focus on class and class struggles does not come at the expense of gender issues, but instead that gender and class are examined alongside one another.

A key criticism of sociolinguistic variation and change studies is the presentation of linguistic differences simply as 'neutral', with the embedded assumption that if only more tolerance is learned, then differences between different speech styles will be non-stigmatised and accepted. Such a relativist argument is politically naïve for feminist sociolinguists. As Cameron points out, such a position overlooks the following:

> To suppose that the problem is intolerance of difference, and that if only we valued women's styles as much as men's there would be no problem, is reminiscent of that brand of right-wing pseudo-feminism which enjoins us to honour the housewife and mother for doing the most important job in the

world, glossing over the fact that her gendered occupation is itself a product of inequality and exploitation. Feminism is not about giving housewives their due, it is about changing the conditions of domestic labour altogether. Similarly, feminism cannot stop at validating the linguistic strategies typical of women; it must also ask why women find some communicative practices more accessible and more relevant than others: a question, as Eckert and McConnell-Ginet argue, of what social practice they are permitted/enabled/ encouraged to participate in. (Cameron 1996a: 44)

Cameron's words draw attention to issues that are still far from resolved. In fact, the advent of post-feminist discourses, as we have seen in Chapter 1, will often echo the exact brand of 'right-wing pseudo feminism' to which she refers, which has arguably become more dominant in popular culture since her work was originally published in 1996.

Cameron's reference to Eckert and McConnell-Ginet highlights the importance of a social practice approach to feminist sociolinguistic studies. This social practice approach is more commonly referred to as the communities of practice approach (CoP). The CoP approach has played a significant role in the theorisation of the sociolinguistics of gender in the last 20 years. The concept of a community of practice has become a focus of much feminist linguistic research since the early 1990s both within sociolinguistics and linguistic anthropology and beyond. Many researchers who use discourse analysis and pragmatics will also draw on a CoP approach (see, for example, Holmes 2006; Mullany 2007; Schnurr 2009).

For many Third Wave feminist linguists, the notion of the community of practice has been important in terms of trying to describe the way that group values affect the individual and their notion of what is linguistically appropriate (Eckert and McConnell-Ginet 1998, 1999). It has proved itself to be a useful notion for thinking through the way that norms become established within groups in a variety of different contexts and the crucial ways in which individuals interact and negotiate with those perceived norms.

The oft-cited and now arguably classic definition of a community of practice is as follows:

> An aggregate of people who come together around mutual engagement in an endeavor. Ways of doing things, ways of talking, beliefs, values, power relations – in short, practices – emerge in the course of this mutual endeavor. (Eckert and McConnell-Ginet 1992: 464)

The community of practice therefore refers to groups of people who are brought together in joint engagement on a task and who therefore jointly construct a range of values and appropriate behaviours. For example, a community of practice might be a group of people who meet to plan an event, or a group of people who go out drinking together. Thus, rather than focusing on the role of an oppressive social system, ideology or patriarchy in relation to individual linguistic production and reception, Third Wave feminists focus on the interactions at the level of

the community of practice: a small group engaged together in relation to a particular task. Individuals hypothesise what is appropriate within the community of
practice and, in speaking, affirm or contest the community's sense of appropriate
behaviour.

A number of researchers, including Cameron (1996) and Holmes and Meyerhoff
(2003a), have pointed out that the CoP framework acts as a complement to social
constructionist conceptualisations of gender as a performative social construct far
more than Second Wave frameworks, which do not place an emphasis upon the
dynamic nature of identity performance, nor do they see interaction as a form of
enacted social practice:

> Throughout our lives we go on entering new communities of practice: we
> must constantly produce our gendered identities by *performing* what are taken
> to be the appropriate acts in the communities we belong to – or else chal-
> lenge prevailing gender norms by refusing to *perform* these acts. (Cameron
> 1996: 45, our emphasis)

From a community of practice perspective, one's choice of words and one's speech
style can be seen as defining one's position within a group or community of practice. McElhinny (2003) and Bucholtz (1999b) both argue that a community of
practice can be seen to be a bridge between analysis of the local and the wider
society. McElhinny (2003) makes the following argument:

> Communities of practice articulate between macro sociological structures
> such as class and everyday interactional practices by considering the groups
> in which individuals participate and how these shape their interactions. The
> groups in which we all participate are, in turn, determined and constituted
> by their place within larger social structures. The notion of community of
> practice thus serves as a mediating region between local and global analysis.
> (McElhinny 2003: 30)

Bucholtz (1999b: 220) neatly emphasises the overarching importance of the
community of practice perspective in terms of bringing together the micro-,
meso- and macro-levels of analysis of gender identities when she argues that,
through CoPs, individuals' 'local identities and the linguistic practices that
produce these identities become visible ... as the purposeful choices of agentive
individuals, operating within (and alongside and outside) the constraints of the
social structure'.

Bourdieu's (1991) notion of 'habitus' has been integrated into the CoP approach
and has thus also been extensively drawn on by Third Wave feminist sociolinguists. 'Habitus' is defined as the set of dispositions which one draws upon and
engages with in order to perform one's identity through discourse. This set of attitudes or practices which are seen as constituting a norm by individuals are then
discursively negotiated in terms of their own perception of what is acceptable for
their own behaviour within a particular community of practice. Eelen (2001),
drawing on Bourdieu's work, argues that we assume that there is a common world,

that is, a set of beliefs which exist somewhere in the social world and which are accepted by everyone, which we as individuals need to agree with or contest:

> On the one hand, collective history creates a 'common' world in which each individual is embedded. On the other hand, each individual also has a unique individual history and experiences the 'common' world from this unique position. The common world is thus never identical for everyone. It is essentially fragmented, distributed over a constellation of unique positions and unique perspectives. (Eelen 2001: 223)

Thus, this view of the relation between individuals and others moves us significantly away from notions of society as a whole influencing the linguistic behaviour of individuals to an analysis of the way that, at a local level, individuals within communities of practice assess what type of language and speech style is appropriate.

Interactional sociolinguistics

In addition to studies of language variation and change, an increasingly significant amount of Third Wave feminist sociolinguistic research has taken place at the level of interaction, beyond the smaller linguistic levels of phonology, lexis and grammar. Such investigations focus instead on men and women in single-sex and mixed-sex groups engaging in face-to-face conversations. This research can be identified under the collective term 'interactional sociolinguistics', very broadly defined as the sociolinguistic study of patterns of interaction within discourse (Wodak and Benke 1997). Indeed, there are many points of crossover between interactional sociolinguistics and discourse analysis; this can also include elements of conversation analysis and pragmatics. Researchers have blended theoretical concepts and analytical frameworks from these approaches together within an overarching interactional sociolinguistic model (see, for example, Holmes 2006; Mullany 2007).

The influence of work from linguistic anthropology has played an important role in the recent theoretical advancements in interactional sociolinguistic work. One theoretical paradigm that has been very influential in recent years is Ochs' (1992) work on gender indexicality. As part of her cross-cultural work on comparing the communicative practices of motherhood in mainstream US society and in Western Samoa, Ochs (1992) brings in the theoretical paradigm of indexicality and argues that gender is either directly or indirectly *indexed* through language. Direct indexicality is defined as examples of language usage where gender is overtly and explicitly encoded, such as in the lexical items girl/boy, man/woman. However, instances of direct indexicality are relatively infrequent. Far more frequent is the indirect indexing of gender, whereby interactional styles come to be encoded or indexed with specific gendered meanings. Individuals' speech styles are viewed and evaluated in light of these gendered expectations. Table 3.1 in Chapter 3, above, presents a good example of the gendered expectations for men and women in Western societies and it is often used as the starting point for studies which adopt the indexicality approach (see Holmes 2006; Marra *et al.* 2006; Mullany 2007, 2010c).

To illustrate indirect indexicality further, the stereotypical view that women are more linguistically polite than men, evidenced in early research in Western cultural settings, should be interpreted as an ideological expectation, held in place by powerful gendered ideologies, which holds white middle-class behaviour for women as the most powerful, hegemonic discourse for *all* women to follow in Western societies. If women should stray beyond the boundaries of this expectation, then they may well be viewed as deviant and/or deficient, and negative evaluation may well result as a consequence of this behaviour.

With particular reference to indirect indexing, Kiesling (2003: 510) states that 'there are one or more social actions ... that come between a linguistic feature and the group that uses it most'. Eckert and McConnell-Ginet (2003) draw on Ochs' (1992) work when they argue that perhaps it is better to see the differences between the fundamental frequencies of children's voices as the result of not only biological differences. They state: 'it is probable that when boys and girls alter the fundamental frequency of their voices they are not trying to sound like girls or like boys but they are aspiring for some quality that is itself gendered – cuteness, authority' (Eckert and McConnell-Ginet 2003: 20). Thus, cuteness indirectly indexes gender in that it is a quality which is associated with femininity.

Japanese provides a particularly interesting example of the ideological indexing of gendered speech styles. Early research on language and gender in Japanese examined the notion of 'women's language' (*onnarashi kotoba*), since Japanese seemed to have 'inscribed gender into its very structure, through the prescribed use of differential grammatical and lexical forms for women and men' (Bucholtz 2004: vii). However, feminists have since 'identified a number of fissures in what had been up until then a seamless and largely unquestioned cultural ideology of how Japanese women ought to speak' (Bucholtz 2004: viii). Other researchers have drawn attention to the fact that Japanese 'women's language' is in fact the stereotypical language used by a particular group of educated middle-class women in a particular sector of Tokyo, and that in the rest of the country there is great variety of language styles. In some rural contexts where local dialects are spoken, this Japanese 'women's language' style is rarely used (Sunaoshi 2004). Thus, in much the same way as in research into English, it became clear that the notion of 'women's language' was a language ideology; that the qualities of polite, gentle, unassertive speech were normative usages rather than being constitutive of actual language practices (Okamoto and Shibamoto Smith 2004a: 4).

In Japanese gender and language research, there has been a great deal of focus on sentence final particles (SFPs), which it was argued are used more by women and seem to be used to indicate femininity; however, as Okamoto and Shibamoto Smith have shown, sentence final particles may indeed index femininity, but they may index a range of other elements as well, for example formality and elegance (Ide 2005).

Okamoto and Shibamoto Smith (2004b) and Inoue (2004, 2006) claim that the notion of 'women's language' has been an important element at the level of the formation of the modern Japanese state. Ide argues that 'the linguistic consciousness of "how women speak" is closely connected with notions of culture and tradition in the assessment that women's language is uniquely Japanese, with unbroken historical roots in an archetypal Japanese past, and inescapably linked with an equally traditional and archetypal Japanese womanhood' (Ide 2004: 57–8). Ide thus argues that Japanese 'women's language' is a product of the contradiction between Japanese traditions and modernity. At a time when Japan was coming to terms with the formation of a state, industrialisation, colonialism and the growth of the military, both gender and language became issues which needed to be dealt with at a national level. Ide demonstrates that 'a metapragmatic category such as "women's language" is never pregiven but is contingent upon historically specific social arrangements in which linguistic forms are motivated and regimented to become an "index" by being mediated through broader political and economic processes' (Ide 2004: 71).

Indeed, Inoue (2006: 1) argues that Japanese 'women's language' is a 'space of discourse' comprised of social practices within powerful institutions where a Japanese woman is 'objectified, evaluated, studied, staged and normalised through her imputed language use and is thus rendered a knowable and unified subject both to herself and to others'.

In contemporary Japanese usage there is a wide range of sociolinguistic speech styles which women can adopt, some of which index femininity, for example the saccharine-sweet 'Burikko' persona where grown women use a feigned childlike naivety, high pitch, swooping intonation patterns and a type of baby talk (Miller 2004), but there are other styles which women use which are more assertive, where pragmatic language features such as honorifics are dropped and 'vulgar vocabulary' is used (Yukawa and Saito 2004: 24; see the section in this chapter on 'Feminist pragmatics', pp. 85–91, below, for further discussion on the importance of politeness in Japanese).

There is also a sense in which, currently, female speakers are experimenting with indexicalised gendered language in order to express their particular sociolinguistic identities. Young Japanese women, for example, are experimenting with different styles of language, using the more masculine first-person pronoun 'boku' (Yukawa and Saito 2004). Business women may use a more assertive, more 'masculine' style in their language use, which has been labelled 'oremeshi onna', 'me food woman', which is a parody of an autocratic husband's command to his wife. In a study examining language and media data in the 1990s, Matsumoto (2004) observed a correlation between gender and age and more experimental language usage. She found that young women and teenagers in Tokyo were using coarse and forceful language stereotypically associated with men's language. However, she is quick to point out that more forceful linguistic forms do not simply mean a shift towards more equality. As we have seen at various stages in this book, there is no simple correlation between the usage of particular linguistic forms and the bringing about of gender equality. Ingrained attitudes and language evaluations based upon deep-seated ideological beliefs make the situation far more complex.

Multilingualism

Other key feminist sociolinguistic research which has taken place beyond Western contexts has investigated multilingualism, including issues of linguistic imperialism, language endangerment and language planning. McElhinny (2007a: 18) refers to Chandra's (2003) work, which presents a historical account of the debates surrounding whether Indian women should have been educated in English in nineteenth-century India. Chandra discusses how local native languages, including Marathi, were perceived as low-status, impure varieties. In contrast, English was seen as the educated, higher-status, international language. However, if women learnt English they were perceived by other women to have become too intimate with their husbands, thus neglecting their duty to other women to establish bonds within the local community.

Chandra discovered that critics of learning English argued that the status of Marathi should be raised, particularly to benefit women from the upper castes, with its promotion seen as essential for its survival as a 'mother' tongue. Marathi thus became feminised in contrast with English, which became masculinised. Critics thus used the threat of language endangerment as a key political tool. However, as McElhinny (2007a: 18) concludes, this is a prime example of policing language which simultaneously also serves as a way to 'police caste and nation'.

At the intersection of sociolinguistics and pragmatics is an approach that has been referred to as 'postcolonial pragmatics' a term coined by Nair (2002) to define the ways in which gender and other areas of identity interrelate with imperialism, assessed in particular by analysing the language politics of multilingualism in context (McElhinny 2007a: 18). McElhinny (2007a) makes particular reference to Nair's work focusing upon the multiple dilemmas faced by postcolonialist feminists when considering women's use of the English language and the imperialist values and status it imbues, in both spoken and written forms.

Nguyen (2007) argues that it is important to focus on multilingual communities in our analyses of language and gender as they 'provide particularly salient cases of the linguistic heterogeneity linked to socio-historical relationships like colonisation, industrialisation, migration, globalisation and war' (Nguyen 2007: 349). Because many Vietnamese-speaking men were killed in the American war, some Vietnamese-speaking women married into families where other languages or dialects are spoken and they therefore had to adopt this language or dialect. Nguyen argues that 'the fact that these Vietnamese women avoid Vietnamese in certain public contexts is evidence of how a historical event like a war interacts with local ideologies of gender to put pressure on a woman's life not only during the war but also long after that' (2007: 363).

Besnier's (2007) study of transgender beauty pageants in Tonga demonstrates that language choice and language skill are crucial in constructing identities within a globalised economy. In Tonga, English is an elite language and in the Miss Galaxy contest, if English is spoken by the contestants, or if they make mistakes in English, they are ridiculed. If they speak Tongan they are seen as less cosmopolitan; he argues that 'globalisation informs and transforms people's lives, creating new forms of agency as easily as it perpetrates structures that are continuous with the past' (Besnier 2007: 425).

Discourse analysis

We are using the term 'discourse analysis' here as an inclusive, umbrella term to refer to a range of different approaches that all have an element of discourse at their analytical core. This will include 'discourse analysis' as an analytical entity in itself, critical discourse analysis, conversation analysis, discursive psychology as an additional branch of conversation analysis and feminist post-structuralist discourse analysis. Some researchers may dispute this classification and argue that their approach stands alone, rather than under an overarching label, but we believe that this is an appropriate and penetrating means through which the subtle differences and similarities between these approaches can be seen from a feminist linguistic perspective. Furthermore, classifying these approaches together under an overarching term of 'discourse analysis' is by no means a new phenomenon. Indeed, it is already established practice to do this. For instance, these approaches are frequently brought together in handbooks of discourse analysis; see, for example, Handford and Gee (forthcoming).

Despite its undeniable usefulness as an umbrella term, before we begin it is important to stress that 'discourse' is used in a wide variety of ways within different disciplines including linguistics, literary theory, psychology and sociology. In the most traditional linguistic sense, it is a term used to signify simply a stretch of text which is longer than a sentence (see Tannen 1989); it can refer to a text or texts which seem to be focused on one particular subject (for example, a 'discourse of femininity'). It can also be used, following Foucault's work (1972), to refer to a set of linguistic practices which shape the way in which something is expressed, a set of unstated rules for expression. To cite one of Foucault's (1972: 49) most famous observations, discourses in this macro sense are defined as 'practices that systematically form the objects of which they speak'. Sznycer (2010: 459) argues that we can see discourse as 'durable ways of presenting'; that is, certain habits of representing and expressing have greater productivity over time than others. For many feminist linguists, it is this Foucauldian definition which has proved very useful, but it is often not entirely clear how 'discourse' is to be disentangled from 'ideology' as both terms are used in very similar ways (Mills 2004).

Feminist discourse analysis

Sunderland (2004: 20) focuses on discourses which are seen to be 'gendered'. She favours 'gendered' as a term, as she points out that it is far stronger than the more descriptive term 'gender-related': 'gendered' explicitly signifies that 'gender is already a part of the "thing" which gendered describes' (2004: 20–1). She draws attention to an overarching discourse, the 'discourse of gender difference', which she identifies as governing societal expectations for gender normative behaviour: 'It is a significant "lens" for the way people view reality, being for most people what gender is all about. Once its "common-sense" status has been contested, "gender differences" can be seen as such' (Sunderland 2004: 52). This discourse is maintained by the deeply entrenched ideology that women and men are inherently different as a result of biological differences that allegedly exist between them (see Cameron 2007a, 2007b for a detailed critique of this position).

There are a whole range of other discourses which operate within the overarching gender differences discourse which provide recognisable narrative pathways for males and females. For example, in Western contexts, Sunderland refers to 'the incompetent father discourse', 'father as line manager discourse', 'the equal opportunities discourse' and so on. Whilst some of these discourses are difficult to compare, since they seem to be very different in kind, nevertheless it is quite useful to be able to track familiar and repeated narrative scenarios which appear to be gendered in some ways.

These discourses can be damaging, but it seems that it is the position of the hearer which determines whether they damage or not; Sunderland argues that 'whereas some individuals may be damaged by sexist discourse, others will recognise it for what it is, resist it, laugh at it and/or become empowered in the process' (Sunderland 2004: 194). Sunderland lays out a range of different strategies in relation to gendered discourses: first, there is meta-discoursal critique, followed by non-use of the damaging discourses and then a stage of rediscursivisation, where the discourse elements are remodelled to be less damaging.

Baker (2008a) also focuses on gendered discourses, particularly in relation to discourses concerned with sexuality; he argues that 'people are often influenced by discourses or ideologies, but ... they also have the ability to challenge and change discourses, imagining new configurations or refusing to go along with the "way things are"' (Baker 2008a: 257). For example, he analyses children's toys and the way that Action Man and Barbie dolls are described. These toys are described in advertising in terms of a discourse of 'gender differences' where their use is described in polarised ways, the toy for boys being described in terms of adventure and action ('he leaps into the unknown') and the toy for girls being described in terms of passivity ('she wears a soft blush-satin gown'). Much feminist discourse analysis has mapped out these differences in the way toys are marketed at girls and boys, but Baker (2008a) argues that these discourses can always be subverted. He describes the actions of the Barbie Liberation Organisation, which, in 1989, stole and swapped the circuit boards of some talking dolls, such as Barbie Teen Talk and GI Joe, and then replaced them in the stores. The modified Barbie dolls when they talked uttered stereotypically masculine phrases like 'Vengeance is mine' and the modified GI Joe dolls used stereotypically feminine phrases like 'I love shopping'. These actions by this organisation draw attention to the way that toys for girls and boys have become increasingly gender-differentiated, and their actions foregrounded the stereotypical nature of the utterances of these talking dolls.

Thus, feminist discourse analysis examines the way that discourses can appear to be gendered, leading to particular types of utterance in particular contexts, but because these are discourses, they are open to subversive potential. Both Baker and Sunderland share similarities in their work with CDA, as do many other discourse-analysis researchers, though, like Baker and Sunderland, many choose not to explicitly identify themselves with a distinct CDA position. Those researchers who have clearly identified themselves as critical discourse analysts will be focused upon in the next section.

Feminist critical discourse analysis

Talbot (cited in Bucholtz 2004: 57) states that the reason we need to analyse texts from a position informed by CDA is that the beliefs that are put forth in the texts of greatest interest to critical discourse analysts are those that encourage the acceptance of unequal arrangements of power as natural and inevitable, perhaps even as right and good. In this way, discourse has not merely a symbolic but also a material effect on the lives of human beings. Lazar argues that feminist critical discourse analysis is 'a critical perspective on unequal social arrangements sustained through language use, with the goals of social transformation and emancipation' (2005a: 1).

This feminist position draws on the theoretical frameworks and methodological approaches developed by critical discourse analysis. CDA takes a position which is informed by political theories and which argues that because our identities and our ways of looking at the world are formed through language, it is through the analysis of language that we can describe and challenge conventional beliefs and representations. Language is focused upon because 'analysis of discourse ... shows up the workings of power that sustain oppressive social structures/relations' and this 'is itself a form of analytical resistance and contributes to ongoing struggles of contestation and change' (Lazar 2005b: 6).

CDA theorists often analyse texts and conversations minutely, focusing on linguistic elements such as transitivity (who does what to whom), nominalisation (where verbs are changed into nouns and thus lose their agentedness) and passivisation (where events are recounted using passive rather than active voice, thus, again, losing agentedness). For example, if a text consistently describes women using a particular transitivity choice, for example, as the recipient of an action, 'He looked *at her*', 'They admired *her*', rather than as the actor, '*She* travelled', then this begins to build up an overall image of passiveness and inaction. A similar effect is achieved if women are consistently presented as 'acted upon' by using the passive voice, for example 'She *was left behind.*' Fairclough (1989) points out that the principle of CDA can be used to examine any level of the linguistic rank scale, but it is at this grammatical level where the detailed close reading practices of CDA theorists have been of most use to feminist CDA theorists (see Wodak 1997, 1998; Wodak and Meyer 2001). CDA has arguably been used most extensively by feminist linguists to produce critical examinations of representations of gender through media discourses (see, for example, Koller's (2004) work on gender representations through metaphor in business media discourses taken from business magazines and newspapers in the US and the UK; Litosseliti's (2006b) examination of the Western media immediately post 9/11; and Lazar's (2006, 2009) extensive feminist critical discourse analysis of advertising discourses in Singapore).

From a CDA perspective Lazar sees gender 'as a category [which] intersects with and is shot through by, other categories of social identity, such as sexuality, ethnicity, social position and geography. Patriarchy is also an ideological system that interacts in complex ways with, say, corporatist and consumerist ideologies' (Lazar 2005b: 1). For feminist CDA theorists, there is a keen sense of the workings of ideology, which they describe as 'representations of practices formed from particular perspectives in the interests of maintaining unequal power relations and dominance' (Lazar 2005b: 7).

Lazar (2005b: 7) argues that 'the winning of consent and the perpetuation of the otherwise tenuous relation of dominance are largely accomplished through discursive means, especially in the ways ideological assumptions are constantly re-enacted and circulated through discourse as commonsensical and natural'. Furthermore, 'a critical perspective on unequal social arrangements sustained through language use, with the goals of social transformation and emancipation, constitute the cornerstone of [CDA] and many feminist language studies' (Lazar 2005b: 1). For feminist CDA, 'our central concern is with critiquing discourses which sustain a patriarchal social order' and what we need to work towards is 'a feminist humanist vision of a just society, in which gender does not predetermine or mediate our relationships with others and our sense of who we are or might become' (Lazar 2005b: 6).

What feminist CDA is engaged in is an attempt to chart the difference between ideological knowledge and what people actually do or are capable of. In terms of gender ideology it is important to be aware of 'the dialectical tension between structural permanence and the practical activity of people engaged in social practices' (Lazar 2005b: 8). This tension leads to 'ruptures in the otherwise seamless and natural quality of gender ideology' (Lazar 2005b: 8). Walsh (2001: 65) sees feminist CDA as seeking 'to connect the detailed analysis of spoken, written and visual texts and intertexts to an analysis of the hegemonic ideologies that operate at the institutional and societal levels of discourse'.

Iyer's (2009) recent innovative work provides a good example of feminist CDA in action in the developing world. Her work focuses on a unique sample of 46 written media texts taken from Indian print magazines and newspapers where the journalistic focus is on female entrepreneurs. Iyer aimed to analyse macro discourses, following the work of Foucault (1991), Fairclough (1992) and van Dijk (2001). She discovered evidence of macro-dominant discourses of femininity and patriarchy in her sample. Alongside these more traditional discourses, she found evidence of a resistant discourse which she termed a discourse of 'being' and 'becoming'. She examines both macro- and micro-structures of discourse and at a micro-level she draws upon the techniques of the analysis of grammatical features including modality and lexical semantics (including synonymy and metonymy) and speech acts to bring out the more subtle ideological textual features. The following examples illustrate an instance from each of the discourse categories:

Discourse of patriarchy:
Nalini was lucky to have a family and husband who supported her from the very first day she went into business. (Iyer 2009: 251)

Discourse of femininity:
She can easily pass off as a model as she sits majestically in the unpretentious environs of her glass cabin. (Iyer 2009: 250)

Discourses of being/becoming:
I know it is not much but I'm proud that my stuff is unique, so there will always be a demand for them. I am still young and this is just the beginning. I feel one should do things because one enjoys doing them. (Iyer 2009: 254)

In the discourse of patriarchy, as the above example demonstrates, women are positioned as being successful in relation to their families, and often this success is represented as only having been achieved because of a supportive husband. Iyer points out that the husband is often seen as the one who sets up the business and is responsible for employment, whereas the wife is responsible for decorating and 'managing' (2009: 251). In the discourse of femininity, women entrepreneurs are presented through reference to 'physical perfection': the modality of 'can easily pass off', in the illustration above, 'establishes ability through looks and posture' (2009: 247). In contrast, the newer discourses of being/becoming provide evidence of women entrepreneurs employing multiple subject positions and gaining some agency for themselves. In the example cited above, Iyer argues that the speech acts here include expressions of agency gained through the empowerment of being an entrepreneur, including the use of 'know, 'proud' 'feel' and 'enjoy'.

Iyer concludes that the media texts often convey rather contradictory discourses of patriarchy, femininity and being/becoming. This represents the changing roles of women in this particular society, which are a long way from the traditional Indian family-only roles for females. She argues that through the discourse of being/becoming a different subject position is allowed but this subjectivity needs to also include 'the ability to align with their given identities of mother, daughter and housewife while valuing their new subject positions' (2009: 257). Iyer therefore demonstrates the overall value of using CDA from a feminist perspective to reveal these different Foucauldian macro discourses and illustrate how changing socio-cultural practices in contemporary Indian society can be viewed through them.

Holmes (2005: 34), in an insightful analysis of the way that gender and power need to be analysed alongside one another, argues that, within the workplace, 'the linguistic forms which express power are often identical to those which reflect solidarity or intimacy'. She observes that 'in contexts where the relative organisational responsibilities of the participants are clear ... managers can issue directives using very inexplicit forms, confident that their utterances will be interpreted as indications of what is to happen' (Holmes 2005: 34). Thus, rather than assuming that there are certain linguistic forms that are powerful, Holmes instead looks at the interpretative process whereby participants assume that certain indirect forms of language are interpreted as if they were directives.

In overall summary, feminist CDA is concerned with the analysis of inequality and the way that discursive means are used to maintain the status quo. Data can be analysed from many different contexts, and CDA has proved to be particularly fruitful for feminist linguistic analysis when analysing texts from the mass media and also spoken language data within institutional settings.

Feminist poststructuralist discourse analysis

Judith Baxter (2003, 2006b) has developed feminist CDA further to create a form of analysis which she terms 'feminist poststructuralist discourse analysis' (FPDA). Giving an example of her own work on the way female students may be disempowered in terms of public speaking she describes FPDA in the following terms:

> [FPDA] takes issue with the traditional feminist view that for example, female students are universally disempowered. It prefers instead to promote an understanding of the complex and often ambiguous ways in which girls/women are simultaneously positioned as relatively powerless within certain discourses, but as relatively powerful within alternative and competing discourses. This ceaseless shape shifting that speakers experience between different subject positions can occur within a single speech event ... The key point is girls/women are not permanently trapped into silence, disadvantage or victimhood by dominant discursive practices; rather there are moments within competing discourses when females can potentially convert acts of resistance into 'new' if intertextualised forms of expression. (Baxter 2006b: 162)

FPDA is therefore very similar to feminist CDA in that it takes an openly critical language-orientated perspective on the analysis of texts and conversations. However, where Baxter differs from many feminist CDA theorists is that her focus is on the way that women can carve out new positions for themselves within the competing discourses. Her approach differs from CA, as she goes beyond the transcript and brings in extra-textual factors, including background contextual knowledge gained via interviews with informants after the interaction had finished, known as retrospective interviews, to help her with her analytical interpretations (see Chapter 5 for further details of retrospective interviews). A handful of other researchers have explicitly taken a FPDA approach, including Castaneda-Peña's (2008) work on competing gendered discourses in pre-school ELT classrooms in Colombia.

Feminist conversation analysis

For many feminist conversation analysts (CA), this approach offers a very careful form of analysis which analyses conversation on a turn-by-turn basis, and attempts to categorise the way that turns are related to one another. Benwell and Stokoe (2006: 8) argue that CA 'resists pre- or post-theorising about the political, historical or macro-cultural implications of any interaction being analysed'. Instead, what conversation analysts are interested in is examining in painstaking detail the way that the conversation participants interact on a turn-by-turn basis. Emmanuel Schegloff, commonly accepted to be the most influential individual in the field of CA, argues that it is the 'technology' of conversation which needs to be analysed (Schegloff, in Benwell and Stokoe 2006: 36), that is, the sequencing of utterances: who speaks and what comes after their talk.

Kitzinger (2008) argues that feminist CA has a great deal to offer feminist linguistics as a whole and that more careful attention to conversational features can be particularly useful in terms of further theoretical advancement away from a simple cataloguing of gender differences, thoroughly discussed in Chapter 3. She believes that CA offers a 'powerful, systematic and contextually sensitive analytical method grounded in participants' *own* practices and actions' (2008: 136, emphasis in original). She argues against earlier studies (for example, Zimmerman and West 1975), as from her perspective they have analysed turn-taking in a manner that is a 'mechanical (mis)application' of the model, 'shorn of its connection to sequential and action analysis in the interests of quantifying gender differences'. There is a warning here that the CA approach should be meticulously followed, and Kitzinger frequently refers to Schegloff's (1992, 2000, 2001) work as providing *the* model to follow if CA is to be applied properly.

Stokoe's (2008) approach accords with Kitzinger's perspective and she makes it clear that, in order for gender to be analysed, it needs to be directly referenced by the participants within the talk itself. From this perspective, feminist researchers should only analyse gender if interactants draw upon directly indexicalised gender categories. However, direct reference to gender is not enough on its own. 'Pure' CA researchers also advocate that these terms need to be examined to see if gender actually becomes the topic of the conversation (Stokoe and Smithson 2001; Stokoe 2008). If it does, then an analysis can be legitimately carried out as the participants are orientating to gender in their own terms. As Stokoe (2008: 147) points out, it should not be that gender categories simply 'crop up in interaction' but instead that analysts should analyse when 'people *do things*' with these categories. She also cites Schegloff to add credence and clarity to her position. If the CA approach is properly followed, then the analyst can reveal how 'participants' production of the world was itself informed by ... particular categorisation devices ... that the parties were orientated to that categorisation device in producing and understanding – moment-by-moment – the conduct that composed its progressive realisation' (Schegloff 2007: 475).

To illustrate, Stokoe (2008) provides an example of a study of police interview data where police officers are interviewing suspects who are accused of beating up a female and male neighbour. The woman being questioned denies hitting her female neighbour and the police thus suggest that if she did not do it then her husband may be responsible instead. She responds to this by stating 'my husband would never hit a woman' (see Chapter 5 for an example of how a CA transcript appears, taken from this police interview study). Stokoe argues that this example shows evidence of the suspect producing a category-based denial where gender is also invoked as a categorisation device as to why her husband could not have hit the victim. The focus of CA is then on how participants 'orient' to all of the categories that they invoke, that is, whether these categories are taken up by others in the conversation, or whether they are disputed, rejected or joked about.

It is in this process of orienting to categorisation that a great deal of gendered work is undertaken in conversation.

To illustrate further, Benwell and Stokoe (2006) draw on CA as an approach in their work specifically focusing on identity. They argue that 'the analysis of "identity" rests on the occasioning of identity categories (for example, nurse, Catholic, heterosexual, man) or person descriptions more generally in talk'. For them, CA analyses 'how identity categories crop up, how they are "oriented" to or noticed by speakers, and what the consequences are for the unfolding interaction' (2006: 8). Benwell and Stokoe (2006) find CA to be of use in such identity analyses as it does not presuppose fixed identities for participants. Thus, 'CA charts the identity work of shifting selves, contingent on the unfolding demands of talk's consequential environment' (2006: 37). This focus of CA on the mutability of the self dovetails with current feminist theory's concern not to stereotype women and men into feminine and masculine roles and to view identity in a more constructionist way. For CA, identity is an accomplishment, something which is achieved or attempted during conversation.

Benwell and Stokoe (2006) examine an extract from the British television show *What Not to Wear* (broadcast on the BBC network), where two expert presenters, Trinny Woodall and Susannah Constantine, give advice to members of the public on how to improve the way that they dress.[2] Benwell and Stokoe focus on the way, in the extract they examine, that the participant, Jane, evaluates her clothing in line with the experts' opinion; from a description of her skirt by the experts as 'nondescript' the woman says, 'I think I've just given up somewhere along the line', which Trinny and Susannah agree with. In this way, turn by turn, the woman is led to agree with the experts that her taste in clothes is deficient, until finally the experts state that 'the real you is so different from the image you're portraying and if it's inside you we've got to haul it out … and you know, put it on the outside' (2006: 2). This is the paradox of this type of television programme: that through assessing someone's clothes, a so-called expert can make a judgement about the 'real identity' of the person, which is in need of transformation by the experts. Various identity categories are explicitly voiced in this interaction, such as those of age and gender, but class is also voiced indirectly, since there is a class difference between the participant and the experts (McRobbie 2009).

Benwell and Stokoe (2006: 4) adopt a social constructionist position which fits in very well with CA; for them 'there is no such thing as an absolute self, lurking behind discourse. A constructionist approach examines people's own understandings of identity and how the notion of inner/outer selves is used rhetorically, to accomplish social action.' They argue, in relation to this example, that 'the very notion of a "real Jane", whether inside or outside, is itself a production of discourse. Who we are to each other, then, is accomplished, disputed, ascribed, resisted, managed and negotiated in discourse' (2006: 4). Here, Trinny and Susannah set up this dichotomy between the outside Jane (wearing unflattering, unfashionable clothes which she has chosen herself) and the inside Jane (which needs to be expressed, and thus externalised, through wearing more exciting fashionable clothes chosen by experts) in order to justify their own actions. Through a CA analysis of the unfolding of the talk, Benwell and Stokoe monitor the way that the participant begins to agree with the opinions of the expert and finally succumbs to their advice to change her clothing style.

Debates within discourse paradigms

Although we have placed a number of approaches under the overarching term 'discourse analysis', there have been debates and often some disagreement between paradigms and between CA and CDA in particular. Debates between CA and CDA have taken place both inside and outside feminist linguistics (see Schegloff 1997; Billig 1999; Wetherell 1998). These debates exemplify a set of key theoretical issues for feminist researchers which we have been discussing here, including when gender is deemed to be relevant, what role gender performs in conversation and how gender interacts with other variables. As we can see from the above discussions of CA, from that perspective, gender should be analysed only when it is talked about explicitly and thus oriented to by participants within conversation. CDA researchers, in contrast, would argue that gender is an omnirelevant feature of conversation (Holmes 1995), a key part of our identity performance and not something that can ever become completely irrelevant. If researchers have to wait until gender is oriented to, then this could be a very time-consuming wait for data, a point made by sociolinguist Joan Swann (2009) – from a CDA perspective many crucial issues of gender and power would be overlooked in the meantime.

As a part of the same argument, Schegloff (1997) believes that critical discourse analysts impose their own notion of what constitutes context onto interactions. He argues that 'discourse is too often made subservient to contexts not of its participants' making, but of its analysts' insistence' (Schegloff 1997: 183). Although context is something which is invoked by speaker and hearer on an ongoing basis throughout the interaction, that does not mean that larger forces are not also at work, and it is these forces that form a fundamental focus of CDA. As Goodwin and Duranti (1992: 6) point out, context is not 'created from scratch within interaction so that larger cultural and social patterns in a society are ignored … Instead … even those participants who are strategically rearranging context to further their own goals invoke organisational patterns that have an existence which extends far beyond the local encounter.'

Although many theorists argue that CA and CDA are rather incompatible, some feminist linguists, including McRae (2009), have attempted to combine elements of CA with techniques more commonly associated with CDA. In her recent work within UK workplaces, McRae (2009) uses valuable analytical elements taken from a CA approach in terms of conversational sequencing and a range of other structural features of talk-in-interaction that a CA approach can bring to a stretch of data. Although she does not explicitly identify herself with a CDA approach, she then takes evidence from the broader socio-cultural context to enhance her own interpretations of her CA data analysis. This includes direct feedback from meeting participants themselves, background information on the companies under study and also general employment statistics taken from the UK context where the data collection took place.

Similarly, Thornborrow (2002) has also attempted to bring together elements of CA and CDA in her work within institutional settings. She analysed the socio-cultural complexity of variables and their meaning outside the immediate context of the transcript, but also produced analyses focusing upon the revealing details of conversational sequencing and categorisation. Mills (2003a: 48) also points out that a logical way forward from debates between CA and CDA would be to use elements of both approaches. This would enable the production of an analysis that covers both 'variables as something engaged with and orientated to within an interaction (CA) and that which views variables as having a material effect on the production and interpretation of the discourse (CDA)'. She goes further, bringing in elements of sociolinguistic study by arguing that such a combined form of analysis should also be fully aware of 'the constraints that class, race, and gender exert on talk, as well as negotiations that individuals engage with in relation to certain stereotypes of these variables' (2003: 48).

Sunderland and Litosseliti (2008) point to potential tensions between Baxter's (2003) FPDA, CA and CDA. They draw attention to Baxter's view that both CA and CDA may have previously overlooked 'the continuously fluctuating ways in which speakers, within any discursive context, are positioned as powerful or powerless by competing social and institutional discourses' – this is the advantage that FPDA offers instead (Baxter 2003: 44, in Sunderland and Litosseliti 2008: 13). Litosseliti and Sunderland point out that both CA and CDA researchers may well wish to contest this viewpoint, particularly as neither CDA nor CA are static entities. However, they rightly point out that the major crux of Baxter's (2003) overall argument is that approaches, including FPDA, should be seen as supplementary to one another instead of being embattled, and a nexus of approaches is put forward by Baxter as the most fruitful way forward for the discipline as a whole. This is a position that very much accords with our own thinking as feminist linguistic researchers. Indeed, a nexus of approaches taking different elements from sociolinguistics, discourse analysis and also pragmatics can be very productive (Mills 2003a; Holmes 2006; Mullany 2007; Schnurr 2009; Mullany 2011).

Feminist pragmatics

Pragmatics is a form of analysis which examines the production of the meaning of utterances in context, analysing the ways in which they come to make sense. Christie (2000) focuses on the benefits of adopting a feminist pragmatics and also discusses the need for pragmatics as a whole to take on board feminist research. By focusing on meaning in context and the way that individuals construct a context within which the other's utterance will be understandable, Christie moves analysis of conversation away from assuming that the meanings of utterances can be found by simply analysing the words in isolation and that the role of gender can be reduced to the sex of the interactants; she argues that 'individuals perform gender and gender identity is perceived as an effect of language, rather than as an a priori factor that determines linguistic behaviour' (Christie 2000: 10).

Christie shows that we can only work out what we think someone means through working through a process of disambiguation; we need to examine the implications and presuppositions of what the speaker has said. In analysing an example where a colleague says to two women, 'I see you two women have stopped gossiping', in order to analyse this as sexist, we need to analyse the presuppositions, where it is assumed that the speaker sees their previous talk as 'gossip' rather than as, say, a business conversation. She makes the following comment:

> It is not just the implication that their speech is trivial that would make this an offensive assertion for the female addressees, it is the way in which such an assertion places the addressees as *typically* female, because it locates them in an ideology of gender that tends to associate all women's speech with both gossiping and triviality. (Christie 2000: 91)

Within a feminist pragmatics, Christie argues that 'language items do not "contain" meaning but can be best seen as triggers that generate meanings' (2000: 91). Thus when researchers analyse language from the perspective of feminist pragmatics, they try to set out the possible range of meanings that a phrase might have, rather than assuming that it has only one meaning. Thus for a sentence such as 'She was 37 but still attractive', it is necessary to access stereotypical presuppositions about women's attractiveness when getting older, in order to make sense of the use of 'but'. It is only with reference to this body of presupposed ideas, which are outside the immediate text of the utterance, that the meaning of the sentence can be inferred.

Christie draws on Sperber and Wilson's (1996) work on relevance theory in order to argue that 'gender is a set of assumptions that are differentially manifest to individuals according to how they represent the world to themselves' (2000: 187). Thus, different people have a variety of perspectives on feminism because of different levels of contact with feminists and access to ideas about women; for Christie, gender can only be seen as a set of assumptions which are drawn on to make sense of utterances.

Christie argues that feminist pragmatics 'alerts analysts to the need to avoid making untestable claims about meaning that are premised on unarticulated intuitions' (2000: 192). This concern with the possible interpretations of utterances does not lead to an endless range of meanings but instead points to 'the meanings that utterances actually appear to have for language users, and function in relation to the needs and goals of their users' (2000: 193).

Cameron (1998a) has also focused on the relationship between gender and pragmatics. She critiques Tannen's (1991) work on gender difference which argues that females and males simply have different speech styles (rapport talk and report talk respectively). This difference of style, attributed to girls and boys allegedly being socialised into different gender-based subcultures, leads men and women to misunderstand each other. Where men use and hear a language of status, women use and hear a language of connection. An example from Tannen's (1991) work is discussed by Cameron (1998a) to show how this model of simple difference leading to misunderstanding is not adequate:

A male and female co-worker are walking between buildings on a cold day:

Woman co-worker: Where's your coat?
Male co-worker: Thanks mom.

Tannen argues that the reasoning behind the male's response is that he has inter-preted the woman to be attempting to use a language of dominance; he feels that she is trying to put him down and treat him as a child. Therefore, he tries to put her down in response by using 'mom' to refer to her. The woman is hurt because she was trying to be friendly and express concern for him. For Tannen, this difference in world-view results in misunderstanding. Cameron reinterprets this anecdotal example and argues that what Tannen leaves out of this discussion is 'the participants' assumptions about gender and about power' (Cameron 1998a: 441). She goes on to ask, 'Why count this as a "misunderstanding" as opposed to a *conflict* about what was meant?' (Cameron 1998a: 441). By drawing on the script of women as carers, indexed by the male co-worker's use of 'mom', 'the man fore-grounds certain gender stereotypical assumptions which could have remained in the background, given that the parties ... have a gender nonspecific relationship as co-workers' (1998a: 442). This foregrounding of stereotypical femininity does not, however, indicate that he misunderstood her intentions. Cameron argues that, instead of focusing on the intentions of interactants, we need to use prag-matics in order to focus on 'the inferential as opposed to the decoding aspects of the process' (1998a: 443). She argues that we need to focus on the process of interpretation, which, for her, 'is also a site where social inequalities and conflicts may have significant effects. It is in the workings of that process, and not only (or even necessarily at all) in the surface forms of discourse that I believe feminists should seek the effects of gender and of power' (1998a: 443).

Thus, she argues that we should focus on conflict rather than on misun-derstanding and difference. For her, 'the question is not whether women and men produce different surface patterns of language use', which they clearly do for Tannen, 'nor whether they have differing general principles for interpreting discourse', which Tannen asserts that they do, but 'whether in interpreting utter-ances they make use of conflicting assumptions about the position a particular speaker in a given situation either is, or ought to be, speaking from; and thus hold conflicting beliefs about the rights and obligations that are normative in the speaker–hearer relationship' (Cameron 1998a: 443). There is a conflict of assumptions about the roles of women and men in society at present, and these conflicts are the result of social changes which have seen women gain powerful positions, especially in previously male-dominated arenas such as the workplace.

Cameron goes on to give an anecdotal example of her own to illustrate this. A friend of hers gave her a brief account of what she termed 'typical male behav-iour'. The friend's father, when his dinner was served, would say to his wife, Vera: 'Is there any ketchup, Vera?' Cameron suggests that there are two possible inter-pretations of this utterance: 'I don't know if there is any ketchup, please tell me', or 'I want ketchup, please get me some.' All of the family members understand this utterance using the second interpretation. Cameron unpacks the inferential process whereby Vera infers that this utterance serves as request for her to go and fetch the ketchup for her husband; the utterance would not have the desired effect if used by any other member of the family. It is only to her husband that Vera has such obligations to serve and it is therefore the service role of traditional women to which this utterance points. Thus, this utterance is not one of misunderstanding, as both participants take for granted this service role.

From a feminist perspective we need to question 'an account [which] sees static (and arguably exaggerated) gender differences' and instead 'it would be more enlightening to see differences of role, status or power (and crucially, conflicts about these) as features of the contexts in which people use language, with the potential to affect the assumptions on which they base their inferences' (Cameron 1998a: 451). This model of interpretation of utterances from a feminist perspective allows for the possibility that a man or a woman can use different speech styles depending on the context, who they are talking to and for what purpose. This approach 'treats the structural fact of gender hierarchy not as something that must *inevitably* show up in surface features of discourse, but as something that participants in any particular conversation may, or may not, treat as relevant to the interpretation of utterances' (Cameron 1998a: 452). The feminist linguist taking a pragmatic approach can therefore make the assumptions and inferences about gender hierarchy explicit in their analysis and need not assume that men and women speak in particular ways. Those assumptions about gender are part of the context.

Another key area of feminist pragmatics research is a focus upon linguistic politeness. Mills (2003a) shows that there is a general presumption within Western societies as a whole that women are more polite than men. In earlier work, Holmes (1995) tends to argue that this stereotypical view of women and men is largely accurate, in her study of a wide range of interactions, although her later work (Holmes 2006), where she has clearly been influenced by developments in Third Wave theoretical perspectives on the field, makes more complex claims about women's and men's politeness use. Mills (2003a) argues that this stereotype is in fact based on the notion that middle-class women's language use is the epitome of politeness. This stereotype that women *should* be concerned more with maintaining harmony within groups and caring for others in the interaction through the use of politeness must be recognised as only a stereotype. Nevertheless, it is a deeply entrenched stereotype which has a major impact on the way that men and women decide what forms of linguistic politeness to use. For example, she shows that many women use the resources of politeness available to them within this stereotype of feminine polite behaviour as a way of strategically achieving their aims in interaction. In one example, she shows how, in a conversation between three women (K, M and D), about a gift from one of the women (K), D *could* be seen as drawing on the resources of politeness in a way which might be seen to be typical of emphasised femininity (Baker 2008a). In this abridged extract, which takes place as D is getting ready to serve a meal to everyone, she thanks K for her gift of a shell from New Zealand, on numerous occasions (see Mills 2003a: 228 for the full stretch of discourse). The frequency of her thanking K seems to be disproportionate to the gift itself. For example:

K: [gives gift of shell to D] when you come to New Zealand you can come
      and pick your own off the rocks
D: [(laughs) just look at that =
M: = beautiful =
D: = isn't that gorgeous
M: [that's a real shell
...

And later on M and D again thank K for the gift of the shell:

M: oh that's lovely
K: [if not leave it behind
D: How nice of you
M: [oh that's lovely =
D: = oh thanks that's really lovely

                                                        (Mills 2003a: 228)

After each thanking episode, K takes the opportunity to begin another turn with more information about this type of shell, where it is found, what colours you can find and so on. D, in an interview, revealed that she was trying to start serving the meal, which was ready, and that she thought that if she thanked K for the gift, that would bring the interaction to a close, to a point where they could begin to eat. D manages to do this towards the end of the extract:

M: I've never seen anything like that (.) really lovely thank you very much
D: RIGHT well I think the easiest thing to do is if I start serving everyone
                                                        (Mills 2003a: 228)

Politeness formulae of thanking which seem to be stereotypically feminine are used here tactically in order to bring the conversation to a close. We therefore need to be careful that we do not conclude that there is a simple correlation between what seems to be excessive use of politeness formulae and the construction of a feminine identity. If politeness formulae are used in this tactical way, as well as constructing gender identity, they also have other functions.

In relation to politeness, Eckert and McConnell-Ginet draw attention to the overarching importance of the way one's utterances are interpreted. Whereas you may intend to be respectful towards another, speakers may well, because of their views on gender, interpret these utterances as deferential. Eckert and McConnell-Ginet discuss the use of questioning intonation on statements, often termed uptalk or upspeak. They suggest that the high-rise terminal, which characterises 'Valley Girl' speech, the speech style of young women largely in California, is often analysed as a signal that those who use it do not know what they are talking about, since statements are transformed by this intonational pattern into what sound like questions. Rather than accepting this negative view of uptalk, Eckert and McConnell-Ginet suggest that questioning intonation may simply signal that the person is not giving the final word on the matter, that they are open to the topic continuing, or even that they are not yet ready to cede their turn.

The notion of politeness has also been essential in discussions of 'Japanese women's language' particularly in relation to indirect indexing, as mentioned above (see the sub-section on 'Interactional sociolinguistics', pp. 72–5). Lexical items which are seen to index femininity alongside the politeness concepts of deference and respect are termed 'honorifics', and the study of honorifics has played an important role in pragmatics research on politeness (Brown and Levinson 1987). The honorifics system was examined as it was claimed that women used more honorifics than men and that this was one of the major features of 'women's language'. Yoshida and Sakurai (2005: 198) demonstrate that the use of honorifics is much more varied than had previously been assumed, and that in their analysis of family conversations, participants switch from the plain style which uses relatively few honorifics to a more formal style which uses more honorifics 'in order to express their role oriented identity'. Yoshida and Sakurai show that the female participants in their study use a relatively plain style in most conversations with their husbands, but shift to the more formal style when they are drawing attention to their role as wives, for example when they inform their husbands that they have completed a domestic task such as cooking a meal:

> *Wife:* Gohan   *desu   yo (formal)*
>   Dinner   COP [ADD.HON] SFP   addressee honorific, sentence
> final particle
>
>   Your dinner awaits you

However, they note that men also shift to these more formal forms when addressing their wives when they have completed their domestic tasks:

> *Husband:* Futon shiki *mashi ta yo (formal)*
> Futon   set   [ADD HON PAST] SFP   addressee honorific,
> past, sentence final particle
> I finished making the bed

Yoshida and Sakurai (2005: 203) ask, if these couples normally talk to each other using the plain style which does not use many honorifics, and if there are no discernible changes in the social or psychological distance between them and the formality of the context remains the same, why is it that, on such occasions, the couple switch to this more formal style? They suggest that in the above example 'the husband's utterance indexes his quasi socio-cultural identity as a wife. In this situational context, this husband is engaged in making the bed, which has traditionally been considered the job of wives. Therefore, he sees himself as a "quasi" wife.' Thus because honorifics may indicate, amongst other things, femininity, this indexing is available to men as well as women to create additional meanings.

As another illustration of recent work in this area of pragmatic analysis of politeness, Herring (2003) suggests that in online communities, women are more concerned with politeness than men. Male users tend to see concern about politeness as censorship or a 'waste of bandwidth' (Herring 2003: 209), whereas women find the establishing of posting rules very important, and sites which are predominantly used by women often have clear rules of conduct.

Herring (2003: 209) argues that 'women participate more actively and enjoy greater influence in environments where the norms are controlled by an individual or individuals entrusted with maintaining order and focus in the group'. On the Internet, where rules for linguistic behaviour are often more fluid as a result of identities being disembodied and contact being remote, not face-to-face, aggression tends to win out over non-aggressive behaviour. Herring (2003: 209) notes that 'male respondents to an Internet survey cited "censorship" as the greatest threat to the Internet, whereas females cited "privacy" as their greatest concern'. However, there is a tendency in Herring's work to tend to revert to treating men and women as monolithic categories. More detailed research on the pragmatics of gender in online communication thus needs to carried out in order to emphasise the importance of this growing area of linguistic development (see Mullany 2004).

A further example of work on gender and politeness is Eckert and McConnell-Ginet's (2003) discussion of the use of compliments, a classic linguistic feature that is frequently examined in studies of linguistic politeness. Rather than discussing whether men or women compliment or receive compliments more, as earlier studies have done (see Holmes 1995), they examine the function of compliments and what role complimenting has in constructing the gender order: 'to compliment a person's looks is to imply that one's opinion of the person's looks should matter to that person. It also implies that how they look is (or should be) an important component of the face they are trying to project in the situation where the compliment occurs' (Eckert and McConnell-Ginet 2003: 150).

Thus by giving a compliment, you are not simply showing the person that you care about them, or that you like their appearance, or even that you count them a friend, but it also determines the make-up of the gender order, that 'institutional and ideological dimension of gendered identities and behaviour' (Eckert and McConnell-Ginet 2003: 5). Eckert and McConnell-Ginet argue that perhaps men, in giving fewer compliments on appearance, are seen as more genuine when they do give them; they go on to say that 'rather than saying that there are gendered rules for complimenting ... it is useful to explore some of the ways linguistic practices such as complimenting ... help produce gendered personae' (Eckert and McConnell-Ginet 2003: 156).

Summary

Thus, we have shown in this chapter that there are a range of different positions which feminist linguists can adopt when they analyse spoken interactions and written texts. None of these approaches is used exclusively by feminists; rather they can be seen as starting points on which linguistic analyses can be based. Most of these approaches can be combined with other positions, and the boundaries between them are very fluid in order to better analyse a particular element, interaction, text or context. In the next chapter, we move on to explore the next step in the research process, methodological approaches to the analysis of data.

5 Methodological approaches

There seems little point to our academic interests if they do not at some stage articulate with real-world concerns and enable us or our readers to identify, for example, certain employment practices as unfair and ill-informed, based more on stereotypes and prejudice than they are on people's actual behavior in the real world. At some point, our research has to be able to travel out of the academy in order to draw attention to and challenge unquestioned practices that reify certain behaviors as being morally, or aesthetically, better than others.

Holmes and Meyerhoff 2003a: 14

Methodologies and methods

Now that we have presented an overview of the different theoretical approaches that can be used in feminist linguistic studies in Chapter 4, it is important to move on to consider exactly which methodological approaches and particular research methods researchers use in order to produce their studies. The aim of this overview is to present readers with a clear idea of the questions that need to be asked and the kinds of decisions that need to be made when designing, planning and executing one's own study, or when critically assessing the feminist linguistic studies of others. We will begin with an overview of current debates regarding feminist linguistic research methodologies that are circulating in the research field.

Qualitative and quantitative methods

As we pointed out in Chapter 1, feminist linguists have recently called for more integrated methodological approaches in language and gender studies, in response to the fact that the field has been largely dominated since the mid-1990s by qualitative methodologies. Before that time, quantitative methods were also popular. As a basic distinction, qualitative methodologies involve detailed analysis of small-scale studies, taking into account the particularities of the context. There is a tendency not to generalise about gender as a whole, but rather to come to conclusions about the particular context in question. Quantitative studies are more broadly based. They involve a greater number of participants and amount of data, and the analysis is controlled in a much more systematic way. Because of the broader base of quantitative studies and the use of statistical analyses, they are more reliable and valid when making generalisations about gender as a whole.

It is useful to give a brief overview of these developments to contextualise the move towards mixed methodologies. The dominance of qualitative research methods came about in response to critiques of early quantitative research, including the sociolinguistic work of Labov (1972) and Trudgill (1974). Their findings were challenged by feminists as they tended to make overgeneralisations about 'females' and 'males' and positioned men and women in direct opposition to one another (see Coates and Cameron 1989; Eckert and McConnell-Ginet 1992). Quantitative research thus tended to assume that women and men were always to be compared and that the search for differences between men and women should be the main focus of research.

Another interrelated reason why studies have tended to focus on small-scale qualitative analyses is that the first researchers in the field of language and gender, most notably Lakoff (1975) and Spender (1980), tended to make broad-brush generalisations about 'women's language' on the basis of little or no data. These anecdotal generalisations were very similar to the stereotypes of white middle-class 'women's language' in Western societies, as seen in Table 3.1 in Chapter 3, above. Although this early work was significant in its political aim of bringing attention to the discriminatory ways in which women were treated in/through language, and the discipline itself arguably began to emerge in response to such early works, it became clear to many that gender and language studies had to move away from these problematic generalisations, which excluded the analysis of many different groups of women and diversity amongst groups of women (and men).

Furthermore, a quantitative approach on its own struggled to produce refined, context-sensitive analyses. To give an example, if you were studying the use of apologies, in quantitative research you would count the number of times 'I apologise' or 'I'm sorry' were used. Similarly, such an analysis would be unable to distinguish between the use of 'I'm sorry' in a genuine apology and 'I'm sorry' used ironically or sarcastically. You would also not be able to tell if an apology was accepted or rejected by the intended recipient.

broad

Researchers thus moved from using quantitative approaches to a more 'punctual', qualitative form of analysis which analysed the language use of particular women in specific contexts. For example, British black women in Dudley (Edwards 1989), linguistic variation amongst women in a Welsh mining village (Thomas 1989), the wedding songs of British Gujarati women (Edwards and Katbamna 1989), McElhinny's (1998) study of women police officers in Pittsburgh, to mention but a few studies. The linguistic differences between and within groups of women, and later between and within groups of men when empirical studies of language and masculinities began to emerge in the 1990s onward (Johnson 1997; Cameron 1997; Kuiper 1998; Coates 2003), became the key focus, rather than having to assume that the language of women as a group differed from that of men as a group. This focus on variation within groups of women and within groups of men was most fruitfully explored via a small-scale qualitative approach.

While this work has produced a wealth of meticulously analysed data in specific social settings, it is often very difficult to generalise from such research findings. Within linguistics, and also humanities and social science disciplines more generally, there has been a shift away from the so-called 'paradigm wars' between quantitative and qualitative methods, where work had been deeply entrenched in one methodological paradigm or the other (Tashakkori and Teddlie 1998). Instead, the development of mixed methodologies has become popular. Indeed, in recent years feminist researchers have started combining elements of quantitative research within qualitative approaches. This has led to a shift in quantitative research, so that it is no longer solely focused on making generalisations about women and men as a whole, in direct comparison with one another. Quantitative data are now often brought to bear on small-scale feminist linguistic analysis.

Holmes and Meyerhoff (2003a) argued that, although quantitative approaches were unfashionable at their time of writing, there are distinct advantages in bringing together quantitative and qualitative work, using quantitative methods to establish initial patterns, which can then be followed up and refined with more detailed, qualitative research. In the introduction to their *Handbook of Language and Gender*, they draw attention to the work of high-profile researchers including Scott Kiesling, Penny Eckert, Ruth Wodak and Ann Pauwels, along with themselves, who all demonstrate the values of using quantitative and qualitative approaches or a mixed-methods approach. Swann (2002) and Swann and Maybin (2008) have similarly argued in favour of using quantitative methods in language and gender research to establish overarching patterns which can then be followed up by more detailed, qualitative investigation.

Indeed, many researchers have now argued that a move towards mixed-methodological approaches, where quantitative and qualitative approaches are combined, will move the field of enquiry forward. This is often seen alongside the 'pragmatist' approach, highlighted in Chapter 1, where methodologies are selected for practical reasons, with particular methods chosen as they best suit a specific line of research enquiry. The days of researchers within the humanities and social sciences having an unquestioned loyalty to either a quantitative or a qualitative approach are thought to be over (Tashakkori and Teddlie 1998).

The advantages of taking a mixed-methodological approach as opposed to a solely qualitative approach include improving research validity and the ability to reach wider audiences (Dörnyei 2007). However, attempting to be proficient across different areas does run the danger of spreading oneself too thinly, and researchers can risk not having the requisite knowledge to be able to carry out mixed-methods research successfully. Feminist linguists thus need to be careful, and researcher reflexivity is important in order to ensure that accountability to more than one method can be achieved (Sunderland and Litosseliti 2008). Working in research teams made up of those with differing methodological expertise can help to circumvent this problem. Sunderland and Litosseliti (2008: 13) also rightly question a free-for-all 'pick-and-mix' approach – some theoretical approaches and thus also the methods that go along with these approaches may not be that compatible, as we have discussed in Chapter 4, and this is also important to consider when deciding upon particular research methods.

There has thus started to be a more observable shift in methodological thinking within feminist linguistics, and this current moment in time represents a period of transition. Studies using more quantitatively orientated methods are becoming more visible. Some language and gender researchers, such as Harrington (2008) and Baker (2008), have questioned the assumption that qualitative and quantitative analyses are mutually exclusive. In the recent *Gender and Language Research Methodologies* (Harrington *et al.* 2008), sections are devoted to mixed methods. This includes using the tools and techniques of corpus linguistics. Baker (2010) points out that a popular misconception of corpus linguistics is that it is solely a quantitative method – in reality corpus linguistics research takes a mixed-methods approach, where overall language patterns are viewed in light of language in context in the form of 'concordance line' data (where specific words are examined within their surrounding co-text; see the section on 'Recording data and the observer's paradox' in this chapter, pp. 109–10, below) and also through the analysis of more detailed stretches of language data.

Baker has shown how corpus linguistics can be integrated with techniques from sociolinguistics (Baker 2010) and discourse analysis (Baker 2006). Other researchers argue for the integration of traditional correlational sociolinguistic methods, similar to those used by Labov (1972) and Trudgill (1974), as a supplementary quantitative analytical method (Hultgren 2008). Eckert (2000) successfully combines quantitative and qualitative methods in her seminal sociolinguistic study of gender, adolescence and social identities in American high schools. These studies will be considered in more detail later in the chapter.

We will now move on to detail other important methodological decisions that need to be made when conducting contemporary feminist linguistic studies. Once we have covered these key issues, we will then define and provide examples of particular research methods in action in feminist linguistics. We will then spend some time detailing successful mixed-methodological approaches that have been conducted so far, including the aforementioned works of Baker (2008b), Hultgren (2008) and Eckert (2000). From the pragmatist methodological approach, it may well be that on some occasions a research question can be best answered and explored by adopting a qualitative or quantitative approach alone. However, the trend towards mixed methods is one that is growing in popularity and also one that promises to move the field of enquiry forward. We predict that this combined approach will make a significant impact in the field over the next few years.

The researcher and the researched: making studies relevant

The importance of research with a specific political purpose, or action-centred research, has been emphasised at various points in Chapters 1 and 2. In order to conduct research which successfully addresses the 'what is to be done?' question, the methodological choices that are made during the research process are crucially important and need to be thoroughly documented, in order to ensure that the findings from projects are of some use and relevance outside the immediate academic audience. Studies of language, gender and feminism should aim to be of applied practical use to those who have either taken part in the research as the community being 'researched' or as research informants, or the findings need to be of demonstrable use to those who are outside the immediate research community but who can nevertheless benefit from the research findings. In order to ensure that these methodological processes are transparent, research reflexivity is required, where investigators offer an open, transparent reflection and documentation of their research process when writing up their studies (see the section on 'Feminist standpoints: research ethics', pp. 114–19, below, and Mullany 2008).

To illustrate, Holmes and Meyerhoff (2003a) make the crucial point that, despite the recent trend away from essentialised notions of gender within language and gender research, it is clear that gender as a social category is still highly prevalent in wider society, and very often it is essentialised, stereotypical gender categories which are perceived to exist. These inaccurate, overgeneralised categories reify gender differences and can have a direct, negative impact upon people's daily lives. As a consequence of this, there is a real need for language and gender research to make itself more relevant to those outside academia. Holmes and Meyerhoff (2003a: 10) encourage researchers to be 'directed by the needs and interests of the communities of speakers studied', instead of simply satisfying their own 'academic appetite'. Therefore, instead of creating knowledge for knowledge's sake, they encourage academics to think very carefully when selecting areas of investigation, coming to final decisions through negotiation with those being researched, in order to find out what would be of use to them. As we have already seen, in the quotation at the beginning of this chapter, which operates as an overarching theme for both this chapter and indeed the book as a whole, Holmes and Meyerhoff (2003a) go so far as to question the overall logic and purpose of engaging in academic research not based upon such principles, using workplace employment practices as one example of a worthwhile, societal concern which warrants investigation.

Feminist language and gender research has always been political in the broadest sense, through its commitment to gender equality. However, Philips (2003: 266) argues that 'there has been a loss of a broader practical political perspective' within recent research which needs to be rectified. In the words of Holmes and Meyerhoff (2003a: 14), academic research needs to be a form of 'social activism', following examples such as Cameron (2003), Talbot (2003) and Holmes and Stubbe (2003).

Holmes and Meyerhoff (2003a) make a further point in relation to research funding. They argue that increasingly academics are being called to account in terms of the research they produce, in that more and more frequently academic work is being held accountable in terms of what it gives back to the community that funds it in the first place (either indirectly through taxation and/or more directly from particular funding bodies). All this suggests that academics have a responsibility to conduct research which is directly orientated towards the political needs of the communities being studied. In UK-based institutions this has recently become known as the 'knowledge transfer' or 'impact' agenda.

However, there are a range of tensions here, and such academic responsibility is far from straightforward when put into practice. For example, academic research which has wider political relevance outside the immediate community of people being studied may be at odds with the aims and needs of those being researched. It is possible, too, that individuals within communities will have different and perhaps incompatible needs. Those being researched may well have a hetero-geneous set of political needs, particularly in institutions where power roles, as well as differing social identities, often result in a range of *different* and often conflicting political positions. Furthermore, the community may have aims that researchers feel uncomfortable with, perhaps conflicting with researchers' own political positioning. The negotiation process is thus extremely complex, and researchers are frequently faced with a number of dilemmas (see Mullany 2008).

Baxter's (2003) work provides a good example of how this process of reci-procity and practically relevant research can work successfully in action. She conducted 'ethnographic-style' fieldwork in a small UK-based dotcom busi-ness (see the sub-section on 'Ethnography', pp. 97–9, below, for a definition). She identified different discourses, following Foucault's macro, pluralised defi-nition (see the section on 'Discourse analysis', pp. 76–85, above), that were significant to the running of the business. Baxter turned these clearly identifi-able discourses, including a discourse of masculinisation, into a 'discourse map' which was designed especially for members of the company who had taken part in her research. The discourse map was presented in a jargon-free, diagrammatic form, which was then used by members of the company as a tool to raise their individual awareness of what could be hampering their effectiveness in business encounters with one another. The 'Language in the Workplace' project in New Zealand, run by Janet Holmes and her colleagues, has numerous examples of activities, events and publications, where the findings of their research, including their numerous projects on gender, have been of applied practical relevance. This includes the hosting of events, including feedback workshops and presentations for those who have taken part in the studies and written publications, including company reports and specially written publications in business and organisational magazines (all of these activities are fully detailed on the project's website (see this book's website for further details).

In linguistics research outside gender and language studies, there is also a critical awareness of the importance of the reciprocal relationship that should exist between the researcher and the researched. For example, sociolinguist Walt Wolfram refers to a principle of 'linguistic gratuity' that researchers need to apply to their work, defined as the requirement to 'pursue positive ways of returning linguistic favors to the community' (Wolfram 1993: 227) . This principle is a good one to abide by when conducting feminist linguistic research

Research methods for feminist linguistic research

Ethnography

Ethnography is an approach to the collecting of data which is employed by a wide range of different researchers from a variety of disciplinary backgrounds. Sociologists Hammersley and Atkinson (1995: 1) identify this method as follows: 'The ethnographer participating, overtly or covertly, in people's daily lives for an extended period of time, watching what happens, listening to what is said, asking questions – in fact, collecting whatever data are available to throw light on the issues that are the focus of the research.' The process of the ethnographer 'participating … in people's daily lives' is more commonly referred to as the methodological technique of 'participant observation'. Stewart (1998: 6) argues that, whilst there can be 'multiple approaches' to the process of ethnographic data collection, participant observation is the 'focal research instrument' of an ethnographic study (see the sub-section on 'Participant observation', pp. 99–100, below, for further discussion).

Early ethnographic studies of gender and language which are now classic examples of feminist linguistic anthropology include Keenan's (1974) work in a Malagasy community and Gal's (1979) work in Oberwart, Hungary. Through participant observation Keenan (1974) found clear evidence of women breaking the norm of indirectness, which in Malagasy was a speech style most valued by men, not women. One reason for this which she discovered through her ethnographic presence was that men often sent women to do the verbal confronting of others within the community for them. This was one of the first studies to show a break with the traditional Western assumption that women use indirectness more than men. This clear cultural difference, which emerged through prolonged exposure to the research site, provides evidence which questions the logic of any biologically essentialist argument which may claim that women are 'naturally' predisposed to use indirect language strategies (cf. Cameron 2007a).

As we mentioned in Chapter 4, Gal's (1979) ethnographic approach enabled her to identify why younger women within Oberwart were engaging in the sociolinguistic process of language shift, favouring German over Hungarian. Prolonged exposure to this community enabled Gal to discover that German was associated with a new urban way of life and employment, which enabled these women to break with the community traditions of engaging in farm labour. Their use of German clearly indexed their rejection of the older ways of life and their embracing of the newer social-economic shifts within their society.

More recently, gender and language researcher Goodwin (2006) uses an ethnographic approach to investigate the speech of adolescent girls in the US. She describes ethnography as a tool which allows us to see how the social order is achieved. One of its key advantages is in making explicit how seemingly simple statements lead to the creation of hierarchies and identities: in her analysis of girls' play, she states: 'within a single utterance a girl can invoke a coherent domain of action, a small culture, one that includes identities, actions and biographies for the participants within it' (Goodwin 2006: 7). The focus of ethnography in her work is to analyse how the girls use language as a socialisation tool to get others to see their points of view. Goodwin points out that through her ethnographic approach, 'children are viewed as agents in the co-construction of events rather than the passive recipients of cultural norms' (Goodwin 2006: 16). The analysis of girls' play therefore focuses on a 'temporally unfolding process through which separate parties demonstrate to each other their ongoing understanding of the events they are engaged in by building actions that contribute to the further progression of these very same events' (Goodwin 2006: 25).

This type of very close, textured analysis is based on fieldwork study of groups of girls in a particular school and the way that they achieve inclusion or exclusion from a group. Goodwin points out that the girls in her study can be witnessed indexing 'social status with reference to events and objects in bids to both assert their position in the group and circumscribe the boundaries of the group' (Goodwin 2006: 156). What is particularly interesting in Goodwin's study of this group is the way that she is able to analyse the exclusion of particular girls from the group itself. She argues that 'one way of constituting and displaying alliances is through affirming similar perspectives with respect to an event' (Goodwin 2006: 195). Here, therefore, talk is analysed for the way that groups are constituted.

In all of these studies feminist ethnographers have focused on gender but tried to explore the complex ways in which gender figures in interaction and language choice. Ethnographers are careful not to assume that interactants can be split into rigid sex-based groups in terms of their language use.

Swann and Maybin (2008: 25) point out that, within British sociolinguistics, there has been a recent trend within language and gender studies towards what they term 'linguistic ethnography'. From this perspective it is more common for researchers to conduct 'ethnographic style' research, a term coined by Green and Bloome (1997) instead of the classic anthropological approach of full-blown, complete immersion in particular cultures which most often takes years to collect data. Mullany's (2007) and Pichler's (2008, 2009) studies provide examples of this and these works are discussed in more detail below.

Participant observation

Duranti (1997) has drawn a useful distinction between the different 'modes' that participant observation can take, ranging from 'passive participation' to 'complete participation' (1997: 99). It is useful to include these terms as part of a feminist linguistic toolkit. Duranti argues that whilst 'complete participation' can be very beneficial to the research process by providing the fieldworker with the opportunity to 'directly experience the very processes they are trying to document' (1999: 100), he also acknowledges that it may not always be possible or ethically appropriate to conduct this kind of research.

Furthermore, he highlights that there is an inherent difficulty associated with becoming a complete participant, in that researchers may become distracted by their own role within the interaction, and lose sight of their task as researchers. Duranti thus suggests that participant observers should resist the temptation to become complete participants. Instead, he argues that it may be more beneficial for the researcher to adopt the position of 'accepted bystander' or a 'professional overhearer' (1997: 101). By adopting these positions as an alternative to being a complete participant, the potential problem of the project's results becoming skewed by the researcher 'going native' and thus arguably running the risk of being unable to say anything that will be of 'wider theoretical interest' (Alvesson and Deetz 2000: 83) can be avoided.

To illustrate these categories in action, Mullany's (2007) ethnographic-style feminist sociolinguistic work in professional workplaces provides a detailed example of how the role of participant observer can fluctuate and shift during the research process in gender and language studies, particularly when a range of different research methods are used. When observing business meetings, Mullany aimed to be a 'complete observer', or a 'professional overhearer', to use Duranti's terminology, sitting in an unobtrusive position, with the intention that participants should carry on as they normally would if she were not present. However, in practice, this was not possible throughout the duration of meeting observation. At the commencement of every meeting, as a fieldworker who was present in meeting rooms, it was important for Mullany as fieldworker to introduce herself, explain her presence and assure participants of complete confidentiality, as well as giving them the opportunity to ask any questions they may have had about the project. Fieldworker presence at the meeting and introductions were frequently recorded in the minutes.

On occasions, participants would also refer to her directly at particular points in the meeting, and often this would involve participation on Mullany's part in order to maintain a good working rapport with her informants. Often this took the form of laughter at the boundaries of meetings, such as the end of a topic or the opening and closing of the speech event, important in order to build rapport with the meeting participants. Within meetings, her role thus fluctuated between complete observer and observer as participant, depending on what was demanded of her in the particular circumstances. Additionally, when she first entered workplaces, the human resources departments set up 'induction' activities for her, so she directly experienced the processes that new employees would go through. When doing ethnographic fieldwork in a manufacturing company, she was required to fulfil a task that all new employees are required to do: make one of the products that the company manufactures. On such occasions, her role as a participant in the activity in hand became primary, as she was required to work on the shop floor alongside all other colleagues fulfilling the same task. These points can thus be classified as at the complete participation end of Duranti's continuum.

Interviews

Using interviews as a research method is a long-established practice in a multitude of disciplines throughout the humanities and social sciences (see Hester and Francis 1994), and linguistics is no exception. As a consequence of the popular nature of this method, there are a number of different forms that interviews can take. There is what is commonly referred to as the 'standardised interview', where researchers ask exactly the same question in exactly the same manner to every interviewee to avoid contaminating the answers that informants produce. In contrast, there is what has been termed the 'active' interview (Holstein and Gubrium 1995), where interviewers will take a flexible approach to questioning and where they ask open-ended and less-structured questions.

The standardised interview is far quicker to conduct and is more commonly associated with quantitative, survey-based studies, whereas the active interview is more commonly associated with qualitative research methods, including ethnographic interviews. Ethnographers have produced various definitions of what actually constitutes an ethnographic interview, but as we have detailed above in the section on 'Defining gender', pp. 42–6, within some recent sociolinguistic studies, although researchers have produced full-scale ethnographic studies in their most definitive sense, as with the two-year fieldwork project undertaken by Eckert (2000, see below), other researchers' work can be classified more accurately as 'ethnographic-style' research, and 'ethnographic-style' interviews have been conducted by feminist linguistic researchers.

Pichler's (2008, 2009) recent work on five British Bangladeshi girls aged 14–15 living in London provides a good illustrative example of this, as well as providing an example of a successful multimethod study. In addition to analysing data from (non-participant) observation, questionnaires and conversations, Pichler (2008) also conducted ethnographic-style interviews. Following the work of Miller and Glassner (1997: 99), she characterises ethnographic-style interviews as 'a display of cultural knowledge by the interviewers'. She argues that this interview format should be used in addition to the analysis of spontaneous spoken data in order to examine the 'interplay between discourse and cultural norms and practices, inflected with gender, ethnicity and religion … [it] seems well suited for a multi-dimensional investigation of participants' own understanding of the practices and categories that they see as relevant, encouraging a reflexive and critical exploration of the perspectives and positions of both researcher and researched'.

In contrast to Pichler's (2008, 2009) multimethod approach, where interview data are used effectively alongside recorded conversational data, many classic language variation and change studies within sociolinguistics have relied upon the interview as *the* speech event where all data collection takes place (Labov 1972; Trudgill 1974). From within the disciplinary perspective of linguistic anthropology, Duranti (1997: 103) argues that analysing data taken from interview data alone is no substitute for observing and recording real-world interactions: it is only by producing analyses of spontaneous interactions that 'a culturally informed linguistic analysis' can be produced, which is of critical concern to feminist linguists (Duranti 1997: 103). Multimethod approaches such as Pichler's can provide a solution to this, if interviews are used alongside methods where naturally occurring interactions (i.e. those which take place in non-artificial settings) are analysed alongside interview data (see also Mullany 2007 for another example of an approach combining interviews with spontaneous interactional data).

Retrospective interviews

Baxter's (2002, 2003) ethnographic FPDA work in British secondary schools (high schools) with pupils aged 14–15 aptly demonstrates the value of including retroactive interviews within a multimethod approach to enhance the researcher's analysis and interpretation of the recorded spoken interactions that have previously taken place. Following video recordings of classroom interaction recorded as part of the students' GCSE examinations (the examinations taken at the end of high school) the children aged 14–15 gave the following assessments of their own performances along with evaluations of their peers in a retrospective interview with Judith Baxter.

Example 1:

1	*Rebecca:*	I was probably more self-conscious in the bigger group in
2		case I would sound a fool. I had a lot of things to say but I
3		couldn't say them because I wasn't picked.
4	*Interviewer:*	So you wanted to speak?
5	*Rebecca:*	Yes, I really did. I really wanted to say my view. At one
6		point I was going to shout out, but I thought, 'No, I'd
7		better behave myself.'
8	*Interviewer:*	Was that affected by the camera?
9	*Rebecca:*	I don't think I would have ever shouted out. That would
10		have been rude and I would have got told off.
11	*Interviewer:*	Did anyone shout out?
12	*Rebecca:*	Yeah. Joe and Damion did because they wanted everyone
13		to know what they thought.

Example 2:

1	*Kate:*	The girls are quieter. The boys say something and the girls
2		just support it.
3	*Cathy:*	The boys say what they think. It's like the husband and the
4		little wife who has to support them.
5	*Kate:*	The girls are like hiding their face in shame that they are
6		actually disagreeing with the boys.

(Baxter, 2002:17)

Baxter uses the material gained in these interviews to enhance her interpretations of the spoken classroom interactions. She draws attention to Rebecca's comment (in Example 1) about not shouting out because 'that would have been rude and I would have got told off' as evidence of her being clearly aware of the different linguistic norms and expectations for girls in the classroom. The boys frequently call out and are not reprimanded by the teacher for rudeness, but Rebecca thinks that she will be if she acts in the same way. In Example 2, Baxter argues that Kate and Cathy are aware of sexual politics and the gender roles of adults and they invoke the heterosexual categories of husband and wife here to explain the dominant linguistic behaviour of the boys and the girls' own complicity in this within the classroom interaction (see also Swann 1998).

Focus groups

Focus groups are very similar to unstructured interviews and it is not unusual for the two terms to be used interchangeably (Benwell 2005). A focus group is based upon 'the collective experience of brain-storming, that is, participants thinking together, inspiring and challenging each other, and reacting to the emerging issues and points' (Dörnyei 2007: 144). Focus groups enable researchers to analyse both the content and manner in which participants speak on a particular set of issues. For focus groups to be successful, a good interviewer is required. Such interviewers are more frequently referred to as 'moderators' (Dörnyei 2007: 145). Focus groups can consist of structured or semi-structured questions posed by the moderator. The moderator's role is also to facilitate discussion, as in open-ended interviews, and monitor the development of discussions, ensuring that all participants get their chance to take the conversational floor. Large amounts of spoken-language data can be generated in a focus-group setting, so it is important for feminist linguistic researchers to have a clear idea of the type of data they wish to elicit before embarking on the data-collection process. Reflexivity is also of importance when selecting who it is that should be moderator. In some situations it may be better for researchers to appoint a moderator who shares certain characteristics with the group members to aid discussion and relax informants as much as possible, rather than the researcher acting as a moderator themselves.

The data that are provided from such focus-group encounters can be analysed in a range of different linguistic formats. One excellent example of how focus-group data can be used in language and gender work is Benwell's (2005) study. She wanted to investigate the discourses and cultural meanings of men's magazines by getting male readers' reactions to these written forms of media. She decided to choose a male moderator for both of her focus groups, which consisted of male university students – one group aged 17 and the other group aged 21. The magazines that Benwell wished to analyse were provided in the focus group to attempt to recreate part of the reading process. The male moderator was thus responsible for using the reading materials to stimulate and guide discussion within the two groups.

Benwell's study would have been much different if she had opted to be moderator of the focus groups herself. By choosing a male moderator her method was arguably more likely to produce a franker discussion, with the young men feeling more at ease than they might with her in the role. In addition to being a woman, she was also their direct superior as a university lecturer and also a known gender studies researcher. Benwell brings together the focus-group approach with tools and techniques from CA. She transcribes her focus-group data and then examines this using classic CA analytical devices including membership categorisation analysis (examining terms such as 'lad', 'slut', etc.), though she moves beyond the classic CA approach in her analysis by focusing not just on the text of the transcript itself. She also uses the focus-group data to show how wider cultural meanings are encoded through particular categories that the informants invoke. As an additional method alongside the focus groups Benwell also conducted a comparative analysis of the written text of four men's magazines in the same month as the focus-group data collection. She found the language that the young men used within the focus groups frequently mirrored the language used within the magazine texts themselves, such as use of 'girl' (to describe adult women), 'guy', 'lad', 'bird', 'boobs', 'arse' and 'shag' (Benwell 2005: 159). For further details on how to conduct successful focus group research see Litosseliti (2006b).

Questionnaires

Questionnaires can be very efficient in gaining access to information quickly. As Dörnyei (2007: 101–2) argues, questionnaires are 'relatively easy to construct, extremely versatile and uniquely capable of gathering a large amount of information quickly in a form that is readily processable'. However, he warns that there is a danger of problems with reliability and validity if questionnaires are not constructed properly. Some obvious things to prevent such problems include: avoiding complex language, ambiguous/loaded words and questions which are likely to be answered in the same way by everyone. There is a limit to the depth of information that you can gain from a questionnaire, and informants also have to fit themselves into the researcher's own subjectivity by the nature of how the research method is constructed. Nevertheless, if used properly it can be a very effective and efficient research tool for discovering general trends within groups of women or men.

For example, Mills (2003b) wanted to discover whether feminist women used their husband's or partner's surnames or whether they retained their own surnames. Mills wanted to discover also what choices these women made about the surnames they gave to their children. She put together a series of questions about surname use, consisting of simple 'yes/no' questions (such as 'Did you take your husband's surname on marriage?') and also more discursive questions (such as 'If you took your husband's name on marriage, could you say what factors contributed to your changing your name'). She sent 20 questionnaires to feminist women that she knew by electronic mail, and she asked these women to forward the questionnaire to other feminist women. By this 'snowball' method she was able to collect 40 questionnaires which reported not only the names which feminist women adopted, but the attitudes that they had to their choice of name. The questionnaire also enabled these women to report on the way that, for some of them, it was important to retain one name for a particular context, for example friends and family, whilst having a different surname for academic purposes or in their work environment.

Overall, the questionnaire analysis revealed that many of the women who had taken their husband's name did so because (a) they preferred the aesthetics of their husband's name to their own; (b) they wanted to demonstrate how serious they were about the relationship; (c) they wished to break with the past. Some of the women who had taken their husband's name remarked on the difficulty of doing this when faced with friends who disapproved of the decision. Although it is difficult to generalise from a small-scale sample such as this, it is possible to discover trends within groups of women in relation to such issues as the surnames they use and their attitudes to surname choice.

In another example, Dröschel (2007) employed questionnaires as a method in her sociolinguistic study examining how gay slang terms have changed over time. She wished to investigate self-referential slang terms as well as terms referring to others. She sent out questionnaires to groups of gay men in England and the US, as well as gaining questionnaire data from heterosexual women and men in England to assess how much of the colloquial vocabulary used by gay men was being used as non-gay slang. The questionnaire was targeted at men ranging between the ages of 20 and 65 and aimed at informants from a variety of socio-economic backgrounds and with a variety of educational levels. One of her aims was to assess how far 'Polari', a form of gay British slang popular in the 1950s and 1960s, had died out and how far it has become influenced by American slang (see Chapter 6 for further discussion and examples of Polari).

The questionnaires consisted of a personal background section, requesting details including age, gender, sexuality, level of urbanisation, proximity to gay culture and level of interest in language. This was followed by a section for inform-ants to list terms that are used to refer to gay men and an assessment of whether such terms had positive, negative or neutral connotations, and whether usage was public, private or intimate. The next section contained 90 lexical items, around 70 per cent of which were taken from Polari. Respondents were requested to tick those that they had heard of, say whether they used them themselves and give a brief definition of those lexical items with which they were familiar. The final section asked for terms of abuse if used by an outsider that would be positive if used by an insider. A third of all questionnaires were returned from gay respond-ents (48 in total). Only 10 were returned from England compared with 38 from American men. The typical respondent was an American male in his thirties. Her questionnaire was thus not as representative as she wanted it to be in the research design process, being more limited in terms of age range and also cultural background. She acknowledges this and points out that further investigation is required. Nevertheless the results that she did obtain enabled her to make some interesting observations.

Her results led her to conclude that it is now inaccurate to talk about gay male slang in a singular way, as was previously the case with Polari in Britain. The questionnaire findings revealed that, instead of gay slang being a communicative form that allowed gay men to identify with other gay men regardless of any social identity/background differences, nowadays slang lexis is unstable and there is a lack of consensual meaning. Meaning and usage differ depending upon age, occu-pation, ethnicity and socio-economic status. There is also evidence that gay slang has made its way into Western heterosexual cultures and that it is often impos-sible to distinguish between them, though identity terms that were pejorative when used by outsiders were alternatively seen as celebratory and positive when used by insiders, including the terms 'queer', 'fairy' and 'fag' (Dröschel 2007: 127; see Chapter 6 for further discussion).

Questionnaires can thus be very useful tools to use when aiming to assess self-knowledge and self-report of usage of particular forms of linguistic usage and cultural linguistic practices.

Discourse completion tasks

Spencer-Oatey (2000) uses discourse completion tasks (DCTs) as a way of analysing politeness, but it is clear that they could also be used in analyses of gender and language. A discourse completion test is administered in the same way as a questionnaire, but it is a half-way house between working with recorded data and using interviews and questionnaires. The researcher constructs a scenario, for example, which would elicit a particular response from the participant. Spencer-Oatey uses discourse completion tasks to assess how participants would respond to unfounded accusations. She constructs a DCT which provides participants with scenarios along the following lines:

> This morning your father went to a clinic for his annual medical check. About a week ago, you overheard your father telling his boss about the date and time of the health check on the phone. However, mid-morning today, the telephone rings and it is your father's boss. He says in an annoyed tone:
>
> *Father's boss: I'm phoning to ask where your father is. He's supposed to be here for our team meeting, and we've all been waiting for him for about 30 minutes. What's happened to him?*
>
> [Please write the EXACT words you think you would say in response]
>
> You: _____
>
> _____

DCTs could be useful in language and gender research, for example if researchers wish to find out how participants think that they *ought* to behave, rather than find out what participants actually do in conversation. Thus, they can be usefully used in analysing features such as swearing, which are sometimes difficult to record, or when you are trying to analyse attitudes towards particular gendered language ideologies.

Mixed-methods research

Although the use of corpus linguistic methods (CL) within gender and language research is still in its infancy, publications have emerged recently which demonstrate the value of using CL for gender research as a mixed-methods approach, such as in combination with sociolinguistics (Romaine 2001; Sigley and Holmes 2002; Murphy 2010b) and discourse analysis (Baker 2006) including critical discourse analysis. Morrish and Sauntson (2007) provide an excellent quotation from corpus linguist Susan Hunston, where she neatly articulates how critical discourse analysis can benefit from corpus linguistics:

> Many of the arguments that critical linguists use depend upon assumptions about the influence upon people and on society of language whose meaning is overt. It seems apparent, then, that corpora are a very useful tool for the critical linguist, because they identify repetitions, and can be used to identify implicit meaning. Because data in corpora are decontextualised, the researcher is encouraged to spell out steps that lie between what is observed and the interpretation of those observations. (Hunston 2002: 123, cited in Morrish and Sauntson 2007: 121)

In language and gender research that has drawn upon corpus linguistic methods so far, researchers tend to use one or more of the following corpus tools and techniques which involve using computerised software to analyse the data. The software package known as WordSmith Tools (Scott 1999) has proved popular. WordSmith enables the production of 'word frequencies', a compilation of how frequently words occur in a raw form within a particular corpus; 'keywords', a list of most frequent lexical items which has been generated by comparing one corpus with another, comparable corpus, known as the 'reference corpus'; 'concordance lines', which we have already defined as when particular lexical items are analysed alongside their co-text; and 'collocation', where patterns of linguistic co-occurrence will be highlighted, often by looking x number of words to the left and x number of words to the right of a particular lexical item. Baker (2008a: 77) suggests that researchers should analyse what he terms 'discourse prosody', that is, 'the tendency for words or phrases to *collocate* with sets of words which express attitudes'. More qualitative-based collocation and concordance line analysis can also be expanded further to include much broader stretches of discourse where particular lexical items occur, akin to the traditional methods of qualitative analysis (see Mullany forthcoming).

Morrish and Sauntson (2007) have used the tools and techniques of corpus linguistics to produce a mixed-methodological CDA analysis of a written corpus of lesbian erotica. The corpus consists of erotic magazines published in the US in the early 1990s. Following Baker (2004, see also Baker 2008a), they employ WordSmith Tools (Scott 1999) and examine word frequencies, keywords and collocation analysis. They use two reference corpora taken from Baker (2004) to compile two different sets of keywords. One reference corpus is on gay men's erotica and the other is on lesbian erotica (see Chapter 6 for further discussion of this study). Morrish and Sauntson point out that a corpus linguistic approach is particularly suitable and beneficial for their study as its survey techniques, combined with qualitative analysis through concordance line data analysis, enable themes, hidden ideologies and semantic associations which are inscribed in the data to be revealed.

Trabelsi (forthcoming) also brings together CDA and corpus linguistics, using qualitative and quantitative analysis in an examination of the representation of Muslim women after the 9/11 bombings in the US. She has found that Muslim women occupy an 'acted-upon' position within newspapers, and, in her visual analysis, she has found that pictures of veiled women are often included when there are reports of conflict in the Arab world.

In a number of recent publications, Baker (2008a, 2008b, 2010, forthcoming) has demonstrated that corpus linguistics can greatly enhance language and gender studies. As one example, Baker (2008b) analyses the way that the gendered terms 'bachelor' and 'spinster' are used in the British National Corpus (BNC), using word frequencies, concordance lines and collocation (Baker 2008b). He shows that there is a frequency bias, with 'bachelor' being used far more frequently than 'spinster' (424 times to 140 times). Baker demonstrates that 'bachelor' tends to collocate with positive adjectives such as 'eligible', 'happy', 'popular' and occurs in contexts which are generally exciting and varied, sometimes related to sex scandals, for example, 'Diana's close friendship with the bachelor was revealed in sensational tapes published this summer' (Baker 2008a: 205). This use of 'bachelor' generally refers to a temporary happy state before marriage; whereas at the same time 'bachelor' can also be used to refer to men who have chosen to be single for their whole lives. This corpus linguistic analysis reveals how the usage of bachelor co-occurs with adjectives such as 'confirmed', 'lifelong', and 'steadfast', suggesting a quiet but contented life. Other usages of 'bachelor' present a less happy picture, where collocates include 'hapless' and 'lonely'. The word 'spinster' in Baker's (2008b) data has fewer collocates overall and these collocates are words with negative connotations (such as 'elderly').

In order to expand on Baker's study, researchers could examine other words which are used to describe single people in contemporary societies. The historically negative connotations of 'spinster' have meant that single women have not used the term to describe themselves for many years, and perhaps the equivalent term to bachelor is 'single woman' rather than spinster.[1]

Harrington (2008) analyses the use of reported dialogue in the conversations of male and female interactants initially using the technique of counting the overall frequencies of reported-speech frames ('she said', etc.). Rather than assuming that on the basis of her overall quantitative analysis males used less reported dialogue than females, Harrington analysed the data more closely so that she could see whether these were hard and fast differences or only tendencies, with overlap between males and females. She argues: 'The combination of quantitative and qualitative methods can contribute complementary perspectives: qualitative analysis helping us to understand the local motivations behind certain language use, how and why it is used the way it is; and careful use of quantitative evidence in understanding the prevalence of such use within larger social groups' (Harrington 2008: 101).

Murphy's (2010b) work brings together sociolinguistics and corpus linguistics in her study on language, age and gender in Irish English. As highlighted earlier in the book, age has been a neglected feature of feminist linguistic analysis, and Murphy's study examines women's talk and looks at generational differences in Irish English using corpus tools and techniques including word frequencies and concordancing to identify different generational patterns of language use. She focuses in particular upon linguistic features including hedges, vague category markers, amplifiers, boosters and taboo words. She has recently started collecting a brand-new corpus of British Muslim women's talk in Edinburgh, Scotland (Murphy 2010a).

Moving on from corpus linguistics, one of the most successful examples of mixed-methods research is Eckert's (2000) study in American high schools. She combined an ethnographic approach with traditional quantitative methods of linguistic analysis to correlate the number of linguistic variables used by girls and boys from different social-identity groupings. Eckert then broadened out her research further to a quantitative, survey approach of a range of different schools, on the basis of the identity categories that she discovered in her detailed ethnographic approach at Belten High School. She terms the survey approach a 'quick and dirty' method: she was able to access a range of different adolescent language data, including gender performances, with rapidity, based upon her knowledge of the 'jock' and 'burnout' categories. Although she was able to collect data quickly by travelling to different high schools in the same Detroit area and asking for the jocks and burnouts, the 'dirty' side of things came when she had to hang about the territories where burnouts were known to congregate and wait around for them.

Eckert (2009) makes the following observations, which neatly provide her own assessment of both types of method:

> Once I had done the work at Belten High, I was able to use the categories jock and burnout from the start in a more survey-like technique. I was able to go into other high schools in the Detroit suburbs and find the jocks and burnouts simply by asking the school principal where their territories were, or by asking who was the biggest jock and who was the biggest burnout. After all, the local salience of these categories makes them ideally visible. ... while using this 'quick and dirty' method gave me access to interviewees and allowed me to sample the speech of jocks and burnouts in a matter of weeks, it did not give me the kind of textured information I gained at Belten, and it certainly did not give me access to particular friendship groups or any kind of systematic view of the in-betweens. So while I developed a picture of how jocks and burnouts use variables across the geographical continuum of the suburban area, I was never as sure of the status of my data as I was in Belten. (Eckert 2009: 150)

Additionally, she highlights the fact that while the ethnographic approach at Belten gave her the time to establish trust with her informants, this was far more difficult with the survey method. Adolescents were not used to her presence in the way they were at Belten, and she documents that the burnouts in particular were far less trustful in this situation, where the researcher (and her motives) were treated with more suspicion.

Recording data and the observer's paradox

Within the broader discipline of linguistics, in order to conduct a detailed legitimate linguistic study of spoken interaction, a form of recording needs to be made. The most obvious choice for researchers, including all feminist linguistic researchers, is between video and audio recording. Duranti (1997: 117) observes that video recording seems far more likely to trigger the effect of the observer's paradox than audio recordings, but audio recordings offer only 'a filtered version of what happened whilst the tape was running'. However, he argues that this method still has 'the power to capture social actions in unique ways' (1997: 119). Milroy (1987: 59) provides a concise definition of the observer's paradox, stating that 'the very act of recording is likely to distort the object of observation'. However, even though recording interaction does have an impact on the way that interactants behave, it is clear that after 5 or 10 minutes of recording, participants do tend to become less concerned about the presence of a recorder. Thus, it may be sufficient to simply not analyse the first 5–10 minutes of any recording.

In the 'Language in the Workplace' project, Holmes and her team came up with an innovative method that gave the participants themselves control over the data that they collected. Individual managers within workplaces were given their own audio and video recording devices and were responsible for turning them on and off (see Holmes and Stubbe 2003; Holmes 2006; see also Coates, 1996 and 2003). As there was no researcher present, this approach arguably diminished the effect of the 'observer's paradox' somewhat.

Researchers who favour a more ethnographic approach prefer to be present at speech events they are recording so that they can make additional field notes, gain further background information and also produce notes and diagrams that help with the process of transcription afterwards, especially if there are multiple speakers (see Mullany 2007). This additional data collection can be invaluable, though arguably the observer's paradox remains more acute if the researcher is present during recording, even if they try and make themselves as unobtrusive as possible. The inescapable fact remains, however, that whatever recording equipment is chosen, its presence can still affect participants' behaviour.

Duranti (1997) argues that the problems raised by the observer's paradox, if they are carried to their logical conclusion, suggest that 'it would be better *not to be there* at all' (1997: 117, emphasis in original). He points out that there are two ways in which such a proposition can be realised. The first option is to abandon the study of people altogether, whilst the second option is to record covertly, not informing participants that their behaviour is being recorded. As he rightly points out:

> The first option is self destructive [as] … it implies that we should not improve our understanding of what it means to be human and have a culture (including a language) simply because we cannot find the ideal situation for naturalistic-objective observation. The second proposal is first of all unethical and, second, impractical under most circumstances outside of laboratories with two-way mirrors. (Duranti 1997: 117)

Therefore, in order to account for the observer's paradox without giving up the day job, researchers can do so by always ensuring that they are reflexive and completely transparent about all of the recording decisions that they have made. Readers of the research are then in a position to assess for themselves how the observer's paradox may have affected the data.

Transcribing and transcription conventions

Once audio or video recording of spoken language data has been made, the data will need to undergo the process of transcription, where spoken text is turned into written form. Unfortunately there is no standard system for transcription in feminist linguistics or in linguistics as a whole, and the type of transcript that is produced and the level of detail that is contained within the transcript will vary depending upon what the analyst is planning to analyse (for instance if you

are not looking at phonetics then you do not need to produce a phonetic transcript). The level of detail that is used also depends upon what theoretical and
methodological paradigm the researcher is working within. To illustrate this, we
will contrast a transcript taken from conversation analysis, where there is a practice of producing meticulous transcription, following Gail Jefferson, known as
the 'Jefferson system', with the other, much more varied forms of transcription
expected in work within interactional sociolinguistics, discourse analysis and
pragmatics.

The following example is a CA transcript taken from Stokoe's (2008: 151)
work on CA and gender categorisation in police interviews, discussed in Chapter
4, along with the list of transcription conventions:

P1:	D'you remember <u>k</u>ickin' 'e:r. =
S:	= No. Not 'er.
	(0.8)
S:	I do the <u>ma</u>:n but not 'er: no.
	(1.7)
P1:	.pt So you've <u>n</u>ot kicked her at all.
	(0.9)
S:	°No.°
	(2.2)
S:	<u>Swu</u>ng 'er about kept 'er off me that's all.
	(2.4)
P1:	D'you remember 'er falling down to the gro:und.
S:	.hhhhhhhh
	(0.3)
S:	↑M: yeah. >See I-< was pulling 'er (.) ar- ar: pullin her arm to k- keep 'er away from me like.

CA 'Jefferson-style' transcription conventions (derived from Kitzinger 2008:
137–8):

[ ] square brackets	overlapping talk
(0.5) time in round brackets	intervals within or between talk measured in tenths of a second
. full stop	closing intonation
(.) full stop in closed brackets	discernible pause or gap, (too short to measure)
¿ inverted question mark	rising intonation weaker than that indicated by a question mark
.hhh	audible inbreath (no. of 'h's indicates length)
hhh	audible outbreath (no. of 'h's indicates length)

:: colons	extension preceding sound (the more colons the greater the extension)
= equals sign	no space between turns
, comma	continuing intonation
<u>here</u> underlining	emphasis
HERE capitals	loud, relative to surrounding talk
<u>HERE</u> underlining and capitals	very loud and emphatic, relative to surrounding talk
- dash	abrupt cut off of sound
°word° degree signs	soft, relative to surrounding talk
°°word°° double degree signs	very soft, or whispered, relative to surrounding talk
$ dollar sign	smile voice
(bring) word in round brackets	transcriber uncertain of hearing
((sniff)) words in double round brackets	sounds or other material hard to transcribe; other comments by subscriber
→ arrow	analyst's signal of a significant line
>word word< <word word>	inwards arrows show faster speech, outward slower

The meticulous detail in this CA transcript can be compared with the much shorter list of transcription conventions from Holmes' (2006) work which analyses gender and language data from the combined perspective of interactional sociolinguistics, discourse analysis and pragmatics. The following example is taken from a conversation between two co-workers in a factory:

Ginette is talking to Francie, the quality assurance checker.

1	Fra:	do you have an NCR for that (box) over there?
2	Gin:	yeah I've I'm waiting for a number + +
3		I need to see Vicky about the NCR thing
4		I haven't got a number for it yet
5	Fra:	oh how would you get it
6	Gin:	when I get to see Vicky +++
7	Fra:	oh how about you just give it to me now +
8		take a copy of that + so I can compare it
9		and I'll take the number then+++
10	Gin:	(where are they) + do you want it right now
11	Fra:	if it's possible [laughs]
12	Gin:	it's just I've left a + I've got um Jennifer's working +
13		going through it as well
14	Fra:	oh okay is it possible tomorrow then?
15	Gin:	I'll get it to you tomorrow morning yeah

(Holmes 2006: 166)

Holmes' (2006: 223) transcription conventions:

<u>yes</u>	Underlining indicates emphatic stress
[laughs] : :	Paralinguistic features and other information in square brackets, colons indicate start/finish
+	Pause of up to one second
xx/xxxx \	Simultaneous speech
xx	
(hello)	Transcriber's best guess at an unclear utterance
-	Incomplete or cut-off utterance
… …	Section of transcript omitted
	All names are pseudonyms

The final transcription example is given to illustrate variation within interactional sociolinguistics and discourse analysis (as well as pragmatics). Coates (1996, 2003) prefers what she terms a musical-score approach to her language and gender transcripts and some of her conventions are different:

Older women [*Pat is talking about her husband*]

PAT: he gives me these little um . notes when he sends me shopping/ you ought to see the notes I get with anything that I don't actually . deal with myself/ like framing bits or anything like that . / you get this long sort of paragraph/ which more or less starts with 'Go out

----

PAT: of the house / proceed down the road' <LAUGHS> you know/
KAREN: I know/

PAT: sometimes there's a map of where the shop is/ and sometimes there's a little drawing of what the thing ought to look like / and I always play to the gallery by going into the shop and showing them the

----

PAT: note/ <LAUGHS>   [and they fall [about
KAREN: absolutely/ [why not/   [about/ that's right/

PAT: dreadful/

                                                      (Coates 1999: 297)

Coates' transcription conventions (abridged from Coates 1999: 311):

-------------------	broken lines mark the start of a stave –
-------------------	lines enclosed are to be read simultaneously like a musical score
/ slash:	end of a tone group or chunk of talk
? question mark:	end of chunk of talk being analysed as a question
[overlapping brackets:	simultaneous speech
= equals signs:	absence of a discernible gap
CAPS capital letters:	uttered with emphasis
hh.	sharp intake of breath
. full stop:	short pause (less than 0.5 seconds)
– dash:	long pause
((help)) double brackets:	doubt about transcript accuracy
<sneeze> angled brackets:	give clarification

Feminist linguistic researchers thus need to ensure that they select a form of transcription which best suits the aims and objectives of their data analysis, as well as the particular research traditions within which they are working. Outside CA, transcription conventions tend to be more varied, even between researchers working within the same linguistic sub-disciplines.

Feminist standpoints: research ethics

There have been numerous debates within linguistics and the humanities and social sciences as a whole in recent years regarding research ethics. In particular, this has focused upon the ethics of using informants. One of the most hotly debated areas is when informants are from less powerful groups than the researcher. Skeggs (2004) comments on the debate about the work of Diane Bell and Topsy Nelson. Bell published an article with Nelson on the subject of the rape of Aboriginal women by Aboriginal men. Bell cited Nelson as the co-author of this article, but she was attacked for co-opting Nelson's words. However, Skeggs argues that perhaps it is necessary sometimes to use different strategies to make visible the needs and wishes of 'subaltern' women. 'If subaltern groups have no access to the mechanisms and circuits for telling and distributing their knowledge, how do others even know they exist?' (Skeggs 2004: 130). Skeggs also points to the fact that the relation between the researched and women researcher is not such a simple one of exploitative power, as she states: 'I know some things about the women I studied that they don't know, just as they know some things about me of which I am not aware' (Skeggs 2004: 131). She goes on to state that 'most of us do empirical work to learn from others, not to exploit and use them' (Skeggs 2004: 131).

Indeed, sociolinguistics researchers more generally have long been debating these ethical issues, both inside and outside of gender and language studies. The unethical nature of covert recording and thus not involving informants in the study at all, let alone making them aware that recording is taking place, has long been discouraged within sociolinguistic research. Following Labov (1981), Milroy argues that as a tape is a permanent record of behaviour, those being recorded are entitled to know that a permanent recording is being made, especially as a person's voice is an important part of their self-image (1987: 88). Additionally, Labov (1981: 32) emphasises that covert recording can also have serious practical disadvantages. Surreptitious recording can result in future access being denied by a group, and furthermore, recording quality will often be too poor to use if recording equipment is concealed. As part of these principles of research ethics a 'general consensus' has now been established for a substantial period of time in sociolinguistics that pseudonyms should be used at all times to protect the identity of those partaking in the research process (Milroy 1987: 91).

In recent years many universities have tightened up their ethics policies for students and staff conducting research with human subjects, and many of these policies now correlate with those within applied linguistics or sociolinguistics guidelines more generally (BAAL 2010). The following are examples of ethics forms currently in use at our UK-based institutions.

Ethics form for non-medical research involving human subjects

Currently used in the School of English Studies at the University of Nottingham:

Ethics Approval for data collection

- [ ] Data gathering activities involving schools and other organizations will be carried out only with the agreement of the head of school/organization, or an authorised representative, and after adequate notice has been given.
- [ ] The purpose and procedures of the project, and the potential benefits and costs of participating (e.g. the amount of their time involved), will be fully explained to prospective participants at the outset.
- [ ] My full identity will be revealed to potential participants.
- [ ] Prospective participants will be informed that data collected will be treated in the strictest confidence and will only be reported in anonymised form, but that I will be forced to consider disclosure of certain information where there are strong grounds for believing that not doing so will result in harm to research participants or others, or (the continuation of) illegal activity.
- [ ] All potential participants will be asked to give their explicit, normally written consent to participating in the research, and, where consent is given, separate copies of this will be retained by both researcher and participant. These consent forms should be submitted as an Appendix, along with this form.

☐ In addition to the consent of the individuals concerned, the signed consent of a parent, guardian or 'responsible other' will be required to sanction the participation of minors (i.e. persons under 16 years of age) or those whose 'intellectual capability or other vulnerable circumstance may limit the extent to which they can be expected to understand or agree voluntarily'.

☐ Undue pressure will not be placed on individuals or institutions to participate in research activities.

☐ The treatment of potential research participants will in no way be prejudiced if they choose not to participate in the project.

☐ I will provide participants with my contact details (and details of the module convenor) in order that they are able to make contact in relation to any aspect of the project, should they wish to do so.

☐ Participants will be made aware that they may freely withdraw from the project at any time without risk or prejudice.

☐ Research will be carried out with regard for mutually convenient times and negotiated in a way that seeks to minimise disruption to schedules and burdens on participants.

☐ At all times during the conduct of the research I will behave in an appropriate, professional manner and take steps to ensure that neither myself nor research participants are placed at risk.

☐ The dignity and interests of research participants will be respected at all times, and steps will be taken to ensure that no harm will result from participating in the research.

☐ The views of all participants in the research will be respected and special efforts will be made to be sensitive to differences relating to age, culture, disability, race, gender, religion and sexual orientation, amongst research participants, when planning, conducting and reporting on the research.

☐ Data generated by the research will be kept in a safe and secure location and will be used purely for the purposes of the project (including dissemination of findings). No-one other than markers and examiners will have access to any of the data collected.

☐ Research participants will have the right of access to any data kept on them.

☐ All necessary steps will be taken to protect the privacy and ensure the anonymity and non-traceability of participants – e.g. by the use of pseudonyms, for both individual and institutional participants.

☐ Where possible, participants will be provided with a summary of research findings and an opportunity for debriefing after taking part in the research.

☐ If working with children 16 and under for a prolonged period of time, I have received Advanced Criminal Records Bureau (CRB) disclosure.

Signed_____

Date_____

Department of English, Sheffield Hallam University

Ethical guidelines for linguistics students

1. Tape Recording Conversation

1. If researchers are planning to record conversations within the department, as part of their research, they need to first discuss the parameters of the recording sessions with the Head of Department and also the uses to which the data will be put.
2. All participants in conversations which are to be recorded must first be notified by the researcher and their permission sought. Recording without notifying the participants is ethically suspect.
3. If the data is to be transcribed and appended to or analysed within a piece of published work, all participants must sign a consent form, following the form below.
4. The participants in the research must be offered the opportunity to see the finished published work. Ideally they will be provided with a copy of the completed research. Some research might benefit from the participants talking over the research with the researcher and their comments incorporated into the research.

Consent form for the use of recorded material

Date: ....

I ....(name)

Address..

give my consent to ....(name)

to transcribe, and use the data which has been recorded by him/her

Signature..

The researcher has explained to me that the transcribed material will be used in the following context .... and I will be given/ shown a copy of the results when the research is completed.

---

2. Ethical Guidelines for the Composing and Delivery of Questionnaires

The Head of Department and Director of Studies must meet with the researcher to discuss the following issues:

- What the questionnaire is trying to elicit
- Which group is being targeted and why
- Whether the questionnaire will deliver what is required
- The number of participants
- Whether the questions which are asked are in any way problematic, for example, asking for too much self-revelation on the part of participants
- Whether the questionnaire demands that the participant devotes too much time to the questionnaire
- Whether the participant incurs any expense because of completing the questionnaire

3. Ethical Guidelines for the Conducting of Interviews

The Head of Department and Director of Studies must discuss with the researcher:

- the reason that interviews are to be conducted
- what it is hoped that the interviews will show
- the reason why a particular group of people has been chosen (it is important to analyse whether interviewing this group is potentially exploitative in any way)
- the place where the interview will take place (in people's homes, in the university, in a community centre, etc.)
- ethical problems which might arise because of the location of the interview (i.e. questions of safety, concerns about or actual sexual harassment must be considered)
- the form that the questions will take
- the amount of time that the interviews will last
- the way that the interview material will be transcribed
- any potential ethical problems, such as enquiring about sensitive issues, encouraging self-revelation on the part of the interviewee
- follow-up (will the interviewees be given copies of the research; will there be a debriefing?)

These ethical guidelines are given to students in order to ensure that they carefully consider ethical dimensions of their proposed research. They are designed to instil the importance of maintaining full confidentiality, the importance of ensuring that trust is not violated and that informants are not deceived as well as the protection of young people and other vulnerable groups who may not be able to give consent on their own.

Feminist standpoints: reflexivity

Hammersley and Atkinson (1995: 16) define a commitment to producing reflexive research as the means by which researchers openly and directly acknowledge that their orientations 'will be shaped by their socio-historical locations, including the values and interests that these locations confer upon them'. Thus, there is a clear rejection of the idea that social research can be carried out in isolation from the social world in which the researcher is studying. There is also an acknowledgement that the researchers are individuals in the social world and that this will influence the research project.

A commitment to a reflexive approach means that feminist linguistic researchers should acknowledge their own orientations, bringing to an end claims that 'objective' knowledge has been produced with the researcher not influencing the research process in any way. Researchers cannot claim to be completely divorced from the social world that they are studying and of which they are a part. Hertz (1997: viii) argues that reflexivity permeates every aspect of the research process, and challenges researchers to be completely aware of 'the ideology, culture and politics of those we study and those we select as an audience'. Callaway's definition of reflexivity summarises the most fundamental aspects of the term, and it is particularly applicable to feminist, action-centred research. She highlights both the importance of self-reflections and of political awareness:

> Often condemned as apolitical, reflexivity, on the contrary can be seen as opening the way to a more radical consciousness of self in facing the political dimensions of fieldwork and constructing knowledge. Other factors intersecting with gender – such as nationality, race, ethnicity, class and age – also affect the anthropologist's field interactions and textual strategies. Reflexivity becomes a continuing mode of self-analysis and political awareness. (Callaway 1992: 33)

Alvesson and Skoldberg (2000) provide a useful outline of four facets to a reflexive approach which can be very useful principles to follow when conducting feminist linguistic studies:

1   *Systematics and techniques in research procedures*. Research should follow some well-reasoned logic in interacting with the empirical material, and use rigorous techniques for processing the data.
2   *Clarification of the primacy of interpretation*. All research work includes and is driven by an interpreter who often interacts with and contemplates other interpreters.
3   *Awareness of the political-ideological character of research*. Social science … is embedded in a political and ethical context. Different social interests are favoured and disfavoured depending on the questions that are asked (and not asked) and on how reality is represented and interpreted.
4   *Reflection on relation to the problem of representation and authority*. The researcher's claim to authority and the texts' claim to reproduce (not to mention

'mirror') some extrinsic reality are undermined: the researching subject and the researched object are both called into question.

(Adapted from Alvesson and Skoldberg 2000: 7–8)

Summary

Thus, we have discussed some of the various debates that there have been within the field of language and gender on questions of methodology. In the next two chapters, we focus on particular areas of research (sexualities and sexism), in order to showcase, in more detail, the sort of language and gender research which is currently being undertaken, using the theories and perspectives described in Chapter 4 and the methodologies described in this chapter.

6 Sexuality

Contemporary issues in language and sexuality

Bucholtz and Hall (2005: 470) define sexuality as 'the systems of mutually constituted ideologies, practices and identities that give socio-political meaning to the body as an eroticized and/or reproductive site'. While we have discussed language, gender and sexuality at various stages already in this book, Bucholtz and Hall's definition is a really useful starting point for this chapter dedicated to language and sexualities, as it brings together a focus on the conceptualisation of sexual identities as well as a focus on the erotic/desire. 'Language and gender' and 'language and sexuality' overlap significantly with one another. Sauntson (2008) points out that it is impossible to separate gender and sexuality from one another in feminist linguistic analysis. Bucholtz and Hall (2005: 471) argue that 'sexuality and gender are most fruitfully studied in ways that explicitly acknowledge how they are imbricated in relations of power'.

Indeed, the significance of social and economic power should not be under-estimated when conceptualising sexuality. Bhattacharyya (2002: 10) argues that 'sexuality is made through the networks of social power; sexual choices are constrained by economics, by social pressures, habit, convention and expectation. Yet despite these many pressures, sexuality retains this possibility of play and magic – a space where dreams can be negotiated if not fully realised.' Morrish and Sauntson (2007: 4) echo this sentiment when they state that 'sexual identity, rather than being an essential, pre-existing property, may be produced in relation to particular material conditions and particular relations of power between those at the margins of society and those whose interests are represented in structures such as government, culture and commerce'. Cameron and Kulick (2003: 115) stress that sexuality feels as if it is the most personal and intimate choice that one makes; it feels as if it is entirely individual. However, for them, 'intimacy is … an interactional achievement. It is a constellation of practices that are publicly mediated even though they may feel like inner discoveries.' Inevitably, this mediation is achieved through language, and thus by studying the language used to express our sexual desires, or used to describe sexual choices and preferences, we can discover a great deal about how sexuality is constructed and viewed. Cameron and Kulick (2003) have played a very influential role in the field, and their seminal work has a central place in contemporary discussions. It is thus frequently referred to in this chapter.

There has been some debate between researchers as to exactly what the focus of language and sexuality research should be. There has been a great deal of discussion as to whether the term 'sexuality' should refer to sexual identity or to sexual desire (Cameron and Kulick 2003; Bucholtz and Hall 2005; Cameron and Kulick 2005). For some theorists, sexuality should be treated as a matter of identity; for example, how individuals signal their membership of communities of practice through their use of particular language styles, for instance by using a coded language which is understood fully only by members of that group – a case in point might be the use of 'the voice' by gay men (see below). However, Cameron and Kulick (2005: 112) draw attention to the problems with 'identity politics', where 'actors ground political claims in their authentic experience as members of particular identity categories and/or communities'. Clearly, here identity is being used in a legitimising way, and whilst this may have positive results, in that it has been crucial for the women's movement and for gay liberation movements, it goes against the grain of recent feminist research which has generally tried to challenge the 'fixity' of identity, as detailed extensively in Chapter 3.

Much research has shown that often desire clashes with the identities which are claimed: 'sexuality is a social and psychological phenomenon that often exceeds and sometimes contradicts the sexual identities people consciously claim or disclaim' (Cameron and Kulick 2005: 113), in the case of married heterosexual men who occasionally have sex with men, for example, or lesbians who have occasional relationships with men. Some theorists, including Cameron and Kulick, believe that it is crucially important to examine the way that erotic practices and desires are reliant upon language for their articulation. It is thus clear that analysis of language and sexuality needs to integrate a concern with identity as well as a concern with erotic desire.

To question the seemingly obvious link between sexuality and identity, in an analysis of telephone sex talk, Cameron and Kulick argue that sex workers manage to 'blur the boundaries between "work" and "play for pleasure" so that what is, indeed, work for one party will be apprehended by the other as something more like play/pleasurable rather than effortful, done willingly and with enjoyment rather than grudgingly just for money' (Cameron and Kulick 2005: 116). They draw attention to the fact that phone sex is premised on illusion; that the people who use phone sex lines know that the sex worker is simulating sexual desire rather than experiencing it and that may in fact be part of the pleasure, knowing that the sexual experience does not entail any responsibility or empathy towards the other person as a real person. Indeed, Cameron and Kulick suggest that the sexual roles that sex workers play are often very stereotypical, precisely because their sexiness comes from their artificiality. The roles they enact are removed from the reality of everyday life and accord more with pornographic fantasies than any situations that may occur in a user's daily life.

They also draw attention to Barrett's (1999) work on the language of drag queens. The use of incongruous language by drag queens is important, as often they will draw on different, clashing styles in their speech. However, rather than seeing this as indicative of a conflicted identity, Cameron and Kulick argue that these clashing language styles can be seen as creative language through which identities and social positions are enacted. Thus, we should not assume that conflict within someone's language indicates a conflict within their sexual identity; rather we should see that the use of a mixture of styles may allow for a certain fluidity of roles.

Cameron and Kulick (2003: 19) argue that it is important to analyse language in relation to sexuality as 'the "reality" of sex does not pre-exist the language in which it is expressed; rather language *produces* the categories through which we organise our sexual desires, identities and practices'. They oppose theoretical discussions on sexuality which focus only on identity, for they argue that if you do this, you risk suggesting that identity is fixed and pre-existing. From their perspective, if sexual identity and sexuality are conflated, there is a tendency to remove sex from sexuality. As we have already highlighted in Chapter 1 in reference to Cameron's sole-authored work, Cameron and Kulick (2003: xiv) similarly question whether identities research has come at the expense of collective political action. They argue that researchers should ask themselves whether 'cultivating and celebrating authentic selves has become a substitute for collective action to change the material structures that reproduce social inequality' (Cameron and Kulick 2003: xiv). However, they are not arguing that we should only focus on the relation between language and desire when we examine sexuality and ignore questions of identity; rather they argue that we should focus on both issues equally, as 'representations are a resource people draw on – arguably indeed are compelled to draw on – in constructing their own identities and ways of doing things' (Cameron and Kulick 2003: 12). Thus they focus both on erotic desire and identity in their discussion of sexuality.

Baker (2008a) draws attention to the fact that it is only relatively recently that 'homosexual' and 'heterosexual' were the primary ways in which people could classify their sexual desires and identities. Foucault (1978) demonstrated that before the nineteenth century, sexual acts did not define one as having a particular type of identity. For the ancient Greeks, for example, sexual acts were characterised as either passive or active rather than heterosexual or homosexual, and even here these acts did not map out a permanent role for either sexual partner. In the nineteenth century, same-sex sexual relations might result in someone being categorised as an 'invert', but this was seen as a pathology rather than an identity. Thus, the notion that one is either a homosexual or not is fairly recent, and even Kinsey *et al.* (1948, cited in Baker 2008a: 6) noted that within this binary divide there were many different choices, for example:

- exclusively heterosexual
- predominantly heterosexual, only incidentally homosexual
- predominantly heterosexual, but more than incidentally homosexual
- equally homosexual and heterosexual
- predominantly homosexual, but more than incidentally heterosexual
- predominantly homosexual, only incidentally heterosexual
- exclusively homosexual.

This complexity suggests that the language which we conventionally use to describe sexual orientation or preference does not map on to the sexual choices that we make, or which are made for us, in real life.

It is important also that when we focus on desire in discussions of language and sexuality, we do not simply focus on pleasure and eroticism. Carole Vance states that:

> [S]exuality is simultaneously a domain of restriction, repression and danger as well as a domain of exploration, pleasure and agency. To focus only on pleasure and gratification ignores the patriarchal structure in which women act, yet to speak only of sexual violence and oppression ignores women's experience with sexual agency and choice and unwittingly increases the sexual terror and despair in which women live. (Vance, cited in McLoughlin 2008: 173)

This is an important point; it is necessary to try to develop a way of discussing autonomous sexual desire for women which does not simply use the structures developed by men, so that we can describe heterosexual and homosexual desire for/by women in ways and using terms which are determined by women. However, we also need to be able discuss sexual violence and the link between power and sexual relations between men and women. Cameron and Kulick (2003: xiv) have made a similar point, arguing that, as well as the positives of the pleasures and levels of emotional satisfaction that sex can bring, there is also a crucial need to look at the negatives. Sex can be the source of 'the most appalling cruelty', misery and abuse. Following the work of Rubin (1984), they view sex as 'a vector of oppression', arguing that it is essential to examine 'the complex of the interactions of power, sex and gender' (2003: xv). As just one example of this, we can come back to one of the contemporary issues which we highlighted in Chapter 2, the rewriting of the marital law passed in Afghanistan in August 2009, that Shia husbands can starve their wives if they do not give them sex at least every four days unless the woman is menstruating. The rewriting of this law legitimises rape within marriage as consent is no longer needed.

The debate about whether language and sexuality research should focus on identity or desire, although at times rather heated, has been a productive one for feminist research. We believe that identity and desire can be fruitfully examined as interrelated components, as long as identity is not seen as fixed and permanent. Researchers therefore do not need to choose between studying the erotic *or* identity, nor does identity research need to be abandoned in favour of research on desire and the erotic.

In summary, contemporary research on language and sexuality focuses upon a wide range of areas, including the following:

- previously marginalised areas of sexual identities (gay, lesbian, transgender, etc.)
- institutionalised discourses of heterosexuality and heteronormativity
- sexual harassment, violence and homophobia
- interaction of sexuality, gender and racialisation
- sexual humour: jokes, teasing and insults
- linguistic constructions of romance and eroticism
- sexuality and political economy

- kinship and family organization
- transgender identities and negotiation of dominant binary sexual systems
- linguistic indexing of normative and non-normative sexual subjectivities (adapted from Bucholtz and Hall 2005: 470–1).

Work which investigates previously marginalised and under-researched areas of sexual identities, as signified in the first bullet point above, does tend to make up the majority of studies thus far (see, for example, Leap 1995; Livia and Hall 1997b). However, as the above list illustrates, a whole range of other areas which bring together crucial themes in language, gender and sexuality research are also being investigated (see Baker 2008a).

Gay and lesbian language?

There has been a focus in much research on sexuality on the language which gay and lesbian people are assumed to speak, presuming that this is different from the language which straight people use. It is clear that in the past some gay men have used forms of coded language. In the UK, this was termed Polari (Baker 2002). However, Polari and other coded languages in locations elsewhere in the world have been as much contested by gays and lesbians as they have been accepted. In the UK, Polari was used when the legal system made it impossible for gay men to be openly gay, and therefore a form of code language developed to refer to other men and to signal one's sexuality. Cameron and Kulick (2003) give the following example of Polari: 'We would zhoosh our riahs, powder our eeks, climb into our bona new drag, don our batts and troll off to some bona bijou bar', meaning 'We would fix our hair, powder our faces, climb into our nice new clothes, don our shoes and cruise to some nice small bar' (Cameron and Kulick 2003: 92).

In Hong Kong, Wong (2008) refers to Mem-ba as a secret coded language which gay Hongkongers use to conceal same-sex desire when heterosexuals and/or overhearers are present. Wong directly links Mem-ba to a time before the decriminalisation of homosexuality in Hong Kong in 1991, which is also the case with Polari in the UK. He points out that its connections with its borrowed form from English, 'member', should not be overlooked. In a series of interviews with non-gay activists in Hong Kong,[1] conducted with gay and lesbian interviewees (10 men and 12 women), he found that some terms from within Mem-ba are still heard/used including '*diu-yu*' (to go cruising), '*yu-tong*' (cruising places) and '*chau-fui*' (to be attracted to white men). However, other terms appear to be used much more infrequently, such as '*wui-so*' (gay bars).

Wong found that the individual term '*mem-ba*' itself operates as an identity marker preferred by his informants – it avoids having to name same-sex desire explicitly as '*mem-ba*' is a multifunctional term. The term '*mem-ba*' can also be used to keep same-sex desire unspecified, depending upon context and is thus a powerful linguistic device. Wong argues that '*mem-ba*' is preferred by his inform-ants as an identity label to '*tongzhi*' ('comrade') which has recently been appro-priated by gay-rights activists as a label to refer to sexual minorities. However, interestingly, the non-activists reject this label, partly because of its associations

with mainland Communist China but also, most importantly, because it explicitly marks individuals out as gay/lesbian, which is something that his informants
wish to keep unspecified. Wong recorded numerous vignettes/comments in his
data about interviewees not wishing to tell their families about their sexuality
and their determination to keep their same-sex desire unspecified. He found that
'Hongkongers do not think that it is necessary to come out to their co-workers,
heterosexual friends, and ... their families' (2008: 281). His informants told him
that their families know about their sexual orientation, but it would never be
openly discussed – they portrayed this as a mutual understanding with which both
they and members of their family were happy. Wong's (2008) work thus raises the
crucial problem of a disjunction between gay and lesbian rights activists appropri-
ating terms such as 'tongzhi' for all sexual minorities, and non-activists who reject
such identity labels that they see as being imposed upon them.

Similarly, Barrett (2004) argues that, in the English-speaking world, most gay
men will actively choose to identify themselves as 'gay' and not as 'queer', despite
movements inside and outside of academia to reclaim 'queer' as a positive identity
label. In an argument similar to that put forward by Wong, Barrett claims that the
imposition of 'queer' has been negatively interpreted for neglecting to take into
account individuals' autonomy to self-name and not be forced to use labels which
are seen as imposed. Barrett (2004: 301) also makes the point that any attempts to
reclaim particular lexical items as positive identity categories such as 'queer' are
'always contested ... because of the gut reaction to the words' citational history
as a potential form of hate speech' (see the section on 'Queer theory and queer
linguistics', pp. 132–4, below, for further discussion of 'queer theory').

There has also been a focus in research on the vocabulary and intonation patterns
used by particular groups of gay men to create in-group solidarity (Gayspeak);
for example, the use of 'she' and female names to refer to other men, a wider
pitch range, hypercorrect pronunciation, hyperextended vowels – this is sometimes called 'the voice' (Barrett 1997).[2] Hayes (1981) argued that '"Gayspeak",
the alleged language of homosexual men', is used to signal one's sexual orientation to other gay men without revealing one's sexuality to heterosexuals, where
innuendo and indirect reference to partners is emphasised. He also argued that it
allows a range of different roles within the gay community, for example the use of
camp as a style. This notion of Gayspeak has been critiqued as it implies that the
gay community is relatively homogeneous and that all homosexual men speak in
much the same way. Not all gay men know this type of coded language or would
want to use it, since it signals a particular type of homosexuality, associated with
campness. Whilst some gay males do use camp language, others do not. We should
not assume that there is one form of gay or lesbian identity, just as we would not
assume that there is one type of female identity. Queen (1997: 238) argues that
'there is nothing specific to gay male speech in terms of its grammar or linguistic
system but there is a unique conventionalised set of meanings attached to some
of the linguistic resources used by gay men. It is the exploitation of these conventionalised meanings that becomes indexical of "gay male".'

Abe (2004) and Lunsing and Maree (2004) have focused on how lesbian
speakers in Japan experiment in the type of first-person pronouns that they use to

express their own identity, some avoiding the use of the more feminine first-person pronoun '*watashi*', some using '*boku*', the first-person, more masculine pronoun, and developing strategies such as referring to themselves by the use of a pet name rather than using a pronoun at all, some using '*jibun*', a rather old-fashioned first-person masculine pronoun, but which is considered to be more neutral, because it is not feminine. Abe (2004: 218) points out that, although some lesbian women use seemingly more masculine first-person pronouns, this does not indicate that they wish to pass as men; rather, it shows that they are rejecting forms which they feel are too feminine or which indicate a particular type of femininity from which they wish to disassociate. Such usage may well be seen as attempting to appropriate 'men's resources, which enable them to express (real or imagined) powerfulness' (2004: 218). These issues will be further discussed in the section on 'Sexist language-change over time: a case study' in Chapter 7, pp. 146–52, below, which focuses on sexist pronoun use.

Cameron and Kulick (2003) are concerned that focusing on the language which gay and lesbian people supposedly use may in fact have been detrimental to research on language and sexuality. However, much research has challenged the notion that gay and lesbian people actually do speak differently from heterosexuals, and it is suggested that often there has been a too easy correlation between the language used in particular contexts and the fact that it is used by people who are lesbian and gay. Straight people in similar contexts, it is argued, would probably use similar language. Cameron and Kulick (2003: 88) also point out that there is a circular methodological logic at play of which researchers need to be aware, if in order to describe a gay or lesbian language, researchers focus only on those they know to be gay and lesbian and then describe their language: 'the fact that gays do X does not make X gay'.

Baker (2008a) examines the language of gay men communicating as avatars on the virtual reality Second Life site. He shows that on occasions they use hypermasculine, stereotypically heterosexual language and on other occasions they use a more stereotypical camp Gayspeak. He argues that we should not assume that gay equals camp, or even that gay equals hypermasculine. He draws attention to those men who identify as MSM, that is, Men who have Sex with Men, but who do not identify as gay. Baker argues that dominant hegemonic masculinity (that is the masculinity associated with white, middle-class, straight males) exerts a pull for gay males as well as other types of identity.

Lesbian language has been significantly under-researched in relation to the research on Gayspeak and gay language. The focus on Gayspeak seems to presume that, for lesbians, there is less of a need to differentiate themselves from the heterosexual community as a whole. Cameron and Kulick (2003: 96) draw on Zwicky's (1997) research to state that 'gay men who use "the voice" are marking a desire to differentiate themselves from hegemonic heterosexual masculinity; this represents a norm which they identify against. Lesbians, by contrast, are more likely to identify with rather than against their gender group, and do not have the same desire to sound noticeably different from straight women.'

Thus, rather than assuming that a particular sexual identity will lead inexorably to a particular type of language use, Cameron and Kulick (2003: 102) try to show that 'instead of seeing gay language as a perverse reflection of a perverse identity, or in 1980s-style scholarship as an authentic reflection of a consciousness-raised, affirmative identity', there should be an emphasis on the way 'language is used to actively construct particular identities and social positions'. Queen's (1997) research emphasises this constructed nature of the language which lesbians use. For her, certain groups of lesbians do choose to mark their speech in particular ways; she argues that 'it is not membership ... in the abstract conception of the lesbian community that makes the language of lesbians unique but rather the fluid contact between a number of styles to which lesbians have access and that carry various "conventionalised" meanings that can be exploited in uniquely "lesbian" ways' (Queen 1997: 239). For her, there is no specific 'lesbian' way of speaking, but perhaps there is a use of different speech styles ironically which marks out a speaking style which lesbians can draw on; 'by combining the stereotypes of non-lesbian communities with the stereotypes that lesbians hold about themselves, lesbians create an indexical relationship between language use and lesbian "identity"' (Queen 1997: 239).

In this way, Queen is able to document the way that certain speech styles may be parodically used (for example hyperfeminine language such as overpolite forms, together with stereotypically non-standard male working-class forms of speech, such as swearing; and also stereotypical gay male speech patterns). She argues that:

> [T]he point then is not to predict when a lesbian will use 'lesbian language' or to offer a diagnostic tool for identifying lesbians but rather to understand that lesbians (like all speakers) have access to a number of special styles, as well as the conventionalised meanings associated with the use of these styles. It is through the recontextualisation and reappropriation of particular features found in various styles that lesbians create new conventionalised meanings and associations and thus, a uniquely lesbian language. (Queen 1997: 242)

This focus on the appropriation of conventions and styles and the ironic use of stereotypes seems a much more productive way of analysing gay and lesbian language than assuming that one's sexual identity determines a particular speech style.

Jones (2009 and forthcoming) has studied the language used by a lesbian hiking group in order to examine the way that the distinction between 'butch' and 'femme' lesbian is handled. Just as Baker (2008a) argues that hypermasculine straight-passing gay men are seen to be more valued than stereotypical gay men who use camp language, Jones asserts that within lesbian communities it is 'butch' lesbians who seem to be represented as more 'authentic', more truly lesbian. Jones' work attempts to chart the contextual construction of identity and the way that individuals align themselves with what they perceive to be the groups' stance on certain issues. The analysis takes in alignment as well as content and shows the way that group identities and relationships are constructed simultaneously.

Thus, Cameron and Kulick (2003) argue overall that focusing on the language used by homosexuals 'has done more to obstruct than to advance our understanding of the relationship between language and sexuality' (2003: xiv). What needs to be focused on is 'the question [of] how speakers take up the ideological resources available in a given community to construct identities for themselves in practice' (2003: 136), which theorists such as Jones (2009) and Baker (2008a) have been attempting to do.

Representations of sexuality

Cameron and Kulick (2003: 12) posit that it is important to analyse 'how sexuality is "done" and how it is represented … because representations are a resource people draw on, arguably, indeed are compelled to draw on in constructing their own identities and ways of doing things'. They argue that it is not only how people use language to enact sexuality and perform sexual identities that should be examined but also how linguistic representations of sexuality and sexual identity are looked at across a variety of different discourse genres. They posit the following as potential data sources for conducting such studies:

- scientific and popular sexology
- the 'Am I normal?' letters in newspaper/magazine problem pages
- pornographic narratives
- romance fiction
- personal ads
- Valentine's Day messages in newspapers
- discussion on daytime talk shows
- sex education materials for schoolchildren
- medical literature about sexual 'dysfunction'
- legal texts defining sexual offences
- radical political literature contesting mainstream representations
- coming-out stories
- other autobiographical genres.

It is important to critically examine the way that gays and lesbians are represented. In the poster reproduced as Figure 6.1, published by the Terrence Higgins Trust and displayed in a wide range of different clinics and health centres in the UK in 2009, the focus of the poster is on the mother of the gay son, Ryan; her image is larger and it is her words which are presented. The strapline 'I love my gay son' may seem a bold attempt to assert positive emotions towards gay people; however, this statement implies that being gay is somehow problematic; there is an implication that 'I love my son [despite the fact that he is gay]', which poses being gay as negative. Furthermore, there is an implied logical link between 'he told us he was gay' and the next sentence 'We reacted badly', as if this is a necessary or inevitable response to your son telling you that he is gay. In the last two sentences this woman asserts that when Ryan said he would leave home, the rest of the family decided to try to keep the family together. Thus 'I love my gay son', read in the light of those last sentences, suggests that she has made a decision to love Ryan in order to ensure that he continues to live at home, and so that the family is not disrupted.

In this example, terms like 'gay' co-occur with other terms and phrases such as 'we reacted badly'. The collocational history of terms referring to gays and lesbians tends to be negative, associated with negativity or excess, and thus this history has an effect on the way 'gay' and 'lesbian' are used. If words keep 'bad company' they tend to pick up negative connotations. As Cameron and Kulick (2003) point out, individuals will draw upon representations to construct their identities and decide upon what is permissible for them in terms of their own sexual behaviour and desire. These sexual behaviours and identities will also influence the form that representations of sexuality will take.

Cameron and Kulick (2003), like Baker, examine the different ways in which heterosexual men and women represent themselves in small ads/personal ads (advertisements for partners which often appear in newspapers and magazines). They note that women tend to stress their attractiveness and state that they are looking for professional men. Men tend to look for attractiveness in women and stress their own professional status. Homosexual men focus on attractiveness, whereas lesbians tend not to. Mills (1995) has shown, in an analysis of personal ads in the *New Statesman* magazine, that heterosexual women tend to describe themselves in terms of their physical and emotional characteristics and they do

Figure 6.1 "Ryan was 17 when he told us he was gay. We reacted badly. But when he almost left home we realised keeping the family together is what matters most. He's still at home and we're closer than ever." (These quotes are real life testimonials)'

Source: Terrence Higgins Trust, 2008.

this in greater detail than males (for example: 'incurable romantic'; 'charming uncomplicated, attractive woman, not slim, not young, feminine'; 'attractive, intelligent, good-humoured, reasonably solvent woman').

Most of the women who advertise are also quite specific about what they want; they do not simply wish to meet an attractive male, but rather a 'personable, caring, retired male, sixty-plus, middlebrow' or 'intelligent, caring man', 'interesting, non-chauvinist, unattached male friend with functioning emotions'. Many of the women in these personal ads indicated exactly what interests the males they were seeking would need to have, for example gardening, cinema, theatre and so on. In contrast, the male advertisers mention that they are interested in sex, or tend to be less specific about who it is they wish to meet: for instance, 'Cambridge graduate ... seeks sexually alert woman also wanting to settle', 'slim attractive male ... wishes to meet attractive woman'; 'lecturer ... seeks woman'.

In one of the personal ads analysed by Mills, the following description of the advertiser appears: 'Rich 1945 Claret with firm strong body, sensuous flavour and adventurous bouquet, handsomely bottled.' Although the advertiser does not reveal that he is male we assume that he is because of the conventions of this type of advert and because of stereotypes of males in heterosexual relationships being older. He says that he seeks 'younger crisp and frisky Chablis, equally well packaged for mulled fun ... with a view to durable casting'. In gay and lesbian personal ads, Shalom (1997) has shown that the advertisers tend to categorise themselves and the person they are looking for in terms of hegemonic masculinity and femininity. Therefore, there is a sense in which advertisers reinforce dominant discourses of gender.

Baker (2008a) has shown how stereotypically masculine qualities are focused on in gay personal ads, for example: 'Good looking, 32, 6' tall, slim straight-acting. Interests: keep fit, weights, badminton, squash ... non-scene, genuine person, wanting to meet similar, straight acting with similar interests.' Baker (2008a: 175) comments that 'here terms like *non-scene* and *straight-acting* indicate a disavowal of the gay subculture or scene'; reference to interest in a variety of sports also seems to be given as an indicator of an 'authentic masculine identity'. He argues that such adverts 'show that the most highly valued identity is traditional heterosexual hegemonic masculinity' and he suggests that gay men who use personal ads buy into 'a set of mores that fundamentally stigmatise the widely held notions of gay identity – that they must be "straight-acting" in order to be highly valued within the gay marketplace' (Baker 2008a: 176–7).

In another study, Shalom (1997) investigated desire in personal ads. She was particularly interested in how the restriction of space affects the lexis selected. In her study, she examined the lexis used to describe the desired other. She discovered that even the most stereotypical lexis is imbued with vagueness and/or sets of resonances in the reader. She argues that a particular, deliberate lexis is chosen to be vague and ambiguous and that this is designed to be an interactive device.

Shalom found that the lexical item 'similar' was most popular with gay men and gay women, which arguably implies a specific gay usage of this word. Use of 'similar' as a strategy also implies a direct link between self and other, though it is also very vague and ambiguous:

> GAY FEMALE, 29, 5′ 6″, slim, attractive, sporty,
> fun-loving, seeks similar for evenings out, clubbing,
> friendship or maybe more. Box 1007.

Shalom also found 'similar age' commonly occurring in the heterosexual women seeking men corpus, as in the following example:

> EVE, 40, arty, Jewish, left-wing, teenage child, seeks tall,
> intelligent similar age or younger Adam, to regain paradise. Box 839.

Arguably the ambiguity of 'similar' acts as a hook, a technique that is designed to draw the reader in. Another of Shalom's findings was that heterosexual men favour the adjective 'attractive', as in the following examples:

> Seeks attractive female
> Seeks attractive intelligent
> Seeks slim attractive

> (Shalom 1997)

Shalom argues that this is a good linguistic strategy to use in order to maximise respondents. She bases this on the view that people like to think they are attractive, so these ads are more likely to attract respondents. Straight women also appear to be aware of the male usage of 'attractive', evidencing the following example, with the introductory use of 'another': 'Another attractive, slim intelligent, blonde, this one a charismatic, young-looking 48.'

Within the constraints of personal ads, it is clear that there is a discursive history, whereby there is a certain range of parameters within which we can construct ourselves as a particular type of person and we can construct our desires for another person only within a certain range of expressions. 'The question is how speakers "take up" the ideological resources available in a given community to construct identities for themselves in practice' (Cameron and Kulick 2003: 136).

Queer theory and queer linguistics

In terms of theoretical framing, sexuality studies are commonly associated first and foremost with queer theory and 'queer linguistics'. Queer theory was developed by gay, lesbian, bisexual and transgender people in order to move away from the focus on heterosexuality as the norm, which seemed to underpin much mainstream theorising. 'Queer' was initially a term of abuse used towards gay men, but in the 1990s the term was reclaimed by gay men and lesbians to be used positively. We have already come across debates about using 'queer' as a label in the section on 'Gay and lesbian language?', pp. 125–9, above. In contrast to Barrett's (2004) perspective, Alan Sinfield states that whilst those negative connotations of the term still endure, 'queer' can be used in positive ways: 'the aggression and ambition in the readoption of "queer" are directly proportionate to the degree to which it proposes to overturn the historic, hostile meaning ... "Queer" says defiantly, that we don't care what they call us' (Sinfield, cited in Baker 2008a: 186). Baker thus argues that queer theory 'focuses on the way that "normal/not normal" identities and relationships are "fixed" and reproduced as binary oppositions in society' (2008a: 186).

Leap (2008: 295) has argued that queer theory has crucial advantages for the study of language and gender. This is based on the fact that 'it does not allow gender to be pushed into the sidelines so that a-historical, highly generic political process can move to centre stage'. Jones (forthcoming) in her analysis of the language of a lesbian community of practice develops further the notion of queer linguistics, so that the field of linguistics is reconfigured, with heterosexual identity no longer being situated at the centre of attention. The most significant contribution of queer linguistics is that it enables 'sexual ideologies, practices and identities' (Bucholtz and Hall 2005: 471) to be discussed as interrelated issues, alongside power relations.

Queer theory is influenced by Butler's (1990) notion of performativity, thoroughly discussed in Chapter 3. The focus of queer theory is on social construction. As Baker (2008a: 187) states, 'instead of concentrating on constructing a "gay subject" (for example by asking "how do gay people use language?") queer theory focuses on deconstructing the underlying logic/rules of a gay subject by examining how the identity itself is constructed through language ("how does language construct gay people")'. Queer theory also sets out to decouple and question the binary opposition heterosexual/homosexual; Baker (2008a: 187) argues that 'queer theory promotes a politics of subversion, a belief that polar terms such as homosexual/heterosexual are mutually dependent, unstable and subject to reversal. One of the goals of queer theory ... is to examine and deconstruct the structures and symbolism inherent in the homo/hetero binary.'

One focus of queer theory has therefore been on the history of the word 'homosexual', which was originally coined in the 1860s as a more positive alternative to the term 'pederast', although gradually it began to be used with negative connotations. Baker (2008a: 187) points out that 'homosexual' was therefore invented before heterosexuality: 'it was only with the creation of "deviant" homosexuality that the concept of "normal" heterosexuality could then be conceptualized'. Baker also looks at sexual relationships in other cultures in order to problematise the binary heterosexual/homosexual. He shows that in the New Guinean tribe the Sambia, all men engage in homosexual behaviour at some stage of their lives. The *hijras* of India, the *yan daudu* of Nigeria, the *kathoey* of Thailand, the *batut* of the Philippines, the Tongan *fakaleiti* and Brazilian *travesti* are all examples of males who do not fit neatly into the hegemonic heterosexual stereotype (see the section on 'Transgendered identities, the body and the "third sex"', pp. 142–3, below). This suggests 'that viewing homosexuality as a minority identity, or even as a stable identity which exists in all cultures is simply incorrect' (Baker 2008a: 192). Not only are identities seen as fluid but also multiple, and Baker (2008a: 192) argues that 'the issues of organizing and theorizing these multiple differences in light of identity politics has led to the call by queer theorists for the abandon-ment of identity as a focus of gay politics'. This has led to Barrett (2002, cited in Baker 2008a: 193) arguing that in some ways 'queer' has no referent, and instead it is 'intended to index an imagined and undefined set of sexual practices ... that fall outside of the heteronormative assumptions of dominant societal discourse'.

However, as we have already highlighted, the term 'queer' is not without its problems or its critics. Mobilising a politics of gay men and lesbians is made more difficult if the very basis of such a politics – gay and lesbian identity – is under-mined by Queer. Furthermore, the very lack of definition which may seem to be one of Queer's strengths, may also be one of its weaknesses. But Cameron and Kulick argue that 'queer theory is not exclusively concerned with people designed as "queer" ... many heterosexuals are also queer – men and women who never marry, women with lovers or husbands who are much younger than themselves, women who openly reject motherhood as an option, men who purchase sex from women, women who sell sex to men' (Cameron and Kulick 2003: 149). In this sense, Queer offers a way of analysing the sexual identities and desires of all those who fall outside the hegemonic dominant sexual categories.

It is important to see that studies of sexuality need to analyse heterosexuality as much as homosexuality to uncover societal norms, boundaries and conven-tions. Through the work of Butler (1990), Barrett (2004: 297) draws attention to the 'incredible power of social normativity in regulating the ways in which we use language and the ways in which language uses us ... social norms *precede* the linguistic forms that reflect social inequalities'. Similarly, Queen (2004: 340) quoting Lakoff (1975: 83), observes that 'a stereotypical image may be far more influential than a (mere) statistical correlation'.

Bisexuality

Bisexuality has been an under-investigated area of language and sexuality research thus far. For example, Chirrey (2007) discusses the lack of referencing of bisexu-ality in a study that examines self-help pamphlets targeted at gays and lesbians from the 1950s to the present. Over half were targeted at both women and men and deal with issues such as how to tell your parents about your sexuality. She conducts a detailed analysis of three leaflets, two specifically targeted at women and one targeted at both women and men. She observes that the term 'bisexual' is not present in any of the women-only pamphlets. Drawing upon Fairclough's (1995) CDA principle that textual absence can be just as revealing as textual presence, she argues that absence of bisexuality signals that it is not available to readers as an identity label or subject position. Chirrey points out that it is quite logical to assume that women readers of these leaflets may very well be ques-tioning their sexuality because they are attracted to both women and men, and are thus looking for advice on this topic. However, she argues that the exclusion of bisexuality acts as an ideological choice from text producers: 'The proscription of "bisexual" as an identity label reveals the underlying ideology of the pamphlets, in which women's sexual identity is conceptualised as a binary choice between lesbian and heterosexual' (Chirrey 2007: 242).

In the remainder of the data, she notes that bisexuality either continues to be totally ignored or treated as other. She cites the example of the leaflet *Telling Your Parents* (1995), addressed to both women and men. Text producers address the reader as 'you' until a paragraph on bisexuality, where pronoun reference shifts to 'they'. Arguably, bisexuality research may have fallen through the cracks somewhat as researchers aim to bring gay and lesbian language issues to the fore to redress heterosexual bias. Bisexuality research could provide some fascinating insights into gender identity performances by the same individuals in different contexts.

Baker (2008a) analyses the way that bisexuality is treated as a sexual orientation. In his analyses of corpora he shows that 'bisexual' is often treated as an afterthought ('gay and bisexual'), rather than an identity in its own right.

Heterosexuality

It is frequently the case that when sex is discussed by feminists, it is lesbian sex which is focused on and heterosexual sex is not considered or examined. Wilkinson and Kitzinger (1993: 1) argue that 'heterosexuality has been largely untheorised within … feminism. Feminist theory tends to assume heterosexuality as a given, developing analyses with women's (and men's) heterosexuality as a taken-for-granted, but never explicitly addressed, substrate'. This results in lesbianism being characterised as an alternative or exception to the norm. In order to expand the research field and give a more comprehensive account of sexuality, it is important to focus upon heterosexuality as well as homosexuality. Heterosexuality should not be viewed as simply the 'opposite' of homosexuality, as heterosexuality brings with it many benefits, for example pension rights and other entitlements.[3] Cameron and Kulick (2003: 7) argue that 'if you are not heterosexual you cannot be a real man or a true woman … sexuality and gender have a "special relationship"'. They comment on the fact that no one talks about the 'straight community', whilst if you are homosexual, it is assumed that you are part of the 'gay community'.

Because of the way lesbianism has often been characterised within feminism as a political choice, for many feminist heterosexuals, there is a conflict between being feminist and being heterosexual, as if having relations with men constitutes a 'selling out' of feminism. As Ramazanoglu (1993: 59) puts it: 'those of us who identify ourselves as both in some sense "really" heterosexual and in some sense politically feminist, come up against a feminist consciousness which is both critical of our most intimate being and entails at least some resistance to close relationships with our nearest and dearest men'. Wilkinson and Kitzinger (1993: 6) argue that for lesbian feminists, 'accepting the label "lesbian" is a defiant act of self-naming, in which we assert our refusal of the heteropatriarchal order, and our commitment to women and lesbians'; however, for heterosexual women 'heterosexuality is not a *political* identity'. Because of the endless focus on romantic love within Western culture, there is often a dissonance between these myths of love and actual relationships between men and women. As Bhattacharyya (2002: 24) argues, 'perhaps it is the omnipresence of heterosexual propaganda that makes lived heterosexuality seem such a disappointment'.

Langford (1997) examines the language used in Valentine's Day messages in the *Guardian* newspaper by heterosexual couples. She notes that many of the messages characterise the love for the other person in very childish terms, constituting the relationship as private and distinct from the 'public world of adulthood' (Langford 1997: 171). As Langford comments: 'While adult humans strive to remain controlled and undaunted in the face of life, death and mortgage repayments, bunnies and bears can snuffle and growl' (1997: 173). Very often the names used by couples are babyish, evoking pets or soft toys ('Fluffy and Higgly'; 'Mootle and Dootle'; 'Bob and Pippy'). She gives as an example a message which states 'Flopsy bunny, I love you. Fierce Bad Rabbit.' Some of the messages adopt childish voices, for example 'Love you Wuggy buggy' and 'Linlin. Snugglebunnies and giggles'. This use of the language of small children and the characterisation of the couple as soft toys tends to make for an asexual representation of love. As one of the respondents in Langford's (1997: 172) study states, this type of representation allowed 'a kind of safe play area where you could still express affection, but it wasn't sexually charged in any way'. For some of the respondents, they found that taking on these personae enabled them to maintain a heterosexual companionable relationship, like two children, rather than as adults.

A rise in oversexualisation in terms of the heterosexual 'marketplace' (see Chapter 2) in public spheres is not restricted to popular culture or to non-professional settings. Evidence of such overt sexualisation can even be found in the highest echelons of power in the public sphere. There is clear evidence of very senior female political figures being subject to overt sexualisation. For instance, in August 2009 during a general election campaign in Germany, Angela Merkel, the German chancellor, was subject to overt sexualisation in a written advertising campaign by a female member of her own political party, the CDU (Christian Democratic Union). In August 2009 the 'Forbes List' of the world's 100 most powerful women awarded its number-one spot to Angela Merkel for the fourth year. On the same day that this was announced, the news agency ARP reported that in the forthcoming elections one woman who was also standing for election within Merkel's own political party, Vera Lengsfeld, had decided to publish a revealing photograph of the German chancellor in a low-cut dress with her cleavage on display, taken by press photographers at the opening of the new opera house in Oslo, Norway, juxtaposed with a very similar picture of herself, in the form of a campaign poster. The slogan at the bottom of these two photographs, strategically placed just above their cleavages, is 'we have more to offer'. Merkel had not authorised this poster.

The official commentator on women's issues from the CDU party, Maria Boehmer, condemned such a 'sex sells' campaign, as outdated. Boehmer was very clear to emphasise that the party and Angela Merkel herself had not been informed of Vera Lengsfeld's poster campaign. Lengsfeld's justification was that following her posters she had received over 17,000 hits on her website – she justified her decision by claiming that if only one tenth of these Internet surfers looked at her policies then this was far more people than she could have reached via the traditional, door-to-door canvassing method. In defence of her actions she claimed that people were lacking a sense of humour – she was merely trying to liven up the election campaign, as so often there are complaints about how dull they are. The deeply ingrained stereotype of the humourless feminist is lurking in the background here. Lengsfeld was reported as stating:

'I find it amazing how little humour some people have shown over this placard. People always complain that election posters are boring and then as soon as someone does something different, people get annoyed,' she said. (*Daily Telegraph Online*, 11 August 2009)

The oversexualisation of women has become so deeply ingrained within Western culture that arguably even the woman who is seen as one of the most powerful in the world is subject to overt sexualisation.

It is interesting to consider the range of reactions to the poster which appeared on newspaper blogs, as reported by the UK's right-wing tabloid the *Daily Mail*, from the perspective of contemporary feminist politics:

'Alex': Fantastic idea. Witty, cheeky and funny. I personally never thought I would see such a daring billboard in an otherwise very respectable and serious German election campaign.

'Lena': This billboard is embarrassing and shameful … how deeply sad that a women [sic] has to attract attention with her breasts because she is incapable of clever words and thoughts. (*Daily Telegraph Online* blog, 13 August 2009)

There is evidence of the reflection of post-feminist discourses in the first blog comment and a Third Wave feminist viewpoint in the second.

Indeed, the original photograph of Merkel had caused previous commentary in the media when it was first taken in April 2008. In the UK, the *Daily Mail* ran with the following metaphorical headline to describe her breasts: 'Merkel's weapons of mass destruction'. In 2006 the *Sun* tabloid newspaper in the UK took a covert photograph of the German chancellor in her bathing suit on holiday and ran with the headline 'Big in the Bum-destag', a rather crass pun on the German lower House of Parliament, the Bundestag.

Coming back to cleavage, in the US, in 2007 Hillary Rodham Clinton's cleavage, and not her political campaign policies, became the focus of a great deal of discussion in certain facets of the media in the run-up to the Democratic Party's presidential leadership campaign. Robin Givhan of the *Washington Post* reported this as follows:

She [Clinton] was talking on the Senate floor about the burdensome cost of higher education. She was wearing a rose-colored blazer over a black top. The neckline sat low on her chest and had a subtle V-shape. The cleavage registered after only a quick glance. No scrunch-faced scrutiny was necessary. There wasn't an unseemly amount of cleavage showing, but there it was. Undeniable. It was startling to see that small acknowledgment of sexuality and femininity peeking out. (*Washington Post Online*, 20 July 2007)

This is a typical example of the lack of focus on the political topic Clinton was actually talking about in Senate. Instead a detailed commentary of Clinton's body and clothing choices ensues. Givhan then goes on to give the reader a direct comparison with Jacqui Smith, a British Labour MP, who, at the time, had just become the first British female home secretary:

> Not so long ago, Jacqui Smith, the new British home secretary, spoke before the House of Commons showing far more cleavage than Clinton. If Clinton's was a teasing display, then Smith's was a full-fledged come-on. But somehow it wasn't as unnerving. Perhaps that's because Smith's cleavage seemed to be presented so forthrightly. Smith's fitted jacket and her dramatic necklace combined to draw the eye directly to her bosom. There they were all part of a bold, confident style package. (*Washington Post Online*, 20 July 2007)

The newsworthiness is not the terror legislation that Smith was talking about but instead that she was showing cleavage in the House of Commons. There was much ensuing discussion about Clinton's cleavage in the days following her appearance in Senate.

Another illustration is in the form of lapel buttons (badges) for Sarah Palin, the Republican Party's vice-presidential candidate in 2008. The buttons had a photograph of Palin's head and shoulders with a slogan describing her as 'The hottest VP from the coolest state'. These were produced by her own political party (presumably with her endorsement) and were given out at the Republican Party's national convention a few weeks before the presidential election took place.

The current 'First Lady' of the US (a term referring to the president's wife, which in itself needs contesting), Michelle Obama, is consistently sexualised in the mass media. On a day when Barack Obama was announcing historic changes to healthcare policy in the US, elements of the UK mass media decided to focus instead upon Michelle Obama's legs in shorts. The *Daily Mail* ran with the following headline:

> From the right to bear arms to the right to bare legs:
> Michelle Obama caught short over her shorts
>
> (*Daily Mail*, 20 August 2008)

These examples illustrate how women's bodies, regardless of who the women are or what status or professional role and responsibility they may hold, become overtly sexualised within a heterosexual matrix and are frequently subject to sexual objectification at the expense of a focus upon their professional skills and abilities. Women's professional expertise will frequently be judged and evaluated upon their physical appearance and sexual desirability.[4] As Foucault (1978) has pointed out, the body is 'the ultimate site of political and ideological control, surveillance and regulation' (Lupton 1994: 23), and women experience this control, regulation and surveillance to a greater degree than men.

As an example of the way that stereotypes of female heterosexuality and submissiveness prevail, we can examine Pocket Girlfriend, a globally available, inexpensive and easily downloadable program available on internet-based smartphones. It is listed under the 'entertainment' category. The Pocket Girlfriend can be purchased for GBP 0.59, or a subscriber can get the 'Pocket Girlfriend Lite' version, which is completely free to download. These applications are visual interactive programs that can be downloaded to internet phones. It was listed as one of the top 25 downloads in November 2009 on UK-based phones, when it was also highlighted as being the top paid entertainment application in India, Mexico, Malaysia, New Zealand and Turkey. There is a note that you have to be 17-plus years of age to access it, but there is no method of enforcing this, as self-report is used in the form of a simple tick box which grants access.

On the home page the following text appears:

> Now she's touchable, tickle enabled.
> Unlike other applications that only offer some random photo gallery of bikini clad girls; Pocket Girlfriend moves, she's interactive, and most importantly she's real. YES SHE'S REAL!!!! She's not some 3D rendered mannequin.

> Key features
> 1. SHE TALKS TO YOU and what she has to say is absolutely hilarious! Amazing one-liners that every guy wants to hear. She's the idyllic girlfriend.
> 2. SHE'S HOT, REALLY HOT!!!! And yes that's a feature!
> 3. SHE'S ANIMATED She engages with you and shows you her playful assets.
> 4. EASILY CREATE YOUR OWN CUSTOM AUDIO CLIPS. Customise her the way you want. She'll say anything you want so use your imagination and be creative.
> 5. SHE'S INTERACTIVE. She'll even miss you when you're gone. She's Accelerometer aware.

The advertising slogan on the main page of the application, is accompanied by a photograph of two men with surprised and excited looks on their faces, gazing at a 3D image of the pocket girlfriend emerging from their phone, scantily clad, in the process of taking off her T-shirt:

> Pocket Girlfriend
> Just like your girlfriend, but funny and hot

The dialogic discourse strategies that are used to attract the attention of the male consumer here, which include the use of deixis, 'your', ellipsis and informality, 'just like', are typical of the strategies used by advertising producers to draw the reader in, as if engaging in a conversation with the reader, arguably fulfilling the role of the 'informed friend' (Talbot 1995). From the perspective of feminist pragmatics, there is a series of identifiable presuppositions contained within the advertising slogan: (a) the reader has a girlfriend; (b) girlfriends are not funny as they lack a sense of humour, fulfilling the deeply ingrained stereotype of women being humourless; (c) the current reader's girl-friend will not be 'hot', that is, will not be heterosexually attractive.

The coarse objectivisation of heterosexual women that is taking place here has arguably escaped any sanctions because the ambiguous nature of humour here acts as a mask for sexist opinions, with women being treated as sexual objects, reduced to a pre-programmed, robotic speech style. This usage of humour accords with similar observations made by Sunderland (2007) regarding the ambiguous and powerful nature of humour. Retorts to feminist protests against such overt sexism in examples such as this lead to the tag of the humourless feminist. However, cases such as these, which are so freely available in mainstream society, where women are being portrayed as objects to be carried around in your pocket and totally controlled by a 'master' who can program speech, send out clear and potentially very damaging signals that this type of behaviour is socially accept-able for heterosexual men.

Some examples of 'her' language use, described in the publicity material as 'one-liners all guys love to hear', include:

Another beer?
I'm very flexible
Love hairy men
More of you to love
Need a hug
Need a massage
Oh poor baby
Special to me

Interestingly, there has been a recent case in the UK where the sexualisa-tion and eroticism of men for target markets of heterosexual women has been the subject of an interesting debate. Whilst huge numbers of erotic magazines targeted at a male audience and full of images of naked or semi-naked women are available in practically any newsagent, a magazine named *Filament*, launched in 2009, was the first to attempt to fill the gap of such publications for heterosexual women. However, following reader demand for photos of semi-aroused men, the publisher of *Filament* ran into trouble. The *Guardian* newspaper reports that although the Obscene Publications Act in the UK does not ban photographs of male erections, the legislation is very vague. *Filament*'s publishers have now refused to publish such images. Arguably this example provides a prime illustration of the fact that women are sexual objects but they are not allowed to have agency and experience sexual desire themselves for males. *Filament* has argued that its surveys and response to their magazine demonstrate that there is a huge market for erotica targeted at heterosexual women with men as the objects. Writing in the *Guardian*, Kristina Lloyd and Mathilde Madden (2009) make the following observa-tion about the disparity between magazines targeted at heterosexual men and those for heterosexual women:

Attempts to even out this disparity often lead to cries that two wrongs don't make a right; that countering the prevalence of eroticised women by adding men into the mix legitimises sexist objectification. But there's nothing inherently sexist about depicting nudity. It's sexist when only women are deemed to signify the erotic; it's sexist when eroticised images of women are so normalised and widespread that women tend to be viewed first and foremost as sex objects – their value inextricably linked to their sexual desirability. The sexism is in the inequality. (Lloyd and Madden 2009)

This is a controversial point – differing feminist perspectives would have differing views on this, and indeed this makes for a very good, provocative discussion point. From our perspective, the most important thing is that all individuals regardless of their sexuality are free to experience desire.

Ehrlich (2003) has noted that in heterosexual sexual harassment and rape trials, there is a tendency for events to be represented from two different perspectives: that of the male rapist and that of the female. She argues that generally the court tends to view the alleged rape from the perspective of the male, colluding with him in presenting male sexual desire as an unstoppable urge, and in seeing women as responsible for leading men on. Eckert and McConnell-Ginet (2003: 211) comment on this: 'the defendant and his counsel but also the judge speak of the male sexual drive as a force external to the man that is (virtually) irresistible and triggered by a woman's "provocativeness"'. When judges view male sexuality as a consequence of natural and unstoppable forces for which the male is not responsible, it is not surprising that so few rape trials find against the male defendants. In the UK alone, at least 100,000 women are raped every year. However, only 6.5 per cent of those tried for rape are convicted (Banyard 2010: 2). This suggests that judges' attitudes to rape collude with the views of rapists rather than their victims.

In the transcripts of a Canadian sexual harassment trial, Ehrlich notes that the male defendant used verbs to describe the harassment with a distinct lack of agented verbs, so that when he describes becoming sexually aroused he uses phrases such as 'it started to heat up', 'things became sexual', where his responsibility for the sexual assault is diminished. This gives the impression that the sex was consensual rather than forced on the woman. He also uses the language of romantic love, describing himself as 'caressing' the woman's hair. Here again, the sexual encounter is represented as consensual. In this trial, Ehrlich notes that the women involved were criticised by the judge because they did not resist the man's advances strongly enough. Thus, responsibility for rape is seen to be the woman's rather than the man's.

Cameron and Kulick focus on the meaning of the word 'no' in heterosexual sexual encounters and the notion of resistance in rape. They argue that saying 'no' to sexual advances is often difficult because there are rarely occasions when sexual acts are explicitly verbalised and requested. Rather, sexual activity tends to be refused more by indirect means such as referring to tiredness or headaches, rather than by explicit refusals. Explicit refusals are dispreferred and therefore are a very marked form of behaviour and consequently difficult, despite the fact that in rape trials much is made of the lack of explicit refusal by the female victims.

There is an additional problem that 'no' can be interpreted within hetero-sexual sex by some men to signify an initial refusal which can be overcome with persuasion or force. Thus, 'a rapist or murderer *can* claim that he legitimately read desire in the words and actions of his victim' and this claim can be supported through reference to the victim's dress, state of drunkenness or words (Cameron and Kulick 2003: 129). Cameron and Kulick also comment on the fact that in sadomasochist sexual acts, 'no' cannot function as a 'safe' word. Words to stop the sexual encounter have be designated, so that it is clear to both parties that one of the participants does not want this particular sexual act. Cameron and Kulick note that one kind of word which is frequently used in sadomasochistic sex is a nonsensical one such as 'pickle'. This is a word which is used instead of 'no', which runs the risk of being misinterpreted.

Transgendered identities, the body and the 'third sex'

In terms of contemporary investigations of transgendered identities, some inter-esting recent work has been produced by Borba and Ostermann (2007) in Brazil, which focuses on the aforementioned group known as *travestis* and their language use. They define Brazilian *travestis* as individuals who are biologically male who engage in a struggle for femininity. They clearly distinguish *travestis* from those individuals who are interested in sex-realignment surgery and attaining biological femaleness. Instead, *travestis*, in Butler's (1990) sense, are engaged in performing feminine identities. The linguistic means through which they perform femininity include the adoption of female names in order to address one another and the use of grammatically feminine gender forms within their Portuguese language system when interacting with one another. In different contexts, they also adopt mascu-line grammatical gender forms, for instance, in order to distance themselves from other *travestis* who display vulgar behaviour.

To illustrate, Borba and Ostermann draw upon data taken from a *travesti* known as Cynthia, who uses masculine grammatical gender when talking about a *travesti* whom she does not deem worthy of any public respect. Masculine grammatical gender thus acts as a face-enhancing device for Cynthia in such a context, as she places social distance between herself and the other *travestis* from whom she wishes to disassociate. As with many studies invoked in this volume, we see again the importance of paying attention to the specifics of the local context of interac-tion in determining linguistic form and function. Borba and Ostermann examine how such linguistic choices are clearly related to an individual's embodiment. This leads them to argue that biological sex needs to be more carefully examined by sociolinguists on account of the fundamental role that the body plays in the identity construction of gender-variant groups.

In another recent work, Zimman and Hall (2010: 166) draw attention within sociolinguistics to what they term the 'third sex', a term used to refer to 'groups whose gender identities and enactments fall outside of socio-cultural norms for women and men'. Drawing on the work of Borba and Ostermann (2007), they argue that if future researchers turn to study the 'third sex' then the research focus will be rightly refocused to examine biological sex, which, from their perspective, has been subordinated because of the dominant focus on the social construction of gender. Their overarching purpose is to demonstrate the 'importance of the body in shaping the relationship between language and identity among gender-variant groups' (2010: 166). However, as we have already seen at various points in this chapter, there is often a disjunction between terms that have been coined for individuals and those individuals' attitudes towards these terms. The category of 'third sex' is no exception to this: Zimman and Hall (2010: 169) point out that 'it is unclear whether transgender people should be discussed as a third sex, particularly given the dissent that exists amongst members of this group on this issue'.

They draw upon empirical research that each individual author has conducted. The first study (by Zimman) looks at gender-variant communities of transsexual men in the US and the second (by Hall) draws upon the aforementioned *hijras* in India (see also Hall 1996). They invoke Third Wave feminist perspectives of sex as a discursively constructed notion as well as gender (discussed in Chapter 3). They are particularly interested in examining the role that language plays in constructing 'female' and 'male' bodies. The US data examines an online community of transsexual men, focusing in particular upon how members discuss their genitals and the gendered meanings that can be seen through these online discussions. Analysis of these data showed that many transsexual men object to any suggestion that their bodies are female in any form: 'instead of consenting to the dominant ideology that having a vagina makes a person female-bodied, these individuals destabilise the boundaries between male and female embodiment through a subversion of the semantics of words for gendered body parts' (2010: 171–2). They give as an example the transsexuals' use of 'dick' and 'cock growing' to refer to female genitalia, which blurs the boundaries between clitorises and penises as well as decoupling 'the specific corporeal characteristics of the penis from the masculinities entailed by words like *dick*' (2010: 173). The analysis of *hijras* demonstrates how they clearly illustrate that they are neither man nor woman by engaging in a specific gesture, a distinctive hand clap. Zimman and Hall argue that both examples illustrate how any analysis of gender-variant groups needs to draw upon the body as a discursive analytical construct. Their work provides some interesting challenges for future language and sexuality research, especially to include a greater focus on the body of gender-variant individuals as sites for discursive identity construction.

Summary

In this chapter, we have aimed to highlight the critical importance of investigations of language and sexuality to contemporary studies of language, gender and feminism. We have shown the importance of analysing the relation between language and sexuality through a focus on language and desire as well as language and sexual identity. We have also shown the importance of the role of language in constituting heterosexual and homosexual desire and identity. In the next chapter we move on to examine our second area of key contemporary study in feminist linguistics, that of language and sexism.

7 Sexism

Introduction: sexism in the twenty-first century

As we have seen at various points in this book, struggles over language use have been crucial in many respects within feminist linguistic research. Sexist language has been one of the key issues within feminist linguistics which has forced people to carefully consider their own and others' language use – to examine, for example, the way that an institution's choice of words in relation to women fits with its mission statements about equality of opportunity or its claims to modernity (Mills 2008).

Sexism is difficult to define in contemporary research, because not everyone agrees about exactly what constitutes sexism. Some argue that sexism is any language use which seems to represent women in a negative way; some consider it as negative generalisations based on stereotypes about men or women (Vetterling-Braggin 1981). Sexism has become associated with conservative thinking about gender roles and seems anachronistic. Sexism is a site of struggle between those who wish women to be treated equally, for example those who want women to be fully integrated into the society where they live, within workforces where they have previously been excluded and so on, and those who are resistant to women's equality or who see differential treatment of women in positive terms.[1] Discussions and campaigns around sexism can be seen as a litmus test for how much societies have changed and also for how much certain groups within societies have resisted the changes in women's roles.

The reason we say that sexism is a site for struggle is that when sexist language is used, it is extremely difficult to resist and to answer back. In a discussion of homophobia, Leap (1997: 70) argues that when someone calls you a 'faggot', you cannot simply respond 'I am not a faggot', because this response accepts a negative view of homosexuality implied in the term. Instead, he argues that we need to try to argue against the negative evaluation of the term, whilst still maintaining membership of the group which is being negatively evaluated. This is a complex process, because in face-to-face interaction it is difficult to challenge the meaning of terms which have been used about you, and in contexts such as advertising, when you disagree with words used about women or gay, lesbian, bisexual or transgendered people, there is no one to take issue with (apart from, as Cameron 2006a points out, bodies such as the Advertising Standards

Authority in the UK and its equivalents in other countries that have such a body). Sexism is also a position which has some institutional support (albeit to differing degrees) in contemporary societies. It is not a view of women that the speaker or writer has invented, but rather just a body of ideas and phrases which others have expressed and which are presented as 'common sense'. Sexism has an agentless feel to it, and because of this, it achieves authority unless it is challenged.

Sexist language and political action

At this moment in time, when studying language and sexism, we need to ask ourselves: what is it we are claiming about the force of sexist language and what actions are feminists proposing to counter sexism? Butler (1997) has asked:

> When we claim to have been injured by language, what kind of claim do we make? We ascribe an agency to language, a power to injure, and position ourselves as the objects of its injurious trajectory. We claim that language acts and acts against us and the claim we make is a further instance of language, one which seeks to arrest the force of the prior instance. Thus we exercise the force of language even as we seek to counter its force, caught up in a bind that no act of censorship can undo. (Butler 1997: 1)

We would take issue with Butler here, because when we make accusations of sexism, we are not simply claiming to be 'injured by language'. What we are injured by is a system which seems to condone such discrimination. Butler seems here to be arguing that any attempt to challenge sexism is simply 'a further instance of language' which does not change the way that language is used or the way people behave. But feminist linguists' anti-discriminatory language campaigns have done more than 'arrest the force of the prior instance'; they have, in fact, challenged the conventionalised thinking which informs such utterances and those discursive structures within society which condone sexist statements (see Kramarae and Treichler 1985; Doyle 1994; Cameron 1992; Mills 2008). Feminist linguistic interventions call not only for a change of usage but also for critical thinking about gender relations, and as such they should be seen as more than an attempt to ban certain language usages. We are not just simply caught up in language – if we attempt to call for reform or change of usage our interventions are, in fact, calling for more than language change. As Cameron (2006a: 16) argues, 'if we take it that no expression has a meaning independent of its linguistic and non-linguistic context, we can plausibly explain the sexism of language by saying that all speech events in patriarchal cultures have as part of their context the power relation that holds between women and men'.

It is the institutionalised aspect of sexism which makes it most difficult to challenge it effectively. Christie (2000: 131) argues that it is 'much easier to generate sexist meanings through language use than to generate meanings that problematise or run against stereotypical notions of gender'. Because sexist meanings are in a sense already established and available to speakers, they depend on presuppositions about gender relations. If feminists wish to change language or to introduce a new word, they have to work very hard for it to become accepted. Christie (2000: 130) demonstrates that 'a speaker's meaning is more easily accessed when it draws on ideas and perspectives that are generally accepted across a community'. She gives the example of 'You think like a woman.' This phrase might be perceived as an insult. But if we simply look at the content alone, we cannot say that it is sexist; it is only through its reference to a body of ideas about women which have become institutionalised that we can see this statement as sexist.

Sexism places you in a negatively evaluated category, for example when an insult term such as 'slag' is used about you which positions you in a role which you do not recognise. Butler (1997: 4) argues that 'To be injured by speech is to suffer a loss of context, that is, not to know where you are. Indeed, it may be that what is unanticipated about the injurious speech act is what constitutes its injury, the sense of putting its addressee out of control.' Sexism therefore 'puts you out of control' in the sense that you are being defined and not defining yourself. However, it is clear that, although the unexpectedness of sexist comments is crucial, we would take issue with Butler that this means that the addressee 'does not know where you are'. In a sense, this is the problem, that you know *precisely* the position to which you are being relegated, but this position is not one that you would choose for yourself.

Sexist language-change over time: a case study

If we look back at magazine articles from the 1950s then we can illustrate how much sexism itself has changed over time in one particular cultural context. In this section we will focus on 'The Good Wife's Guide' published in *Housekeeping Monthly* in the UK in May 1955, where the magazine gives advice to women to put their husband before everything else. We will compare this with a rewritten version of this text published in *Glamour* magazine in 2009. In the original 1955 text, when the husband comes home from work, the wife is advised, through a list of directives, to do the following:

> Take 15 minutes to rest so you'll be refreshed when he arrives;
> Be a little gay and a little more interesting for him;
> Clear away the clutter. Make one last trip through the main part of the house just before your husband arrives.

This stereotypical wife is also advised to light a fire so that 'your husband will feel he has reached a haven of rest and order, and it will give you a lift too. After all, catering for his comfort will provide you with immense personal satisfaction.' Underlying these directives is the assumption that the wife has had to work hard throughout the day to keep the house tidy, prepare the food and look after the children, but that just before her husband arrives home, she should make an extra effort to make all of this work invisible; she is told to 'minimise all noise. At the time of his arrival eliminate all noise of the washer, dryer or vacuum. Encourage the children to be quiet.' Thus, all sense of the woman's labour is erased.

Furthermore, the work that she has done throughout the day is of no importance and should not be discussed: 'Don't greet him with complaints and problems', because 'remember, his topics of conversation are more important than yours.' The descriptions which are given of the care that the woman should show for her husband, to 'greet him with a warm smile and show sincerity in your desire to please him', remind one more of the instructions given to servants and, in the present day, to call-centre workers (Cameron 2000; Hultgren 2008), rather than to someone who is in a companionate marriage. The husband is the one on whom the house should be centred, and the wife and children need to ensure that he can 'renew himself in body and spirit'. The wife is represented as a servant without a sense of self; the meaning of her life comes from serving her husband. He is represented as free in his actions, for he may 'come home late or go out to dinner or other places of entertainment' without his wife, and the guide suggests he should not be criticised by his wife for this. His work environment is represented as a 'world of stress and pressure', and he has to be with 'a lot of work-weary people' but at least he has 'a place of peace, order and tranquillity' to come home to.

It is important to read magazine articles from the 1950s for two reasons. First, we can use these written texts as lenses to gauge how much progress has been made within a UK context in terms of the ways women are viewed and the roles which are seen to be available to them.[2] This representation of women's roles has become so foreign to the vast majority of women today in the UK, mainly because of Second Wave feminist activism around the issue of sexism and equal opportunities for women, and also because of the sheer numbers of women working outside the home, that it would be difficult for most women to put themselves into the position of women in the 1950s, who would have been the target audience for this guide. Second, however, it is arguably important to remember that there was a need for guides to being a 'good wife', precisely because women in the 1950s perhaps could not or would not behave in the way that their husbands and magazines such as this would have liked them to.

This magazine article, with its hectoring tone about the importance of their husbands and the wife's own lack of worth and the sheer volume of the orders to women to make the house a peaceful and welcoming place, indicate quite forcibly, if read symptomatically, the degree of resistance that there was in the 1950s to the unreal expectations imposed on women (Althusser 1984).[3] Through a symptomatic reading, reading against the grain of the text, one can focus on the elements which this text is trying to repress: one can imagine all of the women who complained about their day when their husband returned from work and who were unable and unwilling to spend all day cleaning the house and looking after the children, in order to present a 'peaceful haven' to their husband.

These women may well have resented the fact that their husbands and society in general viewed them and their labour as 'less important than their husbands'. It is crucial to remember that a great number of Second Wave feminists developed their ideas precisely because of the repression that they experienced as housewives and 'the problem without a name', that is, the disjuncture felt by many housewives when expected to engage in unfulfilling work at home, whilst being unable to classify this as work and whilst being unable to gain positive evaluation from society because of this work (Friedan 1963/2010; Oakley 1984). As Skeggs (1997) has shown, British working- and middle-class women were encouraged to take on caring roles within their relationships and within the wider society, and they have developed a sense of their own self-worth through these roles, but society as a whole has not valued caring roles highly, either materially or ideologically.

We would argue that this type of representation, where women are encouraged to see themselves as of less value in relation to men, is clearly sexist, in that it discriminates against women on the grounds of their sex alone. However, most of the current definitions of sexism would not enable us to describe this text as sexist. For example, Vetterling-Braggin's (1981) definition of sexism as 'the practices whereby someone foregrounds gender when it is not the most salient feature' would not classify this text as sexist necessarily. Admittedly, gender is foregrounded, in that the text refers to the man specifically in terms of his sexual difference as being superior to the woman. However, the sexism resides largely at the level of common-sense presuppositions. Althusser (1984) has shown that ideologies are constructed through presenting themselves as if their content is self-evidently true and as truths shared by everyone, through the use of phrases such as 'of course' and 'everyone knows that ...', even if these statements are only implicit in the text.

In *Housekeeping Monthly*, the magazine advises the reader to 'remember, his topics of conversation are more important than yours'. This crucial ideological message underpins the text as a whole, and it is significant that this phrase is highlighted in bold text. The message is represented as being knowledge that the woman already has through the use of the word 'remember'. She simply needs to bring this knowledge to the fore again in her thinking about her relation to her husband. Underpinning this ideological message about women is the expectation that every wife will want to subjugate herself to her husband, since 'catering for his comfort will provide *you* with immense personal satisfaction' (our emphasis).

Vetterling-Braggin's definition of sexism is also inadequate in an analysis of this text as sexist because it also assumes that there is 'someone' who is mistakenly putting forward this sexist message and they are doing this because they are simply misguided. This individualistic notion of sexism fails to recognise that sexism is institutionalised, that is, this type of language use and thought has a history which predates each of us as individuals. Each individual speaker does not invent sexism for themselves, but it exists as a set of options which, at one time, were relatively authorised. These sexist beliefs were accepted by many as common-sense knowledge and were therefore difficult to contest. They were held in place, because they worked in the interests of a great number of men (and some women) and the wider society. This more institutionalised notion of sexism is far more productive as it enables us to see sexism less as something which individual statements possess and more as a set of resources which are available for use in particular political struggles. Nevertheless, whilst holding on to this notion that sexism is an institutionalised resource, we need to retain the notion that individuals make choices about their language usage and are responsible for discriminating against women if they use sexist language.

Thus, we need to be able to think about sexism as consisting of a number of different elements. A sexist statement may well contain a number of linguistic elements which we will be able to recognise as foregrounding 'gender when it is not the most salient feature'; but it will also be sexist at the level of the proposition or at the level of the presupposition, and in order to 'unpick' sexism, we have to analyse this inferential work which the reader needs to do in order to make sense of the statement.

Mills (2008) has termed this type of example, where there is clear and unequivocal evidence of sexism, as 'overt' sexism. However, even here there are difficulties with assuming that this type of text will be read as unequivocally sexist by all readers. For some older women readers who were mothers and housewives during the 1950s and 1960s, this type of representation of women may well depict a role which they themselves cherish and which they feel nostalgia for, something which they feel that present UK society has lost. They may have gained pleasure from being dutiful housewives who ran efficient and welcoming households for their husbands, and their sense of their own self-worth will have been derived from such representations. Furthermore, some younger women have taken on board these ideologies about 'a woman's place' being 'in the home' and have reinvented these ideologies for the present day. For example, in 2007 the BBC network ran a series of programmes hosted by a former TV presenter, Anthea Turner, which aimed to 'revolutionise the running of Britain's households' by teaching housewives how to become domestic goddesses at her country mansion. For example, Anthea takes on Tina, a mother of four, and Tracey, a hairdresser with horrendous hoarding habits, both of whom go out to work but get next to no help from their families at home. Anthea then has the task of crowning the 'perfect housewife'. There are also cookery books, for example UK chef Nigella Lawson's *How to Be a Domestic Goddess*, offering women advice about how to be the 'perfect chef'. These books generally are assumed to be slightly ironic, although it is unclear quite how the irony works, since their advice seems to replicate the type of guides to women that were current in the 1950s.

It is clear that because of feminist campaigns about sexism and consciousness-raising in the 1960s and because of women's entry into higher education and the labour market in substantial numbers in the West, sexist representations like that quoted above from *Housekeeping Monthly* no longer appear in quite the same guise. However, that is not to say that sexism has somehow disappeared. There is a new type of sexism which Mills has termed 'indirect sexism' because it does not seem to operate in the same way as overt sexism (Mills 2008). It works through humour and playfulness and often explicitly evokes these sexist messages from the 1950s in a playful and ironising way.

In the October 2009 issue of the UK-based women's magazine *Glamour*, there is an article entitled 'The (all new) Good Wife Guide'. Here, two columnists, John Perry and Claudia Winkleman, have been asked to update 'The Good Wife Guide' from the 1950s, since, as the magazine puts it, 'Life's changed a wee bit since then.' The photographs accompanying the article are all taken from the

1950s, but all of them have ironising captions; for example, one of the illustrations represents a 1950s woman wearing a checked apron and dancing excitedly. The caption here is 'Guess who's put Ecstasy in her scones again.' This allows the sexist stereotypes of the happy, dutiful housewife to be reinvoked and re-presented to the reader but in a tongue-in-cheek, ironising way. Another illustration shows a 1950s woman smiling, in an apron next to a cooker; the caption here reads, 'Two ovens, a grill and eight burners – shame she could only cook beans on toast.' This allows this model of dominant hegemonic femininity to be mocked, whilst turning the ridicule on the women themselves, rather than on the social system and the ideological pressures which led to women being confined to the home. Through addressing the reader explicitly as 'you' and through the use of humour as a classic ambiguous linguistic device, the article manages to have its ideological cake and eat it, too. It distances the targeted (woman) reader from these ridiculous representations of femininity, whilst also subtly still exhorting women to be subservient to men.

The article is written by a man (Perry) and a woman (Winkleman), and their comments are displayed in the magazine in adjacent columns. Their comments are organised into directives, much as in the original 1950s Guide. For example, Perry advises:

1   Be happy to see him.
2   Tell him he's fit.
3   Let him drive as fast as he likes.
4   Applaud his DIY.
...
8   Sit on his knee.

Perry's column invokes the 1950s stereotypes more than Winkleman's, but, even here, he updates this overt sexism even whilst explicitly making fun of it. For example, he recognises that after years of marriage 'the flames of passion have been reduced to a simmer' and he mocks the notion that therefore women should 'throw on an Ann Summers outfit and ambush him at the door',[4] but nevertheless he still advises women that they should 'sit on his knee'. Sitting on someone's knee seems a particularly infantilising form of sexual encounter. Perhaps most worryingly, there are a number of examples of advice where Perry appears to be trying to update the 1950s stereotype: for example, (6) 'Smile at the furry handcuffs' and (9) 'Let him think he's in charge.' Here, in the text accompanying the advice on the furry handcuffs, women are advised to let their husbands buy them inappropriate sexual gifts, not because they wish to impose their sexual preferences upon them, but because they are inept: 'He wants to buy you nice things, but he just doesn't understand Crème de la Mer and Balenciaga – so he buys you something red from Ann Summers.' Gifts of sex toys are seen, for the husband, as 'a magnificent romantic gesture', so women are advised to 'bite your tongue and feign wonder at his gift'. This is a clear example of raunch culture, in which (as we have seen already in Chapter 2) being openly sexual, albeit entirely within male terms, has been portrayed in popular culture as a sign of 'women's "liberation"'

(Levy 2005: 3), where 'raunch culture is a litmus test of female uptightness'. Thus, if a woman behaves in a conventionally sexualised way in Western culture, for example by pole dancing or going to a strip club, then she is seen to be 'empowered'. Perhaps the very foregrounded sexualisation in this article is the clue that readers are supposed to pick up on, so that they can read this text as ironic and playful. But it is perhaps one of the more troubling elements of the text, since the sexualisation is entirely about pandering to the husband's sexual needs.

In the piece of advice 'Let him think he is in charge', women readers are advised to 'let him read the map, choose the wine, pay for the meal. And most importantly, let him hog the TV remote' and in that way the man will *think* that he is in charge, whilst the woman will be 'making all the important decisions (where to go on holiday, who to vote for on *The X Factor*)'.[5] This is an interesting and complex manoeuvre: women are advised to think that they are, in fact, in control in the relationship, because they really make the decisions on relatively trivial things, whilst they are advised not to allow the man to know that it is women who make the decisions. However, on a day-to-day basis, for ordinary decision-making, the woman is advised to 'massage his ego' and allow him to take charge. Thus the male not only thinks he is in control, he *is* in control. The final piece of advice from Perry is (10) 'Remember, "I do".' Under this heading he reminds readers that their husband promised to 'be there for you through thick and thin' when they married, and he asks the reader to 'Think about all the stuff he's had to put up with over the years: the PMT, the Jimmy Choos you pretended you got in a sale, the way he sat through an entire box set of *Sex and the City* – and remember how much that man loves you. Now go and get him a beer. I think he's earned it.' The same equation between being married to a man and serving him is made here as in the text from the 1950s. If your husband has had to 'put up with' you as a woman, then it makes logical sense within this ideology to go and get him a beer as a recompense.

Winkleman's advice is slightly more complex, and she seems to have taken on board certain feminist ideals about the importance of women's self-determination. However, she also characterises the relationships between men and women as being based on trickery; so the woman reader is advised (1) 'Always be late, as those who are on time are dull and will not be attractive to their husbands'; in a similar vein she advises women to turn their phone off, so that they appear to be less available. She advises (5) 'Be unpredictable', so that the husband is kept on his toes and interested in his wife. She also advises (2) 'Never cook', because 'the people who get over-excited about organic tomatoes also get uptight about husbands'. She suggests that the woman reader should (4) 'Watch *Top Gear*'.[6] Again, like Perry, she advises that women should just feign interest, lie to their husbands about their feelings. In a similar way she advises (7) 'Be happy', because 'men love being with happy girls'. She advises that women should be confident and independent; at first sight, this advice might seem to be inspired by feminism, but confidence is presented as 'the sexiest trait on the planet' and the example of confidence which is given is simply not responding when a drunken girl flirts with your husband. Women readers are advised to 'Look nice', which, at first sight, seems as if it is the expression of a conventional 1950s ideology of femininity, but here Winkleman states 'I know. Who gives a toss, right? You've bagged him, you've had a kid and the new sofa you've always dreamed of. What's the point in washing your hair? Why shave your legs?' The view of relationships which is put forward here, even though ironically, is one where the woman only took care of her appearance in order to achieve her goal of 'bagging' a man, children and material goods. She mocks the notion that beauty lies within and argues that 'a bit of effort makes men feel special and elated. And I know it's pathetic, but it makes them feel important. So put some lipstick on and grit your teeth.' Here, even whilst recognising that this stereotypical view of men is pathetic, women are still urged to make themselves look good for their husbands, as it is important to make them feel special.

Thus, this article, whilst seeming superficially to be critical and ironic about the norms of 1950s femininity, is in fact *reinvoking* those ideologies. This article is a good example of indirect sexism which invokes anachronistic models of femininity and mocks them but which reinvokes those ideologies. Williamson (1986) terms this type of sexism which ironically draws on older forms of sexism, 'retro sexism'. She states that 'retro sexism is sexism with an alibi; it appears at once past and present, "innocent" and knowing, a conscious reference to another era, rather than an unconsciously driven part of our own' (Williamson 1986, cited in Gill 2007: 111).

A further example of indirect sexism is given by Cameron (2006a), when she analyses complaints to the Advertising Standards Authority (ASA), the UK-based organisation which deals with complaints about the media. A great deal of sexist advertising at present depends upon inferencing rather than overt sexism, as it is down to the reader to infer sexism: 'it is open to the producer to deny that what has been inferred was actually intended or intended seriously' (2006a: 35). Thus, if readers and viewers complain about what they perceive to be sexist advertisements, the ASA will not uphold it if they conclude that the sexism is simply inferred rather than intended by the advertiser. Cameron found, in her sample of complaints to the ASA, that the majority of the complaints about sexism and homophobia in advertisements were considered to be 'reflecting the special sensitivities of a politicised minority' rather than reflecting the views of the majority audience.

Pronoun use and naming

We will now examine more fully what linguistic items we can analyse when we want to investigate overt sexism, focusing in particular upon pronoun use and naming. One of the elements which has been investigated by feminist linguists is the so-called generic pronoun. The use of the pronoun 'he' when referring to men and women can be seen as an example of overt sexism. In a similar way, the use of so-called generic nouns such as 'postman' when referring to both men and women and nouns such as 'neighbour' which seem unmarked for gender but which are often used to refer to 'male neighbours' rather than neighbours in general are examples of overt sexism (Cameron 1990).

To give an example of why sexist pronoun use is still an issue and to indicate the resistance that there has been to reform, we wish to quote at some length an extract from the introduction to a book on the Buddhist leader Sangharakshita, because engagement with gendered language practices is instructive in terms of the types of defence that are offered for the continued use of language practices which are seen by some to be discriminatory (Subhuti 1994). Subhuti, the author of the book, states:

> I have given quite a bit of thought to the much vexed issue of the 'gender inclusive pronoun'. Can 'he' be used as a generic pronoun, including women as well as men? Can one speak of 'the individual and his spiritual development' and still be understood as referring to a woman as much as to a man? Should one avoid that usage and if so how? My present conclusion is that there is a problem in the English language that, in general, we have to live with, for it has no easy solution. I have sympathy with those women who moderately inform me that they find themselves identifying more strongly with what is being written about if it explicitly mentions women. At the same time, there are points where one wants to, perhaps even has to, write about a hypothetical single individual, who could be either male or female. This is particularly the case in a didactic work of this kind. English offers only one way in which that can be done that is neither offensive to the eye nor ridiculously verbose. I do not mind the occasional 'him or her' but too many of them become obtrusive and ugly. I have therefore tried as much as I can to mention both men and women when I am talking about both but where I think it is clear I am talking about both and I need a generic singular pronoun, I have adhered to the standard English usage of 'he', 'his' and 'him' as referring to both men and women. Sangharakshita himself follows that standard practice even more strictly. He especially believes that we should not allow the English language to be manipulated for ideological ends. (Subhuti 1994: 7)[7]

Subhuti has clearly been approached by women readers who have tried to explain to him the alienating effect of the use of the so-called generic pronoun 'he', but he has decided to adopt two strategies in response to their concerns: (1) to avoid the use of the singular pronoun in as many cases as possible, and to use the plural so that it is clear that both women and men are being referred to; (2) to continue to use the pronoun 'he' where referring to a singular subject is thought to be necessary. He has decided to continue to use 'he' because he claims that the problem lies with the English language, rather than with his own individual language practice, and that because it is a wider issue we just 'have to live with it'. He implies that the alternatives which have been proposed by feminist linguists are 'offensive to the eye', 'ridiculously verbose', 'obtrusive' and 'ugly' and characterises them (in Sangharakshita's terms) as manipulating the language 'for ideological ends'. Thus sexism is distanced from the author and possible reforms are seen as too difficult – it is the fault of the language; reform is seen in negative terms and he makes a final appeal to authority, someone whose position he admires, Sangharakshita, who uses even more sexist language than he does. This should not be seen as an attack on Subhuti's work, as it is clear that he has given the matter of sexist language a good deal of careful thought; however, it is a good example of the type of strategies which are used when the question of gender-fair language use is proposed.

A further example which indicates the extent to which sexist pronoun reform is resisted is the case of an American law student who posted a blog to complain about the way that her use of pronouns was treated by her lecturer: Lakay writes:

> I was 'dinged' in my first year writing class for using 'they and their' as gender neutral pronouns which I had learned early on in my Women's Studies undergraduate program. For example, when you are referring to a 'client' but not using their name or etc. saying something like, 'When a client experiences an accident as though they were actually there, you can start examining a bystander's case for intentional infliction of emotional distress.' The worst part was that it was so natural to me – it is completely gender neutral – and it doesn't even call any attention to the gender which is irrelevant to the sentence. If you say he/she, it sticks out and people notice – as opposed to noticing what you are saying. But my writing teacher wasn't having it. 'The Legal Profession is conservative and changes slowly.' I didn't change my language though, and the good news is, I wasn't the only person in the class who had the same comments – and didn't change either. (Lakay 2008)

Here, the lecturer is asserting their authority to impose their view of what is an appropriate use of gendered pronouns, but despite the fact that they gave the student a lower mark for their coursework, the student nevertheless continued to use the gender-neutral form.

In Japanese, as we noted in Chapter 6, the gendering of pronouns can be seen in the use of 'I' pronouns where 'boku' or 'ore' are seen by many to be masculine pronouns. Thus, when young women use these pronouns, they are seen as challenging the social order (Yukawa and Saito 2004). 'Watashi' is a pronoun which is considered as feminine and also neutral, but is not generally used by men. However, 'watashi' also carries with it associations of formality and politeness and thus femininity, whereas 'ore' carries connotations of vulgarity as well as masculinity. Lunsing and Maree (2004) note that the use of pronouns for some Japanese gays and lesbians when referring to themselves is seen as a significant element in the way that they present themselves to others. They mention a homosexual informant who used 'watashi' when he was young and then started using 'boku' when he was older. A lesbian informant was shocked when she was not allowed to use 'boku' and therefore adopted a pet name which she used to avoid using the first person.

Others have developed new first-person pronouns such as 'uchi' (inside) so that these gendered usages are avoided (Miyazaki 2004). Miyazaki notes that boys also alter their use of these masculine pronouns depending on how they assess power relations, for example a weaker boy would use 'boku' to a powerful boy, but 'ore' to an equal. Lunsing and Maree (2004) comment:

Gender restrictions seek to normalise sexual relations between female and male, and as part of that project, to prescribe differences in language use for women and men. However, when we view the speech of real Japanese speakers, we witness the extent to which prescription is never fully reflected in actual language use. Speakers' negotiation of language prescription and gender/sexuality norms intersect with their sense of multiple selfhood and with contextual/situational pressures. (Lunsing and Maree 2004: 106)

In Arabic, sexist language use can be seen most clearly in the rules for pronoun use with plurals. If there is a male and female referent, the pronoun used to refer to them will have to be masculine. Hachimi (2001) has shown that in Moroccan Arabic, this is even more complex as there are some feminine nouns which become masculine in the plural, for example:

/wsad/ (sing. fem.) pillow; /wsayd/ (plural masc.)
/xnsa mzwwqa/ (sing. fem.) coloured sack; /xnasi mzwwqin/ (plural masc.)

However, sexism is not simply about the gendered use of pronouns and nouns. As we demonstrated above, the term 'overt sexism' can encompass a wide range of elements (see Mills 2008 for a fuller account). One element of overt sexism is what has been termed by Schultz (1990) the 'semantic derogation of women'. By this she means to refer to the fact that those terms which are associated with women tend to pick up negative and often sexual connotations over time. She notes that words which have been associated with women in positions of authority, such as 'lady', 'dame' and 'mistress' tend over time to begin to be used for women lower in the social order and to pick up negative inflections.

A further discriminatory naming practice can be seen in the way that in many English-speaking countries, women are still expected to change their surname to their husband's if they marry.[8] In the US, the use of double-barrelled names on marriage is much more widely accepted than in the UK. In Israel, the ministry of the interior automatically changes the woman's surname to that of her husband on marriage, but she can change it back to her original name, take a double-barrelled name or the husband and wife can choose a new surname for themselves (Shemmer pers. com. 2009). In Germany, the choices are slightly more complex: most women take their husband's name on marriage, but it is possible for women and men to take a double-barrelled name. However, only one of the partners can take this double-barrelled name; the other has to take the 'married name' and there is quite a lot of prejudice against double-barrelled names since they are seen as pretentious by some and seem overly long and complicated (Esch pers. com. 2009).[9] In other countries, there are different practices; for example, in Spanish- and Portuguese-speaking countries, women retain their own surname and add the surname of their husbands, as the first or second part of a double-barrelled name. However, in these languages, it is generally the male's surname which is the one which is used in shortened versions of the surname.[10]

In English-speaking countries a range of alternative titles are available to women; for example, they can use 'Miss' if they are single, 'Ms' if they would prefer not to reveal their marital status and 'Mrs' if they are married. It is ironic that 'Ms' was developed by feminists so that women would not have to choose between titles revealing their marital status, where men, through the use of 'Mr', do not have to reveal their marital status. Instead, now there are three titles for women to choose from, although some institutions, when sending forms to be filled in by women, often offer only the option of choosing between 'Ms' and 'Mrs'. 'Ms' has been the subject of some debate since its introduction in the 1970s and is sometimes mocked. It seems to have picked up a range of different associations for different groups of people, so that 'Ms' is seen by some to indicate that a woman is divorced, lesbian, feminist or someone who lives with a man without being married to him. Walsh has shown that 'Ms' is often used to refer to women politicians when they are being ridiculed (Walsh 2001).

These examples have given only some indications of the ways that overt sexism currently manifests itself in language. There are many other elements apart from pronouns and naming which can be analysed when examining sexism in language, and each language will manifest its concern with differentiating women from men in different ways.

Feminist linguistic reforms

Feminist campaigners have tried to draw attention to the way that language use can signal stereotypical views about women, gay, lesbian, bisexual and transgendered people, ethnic minorities and disabled people. Discriminatory language can signal a wish to categorise someone as a member of a stigmatised group rather than as an individual. These ways of thinking and language use can be seen by some as indicating fairly old-fashioned views about women's position in the world and suggest that those who use them are not open to change. As Hellinger and Bußmann (2001) have argued:

> Gender-related language is a reaction to changes in the relationships between women and men which have caused overt conflict on the levels of language comprehension and production. Reformed usage symbolises the dissonance between traditional prescription such as the use of masculine/male generics and innovative alternatives. In most cases it explicitly articulates its political foundation by emphasising that equal treatment of women and men must also be realised on the level of communication. (Hellinger and Bußmann 2001: 19)

For these reasons, feminists have argued that language use which could be interpreted as indicating views of a stereotypical nature should be avoided and more positive inclusive language should be used instead. For some, this has been characterised as simply suggesting alternative terms for sexist terms, but language reform aims to be far more wide-reaching than this.

Language reform began in the 1970s and 1980s in the UK and focused particularly on the workplace. Many feminists working in institutions tried to encourage their institution to adopt explicit guidelines and policies on sexist language use.[11] Publishers, trade unions and educational institutions adopted guidelines and implemented them to a greater or lesser extent. As an example, non-sexist guidelines on language use were adopted by many universities in the 1990s, and although they generated a great deal of criticism, they did draw attention to language use which seemed to many women to be aiming to erase their presence from the workplace (Cameron 1995). Mills (2008) has argued that sexist language use can create a 'chilly climate' for women working within traditional, male-dominated workplaces, that is, they can feel that they are being asked to masquerade as men in order to do their job and are thus encouraged not to draw attention to their position as women within the workforce (see also the section on 'Gendered identity categories', pp. 50–7, in Chapter 3, above).

Many of the anti-discriminatory language guidelines which were introduced into the workplace in the UK from the 1970s onwards are now no longer in use. This may be because discriminatory language, at least in relation to racism, now can be dealt with through recourse to the law (for example, in the UK, the Equality Act, 2010). The lack of guidelines in the UK workplace may indicate the extent to which overtly sexist language has been recognised as problematic by employers and employees alike. The lack of guidelines could therefore be a positive sign that there is no longer a need for such measures.[12] However, the guidelines which do still exist seem to be very watered down in comparison to the guidelines of the 1980s (see Mills 1995). Here is an extract from a publisher's guide to authors (2008) on sexist and racist language:

> Sensitive language
> Try to be sensitive in your use of terms that may cause offence, e.g. use 'Native American' rather than 'Indian'; 'White' and 'Black' are preferable to 'Caucasian' and 'Negroid'; use 'Humanity', 'people', 'humans' rather than 'Man' to describe the human race; use 'him/her' or 'them' rather than 'him' (but we prefer that you rewrite to avoid excessive use of 'him/her').

Here, authors are being advised to be 'sensitive' about their language rather than to be 'anti-sexist', 'gender neutral' or 'anti-racist'.

However, simply advising the substitution of one language item by a more progressive one is not the only strategy adopted by language reformers. For example, writing or spray-painting on adverts has been a strategy adopted by feminists since the 1970s. In Australia, on an advertising hoarding for 'Heaven' chocolate truffles, which, like many chocolate advertisements, targets women consumers, feminist activists objected to the fact that the advertisement featured a naked woman. The advertising poster is headed 'Chocolate truffle heaven' and activists have subverted this by spray-painting over this with the text 'sexism heaven'. They also partly obscured the message of this advert by drawing attention to the fact that the woman is naked. Over the woman's body, they sprayed another statement, operating as the voice of the naked woman, stating 'I'm in far too little clothing.' Although this type of spray-painting was far more common in the 1980s, there are still examples of spray-painted slogans on advertisements on the London Underground network in the UK (cf. Talbot 2003).

In recent years, as we have seen already in Chapter 2, there have been concerted campaigns by OBJECT campaigners in the UK to subvert the so-called 'soft' pornographic images of women in 'lads' magazines'. By placing the offending magazines in brown-paper bags and writing their own political commentaries (see 'The role of feminist linguistics', Chapter 2, pp. 25–8, above) they have successfully satirised these magazines. Thus, although many feminists have campaigned to change the way that language is used through trying to introduce language policies in the workplace and in parliaments, they have also tried to tackle this problem through direct political action.

Effectiveness of feminist language policies

It is quite clear that feminist language policies have made an impact on a range of different contexts, and this has meant, for example, that it is now rare to find an example of overt sexism in university and trade union documentation and in published books, since most organisations have at some stage developed policies themselves to deal with discriminatory language (Greater Manchester Police 2001a, 2001b).

However, even where feminist reforms have not been wholeheartedly adopted (see the Subhuti example, above), feminist campaigning on this issue has at least managed to draw attention to the problematic nature of language use, and has perhaps made individuals and organisations more mindful of the effect that their language use has on others.

Pauwels (2003) has commented on the overall success of many feminist language reforms, particularly in relation to the use of 'Ms'. She shows that 30–45 per cent of women use 'Ms' in the US and 36 per cent in Australia. However, she does note that, even though it is widely used, it does not have the same meaning to all who use it. She argues that 'non-sexist language reforms can be considered truly effective if there is not only evidence of the adoption of non-sexist alternatives but also evidence that these alternatives are being used in a manner promoting equality of the sexes' (Pauwels 2003: 566). In her research, she found that the 'generic he' pronoun was used much less widely now and sex-specific terms such as 'barman' have been replaced by the use of words ending in '—person', even though some people use this affix in an ironic or mocking way. In many languages, this strategy of gender neutralisation has been very effective, although in some languages it is more difficult than in others. Whereas in Dutch it is possible to use gender-neutral forms, such as '*de advocaat*' (the lawyer), in other languages, such as Italian, it seems that developing a feminine form from the masculine form (for example, '*avvocatessa*', female lawyer, from '*avvocato*', male lawyer) is preferable to women referring to themselves using the masculine form. However, this new feminine form is often viewed very negatively.

Hellinger and Pauwels (2007) describe the major changes which have been brought about in the legal and administrative documentation in Germany and Switzerland, in the European Parliament and in the Council of Europe in terms of using gender-neutral language. Thus, it is clear that, in each language, women have argued that their increased visibility in the workplace should be reflected in

the terms which are used to refer to them and this has brought about great struggles and sometimes discomfort about what to call women. In each language it is
necessary to decide whether it is better to (a) argue for getting rid of the female-
specific forms, which are often negatively viewed; (b) to insist on using them to
make women more visible; (c) try to develop neutral terms which will refer to
men and women without specifying their gender.

As we have shown above, reforming campaigns have responded to sexism and
racism and have tried to draw attention to the way that offence can be avoided.
However, one of the responses to anti-sexist campaigns has been the development of the terms 'political correctness' and 'political incorrectness'. Both of
these terms are problematic; they are media-invented terms to refer to campaigns
by feminists, ethnic minority activists and disability rights activists. These
campaigns are often represented in a negative way. Thus, as Mills (2008) has
shown, 'political correctness' is generally used within contexts where its aim is to
ridicule campaigns over language; the term 'political incorrectness' is generally
used in contexts where the aim is to applaud laddish behaviour. Thus anti-sexist
campaigns already have to compete to ensure that they are represented in their
own terms rather than being characterised as concerns with political correctness,
which is seen as trivial and concerned only with language issues.

New forms of feminist analysis of sexism

What contemporary feminists need to be aware of is that sexist stereotypes are
not stable; as Gill (2007: 111) argues: 'new stereotypes have not necessarily
displaced older ones but may coexist alongside these or perhaps merely influence
their style'. However, we need to be aware that sexism may have changed but that
it is still there and needs to be dealt with, using new forms of analysis. For Gill
(2007: 271) it is important that 'the notion of sexism ... [is] held onto and revi-
talised'. Thus, feminists need to analyse the transformations within sexism and
develop new, more complex forms of analysis, so that sexism is no longer seen as
something which is inherent in a text, but something which makes sense because
of the discursive structures which inform the text. Feminists can make an impact
on those discursive structures through their analysis.

By turning to the context of the text, it is possible to analyse sexism in more
productive ways. As we have seen in Chapter 5, Baker (2008a) draws on corpus
linguistics to broaden the analysis from the word or phrase to a concern with
collocation, or the way that a word means or has a particular connotative meaning
because of the company it keeps within the text through concordance line analysis. He makes the crucial point that 'words are "primed" for use in discourse due
to the cumulative effects of our encounters in language' (Baker 2008a: 77). By
this he means that words accrue particular associations with certain contexts of
use, and because of that they begin to develop certain types of connotations or
meanings.

By moving away from the type of analysis which focused only on words in
isolation and which assumed that words always have one particular meaning,
and adopting instead a mixed-methods approach through techniques such as

corpus linguistics, we can develop a form of analysis of sexism which can examine the way that emotive connotations accrue over time to words associated with women. We can also be aware of the role of context in the development of these meanings, so that we can recognise that simply replacing words with more neutral terms will not solve the problem.

Summary

One of the key aims in this chapter has been to illustrate the complexity of sexism. Current feminist work demonstrates that sexism is as much a struggle over the position of women in society as it is a struggle over meaning. Debates about sexism are clearly also political debates about the rights of women, and these debates are context- and culturally specific. Thus, concerning ourselves with the use of discriminatory language in the world's many different language systems also involves us in struggles over wider discriminatory beliefs about women and behaviour towards women. It is for this reason that it is important to continue to analyse sexism in contemporary research. In the concluding chapter which follows we examine the possible future directions for feminist research in the field of language and gender.

8 Future directions

Theory, methodology and political activism

From a theoretical perspective, it is clear from what we have written in this book that, for us, the most important theoretical aspects of feminist gender and language research have been influenced by the developments most commonly associated with Third Wave feminism. Additionally, the recent resurgence in feminist thinking within popular culture in Western societies and the emergence and continuation of different waves of feminism in countries all over the world have demonstrated the importance of the underlying principle of the overwhelming need for political action to be the basis of all academic research on language, gender and feminism.

It is useful at this point once again to come back to the title of bell hook's book, quoted at the very beginning of the volume, *Feminism is for Everybody*, the principle that we have placed at the centre of this work. If feminism is overtly theorised with this principle in mind, then the aim is for action-centred academic research to be of practical use and relevance in the wider world beyond the ivory tower, to men and to women. We have argued that interdisciplinarity is one step towards this, with feminist researchers working both within and outside academia, including journalists and activists such as Kristof and Wudunn (2010) and Banyard (2010), whose work we have included at various stages as a central part of our overarching 'importance of feminism' argument. Only by working together, as part of or alongside political organisations, can analyses of language play a continuing part in the emancipatory aims of feminism as a political movement.

One of the key aims of this book has been to stress the overarching importance of academic feminist language and gender research, making clear its political research goals and having what Cameron (2009) terms the 'what is to be done?' question right at the core of gender and language research projects. It is our intention that the interdisciplinary approach laid out in the book, given in particular detail in Chapters 1 and 2, has demonstrated the importance of feminism in all of its different varieties, especially at this particular moment in history, for societies worldwide.

From a methodological perspective, it is also worth echoing here a crucial point from Holmes and Meyerhoff (2003a) that we initially made back in Chapter 5 as the theme for this methodological chapter and also as a theme for the book as a whole:

> There seems little point to our academic interests if they do not at some stage articulate with real-world concerns and enable us or our readers to identify, for example, certain employment practices as unfair or ill informed, based more on stereotypes and prejudice than they are on people's actual behaviour in the real world. At some point, our research has to be able to travel out of the academy in order to draw attention to and challenge unquestioned practices that reify certain behaviours as being morally, or aesthetically, better than others. We should never cease to engage actively with and challenge assumptions about gender norms and loudly draw attention to the way power, privilege and social authority interact with and are naturalised as properties of independent social categories. (Holmes and Meyerhoff 2003a: 14)

We have quoted Holmes and Meyerhoff again at length, because this seems to us to be the most crucial aspect of future feminist theorising and practice. The importance of carefully planning exactly what research questions we wish to pursue on the basis of the political and social contexts in which we find ourselves as researchers is crucial to the future success of the discipline. It is also crucial that such studies can be viewed as a force that, alongside research from other disciplines and in conjunction with activists, journalists, politicians, feminist and human rights groups, can aim to influence the wider society outside the ivory tower and continue to aim to fulfil its emancipatory aim.

As we have already highlighted, researchers should also be careful and self-reflexive. Feminist theorising needs to inform our methodological practices when we construct research to test the role of gender. We should follow Sidnell's (2003) advice that we need to be vigilant when constructing research projects on gender and language in order to avoid the following methodological problems that Sidnell has found with earlier research:

> Researchers do not discuss the ways in which, given the mandate to record male or female conversations, settings were constructed and managed to assure that this was accomplished. Moreover the researchers do not acknowledge the possibility that, given a mandate to find women's or men's talk, the people collecting the data might already be predisposed to producing features of talk in interaction consistent (or otherwise) with its stereotypic understanding. (Sidnell 2003: 330)

Thus, within the new wave of feminist work on gender and language, our methodological design and our research questions need to be very carefully thought through. It is no longer adequate, within Third Wave theorising, to compare and contrast the language of males and females in a particular context. Instead, we need to consider carefully what we are trying to discover and why, and whether our experimental design will provide us with data which test out our hypothesis, or whether the results are determined by other factors than gender alone. We need to be clear about what exactly it is we are referring to when we talk about 'gender'.

Thus, we need as researchers to be very careful about interrogating our own sense of what it is we are looking for when we analyse women's and men's inter-action. Sidnell (2003) analyses a rum shop in Guyana and the way the group constitutes itself as an all-male environment. He shows the way in which the rum shop is constituted as a place where respectable women cannot go, through the telling of narratives by the males. These narratives indicate to the hearers that the previous story had been attended to, accepted and understood: 'this is one way in which gender is woven into the taken for granted, seen but not noticed backdrop of everyday life' (Sidnell 2003: 343). The content and sequencing of the narratives is intended to constitute the group as gender-exclusive. Thus 'prac-tices of speaking are not necessarily linked to gender in any straightforward way. Rather gender emerges as a recognisable feature of social settings ... within situ-ated activities' (Sidnell 2003: 345). In order to construct research projects on gender and language we need to ask ourselves about the constitution of gendered groups and how they maintain their gender-exclusivity.

Debates regarding the navigation between stereotypes, gender ideologies and normatively gendered behaviour in the wider society and the role that these elements play in future research will continue to take place. The most important thing to bear in mind is that there is still a real and urgent need for gender and language research. The theories and methods that researchers use to navigate their way through these complex issues may vary, but ultimately the field should be seen as united in its common aim of emancipatory research.

Problems and issues for current research

As we have seen at various stages throughout this book, there are important theo-retical and methodological issues which are currently being addressed, but which need to continue to be examined and developed in future research in order for the discipline to continue to move forward. We will here focus in particular upon the role of gender and the problem of essentialism.

In terms of the role of gender, if we see gender not as a determinant of linguistic difference but rather as an effect of language use, then we need to continue to define and analyse gender differently. As Christie (2000) has stated, 'seeing language use in terms of ideology would entail seeing an utterance as a way of *representing* gender relations, seeing it in terms of discourse would entail seeing an utterance as a way of *realising* gender relations' (2000: 50). This newer view of gender sees utterances as the means by which interactants attempt to achieve their gender.

We also need to continue to be very careful about the assumptions we make about gender. As Trechter (2006: 424) argues, 'there is some risk in assuming the gender (or ethnic) identity of participants as obvious or given as we look to their interactional strategies in constructing such identities'. This issue is a deeply complex one for the field, as we have seen in Chapters 3 and 4, and it will continue to be debated for quite some time yet (see also Swann 2009). As we have seen, the manner in which gender is analysed depends to quite an important degree upon whether researchers view gender as an omnipresent feature within interaction, which often tends to accord most strongly with an indirect indexicality approach, where language is encoded with gendered meanings at a macro, societal level, most commonly associated with interactional sociolinguistic feminist discourse analysis, including FCDA, FPDA and feminist pragmatics (Eckert and McConnell-Ginet 2003; McElhinny 2003; Mills 2003a; Holmes 2005, 2006; Mullany 2007), or whether researchers follow the theory that gender is something that can only be first enacted by direct indexicality and then also becomes the topic of the conversation itself, such as those who follow a CA approach (Stokoe and Smithson 2001; Stokoe 2008).

A related point is the need to continue to move beyond stereotypical notions but be aware that they still play a crucially important role in the way that interactants see themselves in relation to others. Similarly, when we analyse the ways that gender is represented within the mass media in both spoken and written forms, we need to continue to move away from the assumption that these representations have some direct and unmediated impact on the construction of identities. However, if we are critical of these assumptions, we have to find some way of accounting for the impact that they *do* have. Freed (2003) makes the following, crucial argument:

> [T]he public representation of the way women and men speak is almost identical to the characterisation provided 30 years earlier. These deeply entrenched gender-specific linguistic stereotypes apparently serve critical social purposes; they appear to maintain not only a status quo that advantages men over women and heterosexuals over homosexuals and lesbians, but one that helps establish and maintain rules of feminine and masculine behaviour even if these generalisations fail to reflect social or linguistic reality. (Freed 2003: 706)

Thus, when, in our theorising, we attempt to move beyond binary differences, we need to be continually aware that, for the interactants or texts that we study, these stereotypes of gender play an important element in individuals' everyday lives and can never be fully escaped, even when they are being resisted and/or challenged. However, at the same time as acknowledging that stereotypes have an impact on individuals' assessment of their own gender identity, we need to recognise that stereotypes are not necessarily the same for everyone and that our hypothesised stereotypes of gender are shaped by many different social forces.

Moving on to the interrelated issue of essentialism, it is important in future work for researchers to continue to try to develop a way of talking about the very real way in which gender impacts upon the lives of women without resorting to essentialism. However, we need to be able to make generalisations without assuming that this will necessarily lead to essentialism. Essentialism is used as a very negative term in much Third Wave feminist theorising. As Holmes and Meyerhoff (2003a: 10) state: 'if we truly believed a radical version of the anti-essentialism that has recently become an axiom of the field, then we would put away our pens, our tape recorders and our notebooks and the field of language and gender would disappear'. Clearly, we need to develop ways of discussing gender difference without resorting to binary opposition and without assuming that there is no difference at all. This comes back to Cameron's (1992) classic pronounce-ment that we need to look at the difference gender makes.

It is essential, therefore, to continue thinking through ways in which we can generalise about the way gender works, across a range of contexts. As Holmes and Meyerhoff (2003a: 10) remark: 'No matter what we say about the inadequacy or invidiousness of essentialised, dichotomous conceptions of gender, and no matter how justifiable such comments may be, in everyday life, it really is often the case that gender is "essential".' If, by this, Holmes and Meyerhoff mean that a general conception of fundamental gender difference is brought into play in many situ-ations, that is, it is employed discursively, then we would agree with them. In future theorising of gender, this is clearly something which continues to need to be addressed.

Future aims and directions

There are many future areas of research that need to be conducted within femi-nist language and gender research. As we pointed out in Chapter 1, Sunderland (2009) has drawn attention to how feminist language and gender studies are significantly under-researched in African contexts. However, she points to a handful of sociolinguistic studies investigating language variation and language styles as good examples of initial research which is starting to emerge in a context that needs more thorough investigation. This includes a study by Pearce (2009) examining language variation in terms of gender and tone in Kera (Chad), the use of 'Student Pidgin' by young women in Ghana (Dako 2002) and certain dialect usage, including Hlonipha in Sesotho, which operates as a 'language of respect' as investigated by Hanong Thetela (2002). This dialect significantly disadvan-tages women as it holds expectations that women will not use lexis associated with sex, and alternatively they are expected to use 'baby language equivalents' (Sunderland 2009: 128). This gendered language expectation acts as a barrier when women try to report sexual assault.

Furthermore, McElhinny (2007a: 18) summarises some key areas for future language and gender research in the introduction to her volume on language, gender and globalisation. She makes the crucial observation that 'in bilingual or multilingual societies, in areas where national boundaries have been drawn and redrawn, in postcolonial contexts, and in diglossic linguistic situations, it is often the use of, or access to, certain languages which differentiate the speech of men and women, or more elite and less elite men and women'.

Many other parts of the world, not excluding Western locations, are still in need of a series of sociolinguistic investigations on a whole range of topics including assessment of the roles that languages, dialects, accents, speech styles, language attitudes and their associated gendered language expectations play in maintaining gender stereotypes and disadvantaging women in monolingual and multilingual settings across the world. An interrelated issue that needs to be addressed for the research field also is the continued dominance of the English language and how this seals off opportunities for those who do not have access to global English in their linguistic repertoire. When the journal *Gender and Language* was launched in 2007 it stated that it would publish in languages other than English. It has yet to do so, but the fact that this commitment is there should be viewed as a positive step forward. This whole point opens up a much broader set of issues of language policy and language planning, but it is important for English-speaking feminist linguists not to lose sight of the fact that learning other languages such as Chinese or Japanese or many others could open up access to pre-existing arenas of research which have yet to make it into the dominant mainstream through the medium of English.

The following sub-sections make some suggestions for future research foci.

Exceptional gender

Following on from Hall's (2006) work on exceptional speakers, researchers could examine the way that those who are positioned at the margins of gender identity might be seen to be as much part of what gender means as those who are seen to be more central or mainstream. Hall discusses the gender identity of 'tomboys' and 'sissies' and the way that they are seen as marginal or exceptional. Barrett remarks that 'drag queens are not acting like women, they are acting like drag queens' (Barrett, cited in Hall 2006: 374). Hall argues that 'we need to discuss the conversational practices of all sexual identities … as potentially felicitous on a … localised level' (Hall 2006: 374–5), rather than assuming that they take their meaning solely in relation to other practices, which they can only imitate rather than perform successfully.

The third sex

Following on from Zimman and Hall's (2010) work detailed in Chapter 6, if their perspective of the importance of researching the concept of the third sex is followed, then there is a need to bring biological sex back to occupy a more central position in order to fully interrogate the crucial role that the body plays in shaping the relationship between language and identity. This focus will also produce more work on the under-investigated area of gender-variant groups, which in turn, can also influence studies of 'exceptional gender' discussed above and could help to foster new interpretations of performativity and femininities and masculinities, discussed below.

Communities of practice

Another future direction for gender and language research will be to continue attempting to relate small-scale contextualised studies more to their wider social context. At the present moment, the field is still dominated by studies of language use at the level of the community of practice, but few relate the norms established within communities of practices to wider social structures and norms or global communities of practice (Eckert and McConnell-Ginet 1999). However, we need to be careful about using this approach uncritically. As Trechter states, it runs the risk of tautology: 'linguists simultaneously try to define the practices of a linguistic community while maintaining that the community as an entity is defined by its practice' (Trechter 2006: 429).

Performativity

If we take on board Judith Butler's work on performativity and see 'gender' as a verb, it is clear that future work in feminist linguistic analysis will need to map out more clearly the range of possibilities for performing gender. Thus, the way that individuals perform their gender identity and, perhaps, also have their gender identity restricted or enabled by particular communities of practice will be a critical topic. This notion that gender is not only performed by individuals but that the boundaries of what is possible for individuals are mapped out by groups of people will be an important revising of Butler's work. For example, it might be useful to examine the way that a largely heterosexual community of practice might constrain the way that a lesbian member discusses her partner (and the heterosexual members of the group might also feel constrained in their discussions of *their* partners). Further, we might examine the way that community of practice norms about what constitutes an authentic lesbian might also constrain (and enable) the expression of particular identity positions for lesbians within a group (Jones 2009).

New models for analysing femininities and masculinities

Researchers could continue to investigate the way that femininities and masculinities need to be further decoupled from the concepts of powerfulness and powerlessness, which has been explored so far by Holmes (2006) and Holmes and Schnurr (2006). An analysis of the gendering of social spaces may continue to run the risk of entrenching the association of femininity with powerlessness. As Kendall (2003: 604) argues, 'women in positions of institutional authority who linguistically downplay status differences when enacting their authority are not reluctant to exercise authority, nor are they expressing powerlessness; instead they are exercising and constituting their authority by speaking in ways that accomplish work-related goals while maintaining the faces of their interlocutors'. Holmes and Schnurr's (2006) recent work is also careful to point out the distinct advantages of speech styles stereotypically associated with femininity in effective leadership talk when used by women and men managers. Baxter (2010), too, highlights how what she terms 'gender-progressive businesses' positively value speech styles stereotypically associated with femininity. She thus also illustrates a break with the traditional 'femininity equals powerlessness' correlation. The key here is to ensure that women and men are not being evaluated and assessed differently, even when using exactly the same speech styles. Mullany (2007) found that normatively feminine discourse strategies were dominant in both businesses where she conducted ethnographic fieldwork. However, while male managers were positively valued for using stereotypically feminine strategies, some female managers were still experiencing negative evaluation for being too feminine in their speech.

A potentially different way to approach this would be to consider that when women hold powerful positions they use language which has been classified in the past as conventionally masculine or feminine (or a combination of both). Perhaps new terms could be developed to refer to these styles of speech which do not associate them with gender. Similarly, when we discuss workplaces as gendered and we associate 'feminine' workplaces with those which are more informal and where much small talk is permitted, a different approach would be to develop terms which are not gendered, and term them informal workplaces rather than imposing a gendered view of the workplace.

However, such an approach of developing non-gendered terms risks ignoring the meanings that these styles still have for many of the interactants – it may well be that this gendered view is one which is shared by the workers, which could be gleaned via an ethnographic style approach. Such an alternative approach would also depend upon researchers' theoretical positioning towards whether gender is omnipresent or not and how and when gender becomes relevant in an inter-action. Holmes (2007: 56–7) makes the crucial point that 'if we wish to make political progress, it makes strategic sense to acknowledge that most of the world continues to treat "women" and "men", "female" and "male" as fundamental social categories, not least in describing interpersonal communication style'.

In specific relation to the workplace, she points out that 'nowhere is the gender order more apparent that in professional workplaces where lip service is paid to equality of opportunity … many professional workplaces are still rife with exam-ples of systemic gender discrimination in which language plays an important role … *stereotypes rule*' (Holmes 2007: 53, our emphasis). Furthermore, she goes on to argue that the workplace is a context where gendered expectations about norma-tive ways of speaking are deeply entrenched and continue to persist. To ignore this would be to miss out a crucial step in the analytical process, particularly when attempting to engage in politically active research, which challenges the wider, macro processes of social structuration.

Language, gender and age

Although there are a number of studies which examine gender and language amongst groups of older people and amongst children and adolescents, this is an area which needs more thorough investigation (Goodwin 2006; Eckert and McConnell-Ginet 2003; Murphy 2010b). Goodwin (2006), by focusing her anal-ysis on groups of female children in playgrounds with groups of male children, has managed to analyse the specific dynamic associated with children, rather than assuming that all groups of women and men will interact similarly because of a stable gender identity. The linguistic behaviour which she describes in these groups of girls is very different from the dynamics within adult women groups. Thus, what her study draws attention to is the fact that one's gender identity changes over time.

Language, gender and race/ethnicity

Trechter (2006) has shown that the relation between gender, language and ethnicity is not a simple one. She asks 'how do some features of gender or ethnicity become iconic / ideologically part of a community as easily recognisable and interpretable features that are then taken as natural' (Trechter 2006: 424). This is one of the key challenges facing race/ethnicity researchers, as well the crucial challenge of establishing race/ethnicity research far more centrally within the discipline instead of at the margins, where it continues to remain. Morgan (2004: 252) makes the following, crucial points, that 'scholarship on women of color has actively asserted that the interrelationship between race, gender and class is integral to understanding both race and gender. Paradoxically, rather than social science and linguistic canons and paradigms shifting in light of the extensive writings on African American and other non-white and working-class women, academic theories have simply shrugged in disregard.' She continues by pointing out that there are little more than 'occasional' and 'half-hearted inclusions' within the field of study. She refers to this as 'a big tease that refused to include race, ethnicity, and class while romancing gender and sexuality' (Morgan 2004: 253).

Coming back to the issues raised in Chapter 1 about who has the right to study which group, all researchers should ask themselves careful questions regarding the topic they select for analysis. Does the field, dominated by white, middle-class academics, really need another study of white (often middle-class) women? Could collaborative research with other groups from different racial and ethnic backgrounds be conducted instead? This is also a challenge that must be taken up by journal editors and publishers, to ensure that this disparity does not continue.

Language, gender and social stratification

Questions of the relation between class and gender have now developed into wider concerns for the way power and stratification connect with issues of gender. It has been the realisation of many feminists that class is not the only way that social groups are divided. In many countries, class is not significant; instead issues of caste, tribal grouping, religious, cultural or geographical allegiance, or even income, are seen as more significant. Western feminism needs to reconsider its conceptualisation of social divisions when analysing gender, particularly within Western countries, since class is no longer the clear determinant of social position that it was in the past. Thus, in turning away from a simple acceptance of the term 'class' we are not also turning away from analysing the clear economic, material distinctions within societies and the impacts that those differences make on individuals. Instead, an analysis of stratification might consider the linguistic differences between, say, relatively privileged women and less privileged women and the way that these differences are maintained and challenged in the styles that they adopt, both when they talk to their own groups and when they talk to members of other groups. The power differences between the two groups are always ceaselessly shored up and challenged through the use of particular styles.

Language, gender and sexuality

The analysis of gender and sexuality has become much more wide-ranging since it has moved away from the question 'How do gay people speak?' As we have seen in Chapter 6, the focus of attention is instead more on the way that individuals achieve or try to achieve a sense of their own sexual identity, and also, as we have further seen in Chapter 6, express their sexual desires through the language resources available to them. What is most interesting to research now is not only the language used by particular individuals who identify in a particular way (although that still needs to be done), but rather two slightly different enterprises: the mapping out of the linguistic resources available to individuals and the use that individuals make of those resources.

It will not be assumed that all individuals will identify as either straight or gay through their use of language, but rather that individuals will be able to make use of these distinctions within language styles to identify by aligning themselves as more in line with hegemonic masculinity/femininity or other styles of masculinity/femininity. In this way, individuals can craft for themselves, out of the language resources available, a particular range of identities: a heterosexual male can signal his particular identity by adopting a camp style in his interactions with women friends, but adopt a more hegemonic masculine style with his male friends (Baker 2008a). These uses of styles will also be judged by others in ways which are beyond the individual's control. The analysis of this process of choosing identities out of the myriad choices available is one which still needs to be more thoroughly researched, as does the process whereby these provisional identities are assessed by others.

Language, gender and sexism

As we have seen in Chapter 7, it is no longer adequate to discuss linguistic sexism as if it were something on which everyone agreed. Sexism is the site for linguistic struggle in all languages worldwide, and thus all perspectives on sexism need to be explored and described. Researchers could produce more analyses of the benefits that sexism confers on those who are sexist. Following on from Wetherell and Potter's (1992) analysis of the benefits which accrue to those white people in New Zealand who are racist, we need to examine further the benefits of sexism for sexists. Cameron's (1998a) article, which insisted that feminists need to focus on the underlying conflict between women and men in the workplace, rather than assuming that linguistic differences were due to essential differences or misunderstanding, can form the basis for such an analysis. Only when we can fully understand the motivations for sexism (for instance, the precariousness of power and the fear that that power is being challenged), will we understand the politics of sexism. Reforming individual language items will not reform sexism out of existence, but it does constitute a staking out of territory, a clear statement that women can also use language as a tool in this conflict.

Overall conclusion

Throughout this book it has been our intention to highlight that the current state of the field of feminist language and gender research is very positive and it is one that promises much for future development. The discipline is clearly in the process of developing more complex theoretical perspectives and innovative methodologies which feed into practices both inside and outside academia. The complexities of the construction and maintenance of gender are now far more intricate than ever before, and language plays a crucial role in this, demanding more careful and nuanced linguistic analyses. The continuing moves towards a more global, international perspective have also changed the way that the field is developing, and through this, feminists will develop a new self-reflexivity. We need to use this self-reflexivity to develop new perspectives on gender and language and new alliances with feminists and pro-feminists both inside and outside academia and in a range of different cultural contexts worldwide in order to continue this productive and essential dialogue towards the ultimate feminist goal of gender emancipation.

Notes

Chapter 1

1   A more positive definition of post-feminism might be that it is a theoretical position, which works on the assumption, not that feminism is irrelevant, but that all theorising must take the achievements of feminism as its grounding. However, we have not found many theorisations which have used this more positive definition of post-feminism.

2   It is worth noting here that liberal feminism argues for equal rights and opportunities, whereas radical feminism argues for the differences of men and women and draws attention to the way these differences are emphasised and form the basis of discrimination (see also the section on 'Feminist models' in this chapter, pp. 13–17, for further discussion of feminist models).

3   This is not to say that there were no feminists before the eighteenth century (see Hobby 1988).

Chapter 2

1   International Women's Day first started as a part of the socialist trade union movement, with women's demands for better rights as manual labourers in the workplace in the US. It is officially recognised by the United Nations and it is also a national holiday in over 20 countries in the world. It was first observed as a national holiday in the Soviet Union following the Russian Revolution in 1917.

2   The Financial Times Stock Exchange Index (FTSE) is a share index of the 100 most highly capitalised companies in the UK, as listed on the London Stock Exchange.

3   In Sheffield, for example, there is a Sheffield Feminist Network which organises discussion groups and a group called Sheffield Women in Black which organises protests/demonstrations. UK Feminista is a British group, organised by Kat Banyard, which co-ordinates campaigns (for similar groups, see the list of websites of organisations in this book).

4   In early feminist conferences where women and men attended, it was found initially that some men did try to dominate the speaking time, and this did become a crucial issue in deciding whether men could be admitted to feminist conferences (Whelehan 1995). Many conferences now are open to both women and men.

5   It is also vital for campaigning and policy changes to represent LGBT families, single-parent families and any other family that does not reflect the traditional two-parent model, as well as those who are working as carers for adults in the home, not just children (see Redfern and Aune 2010: 133).

Chapter 3

1 However, it is worth noting that Cameron (2005) favours the terms 'modern' and 'post-modern' over 'waves' as she feels that the baggage that goes along with the modern–postmodern distinction can be viewed as adding an additional layering of detail. She argues that the broader knowledge which individuals may have surrounding the term evokes a number of relevant 'theoretical stances' which are helpful to conceptualising a contemporary approach to language and gender research. These particular stances of postmodern thinking include 'an emphasis on diversity, a sceptical attitude to "grand" narratives, an urge to deconstruct binary oppositions and a tendency to treat apparently fixed and natural categories as constructs whose ontological reality may be called into question' (Cameron 2005: 81).

2 Heteronormativity is the ideology which poses heterosexuality as a norm, whereby, for example, it would be assumed that if a woman referred to 'my partner' she was referring to a male partner.

3 These are not the only interpretations of this type of feminine behaviour, but it is an indication that certain language styles can signal certain identities to others and be interpreted by them in a range of ways.

4 This is a slight oversimplification of Butler's work, as she has stated that gender is not simply a question of choice, as we show; however, it is useful to think of gender as a performance, a set of decisions one makes about what sort of women or man one wants to act as. This does enable individuals to see that they have a choice about whether to 'buy into' stereotypical constraining gender roles. The language style that an individual adopts is crucial in terms of displaying to others the role, or resistance to a role, that a subject has decided upon.

5 This also means that if we can bring about change in the way that individuals think about the language that they use in interactions, then we are also bringing about a change in the social system.

6 A locally organised group called Tostan is making inroads on this practice in Senegal by organising locally, involving both males and females, as part of a wider long-term educational programme concerned with health, hygiene, democracy and human rights: www.tostan.org.

7 A community of practice approach examines the type of talk which is generated by groups focused on a particular task. Thus small-scale groups are analysed rather than wider communities of speakers. See Chapter 4 for a fuller definition/discussion.

8 Some may argue that this use of 'feminine' and 'masculine' to refer to speech styles and settings is not productive, since it seems to reify femininity and masculinity, to assume that they are stable and unlikely to change. This use of femininity and masculinity could also be critiqued on the grounds that it seems to accept the problematic link between masculinity and professionalism. However, it does foreground the gendering of styles within particular contexts and may well lead to a critique of this gendering rather than an acceptance.

9 However, in other contexts of intimate conversation, research has shown that males may in fact engage in combative displays of aggression and verbal play (see the essays in Johnson and Meinhof 1997).

10 Those in positions of institutional power in Diamond's study can 'afford' in a way to use indirectness, because others interpret their indirectness in relation to their status; thus, their indirect suggestions may well be interpreted by others as having the function of commands. Thus, if we are truly to analyse the local context, we cannot simply ignore the force of institutional status as Schegloff and other conversation analysts insist that we do, paying attention only to the way that participants orient to status within the interaction (Schegloff 1997).

11 The origin of the term 'chav' is fairly obscure but it is asserted that it might have originated from the Romany word for child – 'chav' (Tyler 2008).

12 'Lurgy' is a slang term for 'illness' in British English, often referring to non-serious illnesses such as cold and flu; 'flobbed' is a slang term for spitting.

Chapter 4

1 'Symbolic capital' is a term which was developed by Bourdieu (1999) in an analogy with actual economic capital to describe the power and value that one can accrue to oneself through knowledge of and use of elements which seem to be valued within your culture.

2 For a very critical view of *What Not to Wear*, see McRobbie (2009), who argues that issues of class need to be analysed in this type of programme, where the cultural capital of the presenters is drawn on in order to ridicule largely working-class women for their lack of 'taste'.

Chapter 5

1 We might perhaps also analyse words using corpus linguistic techniques developed to describe being a single female which have more positive connotations, for example in the 1970s and 1980s 'bachelor girl' and in the 1990s 'singleton'.

Chapter 6

1 Wong (2008) revealed his own same-sex orientation to informants before interview, and he let the interviews take place in any space chosen by the interviewees where they felt comfortable. Most chose cafés or restaurants.

2 Baker (2008) remarks that not all men who use 'the voice' are gay, as many heterosexual men also draw on features of this style, for example the UK television celebrity Russell Brand.

3 However, with changes to legislation in the UK, Canada and other countries, it is possible for gay and lesbian couples to marry in civil partnerships and thus have all of the legal entitlements of married heterosexual couples.

4 Nonetheless, it is important to point out that male political figures who are homosexual or are 'outed' as having homosexual experiences are also subject to bodily scrutiny in a way that is not imposed on their heterosexual male political counterparts. Morrish and Sauntson (2007) provide an excellent analysis of how Peter Mandelson and Michael Portillo were 'outed' in the mass media and subjected to substantial negative evaluation on the grounds of their sexuality.

Chapter 7

1 For example, those who see women as very different from men (culturally and biologically) are likely to advocate the differential treatment of women, and some elements of what is termed sexism by others will not appear discriminary to them. For example, conservative women might find that the use of the term 'lady' to refer to women is unproblematic, because it seems to them to be a term denoting respect rather than condescension.

2 Indeed, a 2009 BBC Radio 4 programme questioned whether the concept of 'wife' still existed, since there are now in Britain fewer marriages than there have been in the past. Soon, less than half of the adult population will be married, since many people opt to be single and divorce has risen (Geraldine Bedell, 'What is a wife?', Monday 16 February 2009: www.bbc.co.uk/radio4). Bedell suggests that in Britain, rather than there being a husband and a wife in a marriage, there are now two husbands.

3 A symptomatic reading is a type of Marxist reading which viewed texts as a mass of contradictions which were caused by the impossibility of ideology holding everything together. In a sense ideologies tried to present a unified, seamless vision of reality, but the sheer impossibility of this effort meant that texts manifested contradictions and inconsistencies. It was the task of the Marxist critic to track down these

contradictions, to expose the 'symptoms' of the text in order to describe adequately the way that ideology and texts work.

4   Ann Summers is primarily a lingerie retailer in the UK, known for its revealing and explicitly sexualised products. It also sells sex toys.

5   *The X Factor* is a crass but nevertheless highly popular reality television show where contestants who are 'ordinary' members of the public compete with one another as singers for the prize of a recording contract.

6   *Top Gear* is a motoring show shown on the BBC network, with male presenters and largely male audience.

7   It should be noted that only in recent years has there been complete gender equality amongst Buddhist adherents in the UK, and the use of the 'he' pronoun for generic use is perhaps a vestige of that inequality.

8   Whilst many women choose not to marry, and whilst many women who marry retain their own name, there is still some pressure from the media and families to conform to this practice.

9   Esch comments that 'If you ask people which party has the most female members with double-barrelled names, I'm sure they will say the Green Party. It fits perfectly into the stereotypical image of a Green Party member. However, according to a list on the Internet there are more "double-name women" in the SPD (Social Democratic Party of Germany), which surprises me' (Esch pers. com. 2009).

10   Although this depends on the country and the level of feminist activity, since in mainland Spain, for example, it is now legal for women to choose which of the family names comes in which position in her surname and which one she uses as a shortened surname (Castro pers. com. 2009).

11   Policies were also adopted which dealt with racist language use and language use which discriminated against disabled people.

12   However, see Mullany (2007) for examples of unreconstructed sexism in the workplace.

Websites of organisations and other sources

African-American Communication and Gender
www.africanamericanfemalecommunication.com/

Apne Aap
Battles against sex slavery in India.
www.apneaap.org

Carnival of Feminists
www.feministcarnival.blogspot.com

Chinese Language and Gender: Majorie Chan's Online Bibliography
http://people.cohums.ohio-state.edu/chan9/g-bib.htm

Chinese Women and Gender Issues: Bibliography
http://people.cohums.ohio-state.edu/chan9/g-bib.htm#women-bib

Engender Health
Focuses on reproductive health issues throughout the world.
www.engenderhealth.org

Equality Now
Lobbies against the sex trade and gender oppression throughout the world.
www.equalitynow.org

F-Word
www.thefword.org.uk

Fawcett Society
Campaigning group for equality between men and women in the UK on pay, pensions, poverty, justice and politics.
www.fawcettsociety.org.uk

Feministing
Jessica Valenti's feminist website.
www.feministing.com

Global Fund for Women
Venture capital organisation funding women's groups in poor countries.
www.globalfundforwomen.org

Guerrilla Girls
Exposing sexism, racism and corruption in politics, art, film and pop culture.
www.guerrillagirls.org

International Gender and Language Association
www.lancs.ac.uk/fass/organisations/igala/Index.html

International Women's Health Coalition
Reproductive health rights throughout the world.
www.iwhc.org

London Feminist Network
www.ldnfeministnetwork.ik.com

London Pro-Feminist Men's Group
www.facebook.com/group.php?gid=143650195564
http://londonprofeministmensgroup.blogspot.com/

Manifesto for 21st Century Feminism
Launched on the hundredth anniversary of International Women's Day.
https://counterfire.org/index.php/features/78-womens-liberation/3901-feminism-a-21st-century-manifesto
See also
www.guardian.co.uk/commentisfree/2010/mar/08/international-womens-day-manifesto

Men against Violence to Women
www.whiteribboncampaign.co.uk

Men and Feminism
Discussions on the interplay between the two topics.
www.menandfeminism.org/

MenEngage
A global alliance that seeks to engage men and boys to achieve gender equality.
www.menengage.org

Million Women Rise
Coalition of women from the voluntary sector to organise demonstrations against male violence which coincide with International Women's Day in March.
www.millionwomenrise.com

OBJECT
Challenges sex-object culture – the sexual objectification of women in the media and popular culture; opposes lap dancing and lads' magazines.
www.object.org.uk

Rights of Women
Works to attain justice for women.
www.rightsofwomen.org.uk

Stonewall
Works to achieve equality and justice for lesbians, gay men and bisexuals.
www.stonewall.org.uk

Stop Porn Culture
Challenges the pornographic industry.
www.stoppornculture.org

Tostan
Works on female genital cutting in Africa.
www.tostan.org

UNIFEM
Women's Organisation at the United Nations.
www.unifem.org

Vagina Monologues: V-Day
To end violence against women.
www.vday.org/home

White Ribbon Alliance for Safe Motherhood
Campaigns against maternal mortality throughout the world.
www.whiteribbonalliance.org

WOMANKIND Worldwide
Works in developing countries to enable women to achieve their legal rights.
www.womankind.org.uk

Women, Motherhood and the Workplace.
www.mumandworking.co.uk

Women of Color: Women of Words
Black women and theatre productions.
http://comminfo.rutgers.edu/~cybers/home.html

Women Thrive Worldwide
Focuses on the needs of poor women worldwide.
www.womenthrive.org

Women's Aid
Working to end domestic violence.
www.womensaid.org.uk

Women's Library
An extensive collection of women's history.
www.londonmet.ac.uk/thewomenslibrary

Bibliography

Abe, H. 2004 'Lesbian bar talk in Shinjuku, Tokyo', in S. Okamoto and J. Shibamoto Smith, eds, *Japanese Language, Gender, and Ideology: Cultural Models and Real People*, Oxford and New York: Oxford University Press.

Afshar, H. and Maynard, M. 1994 *The Dynamics of 'Race' and Gender: Some Feminist Interventions*, London: Taylor and Francis.

Ahlers, J. 2008 'Language revitalisation and the (re)constituting of gender', paper presented at IGALA5 Conference, Victoria University of Wellington, New Zealand, July 3–5.

Althusser, L. 1984 *Essays on Ideology*, London: Verso.

Alvesson, M. and Deetz, S. 2000 *Doing Critical Management Research*, London: Sage.

Alvesson, M. and Skoldberg, K. 2000 *Reflexive Methodology: New Vistas for Qualitative Research*, London: Sage.

Amnesty Magazine 2008 'Women and human rights', March.

Armstrong, J. 1997 'Homophobic slang as coercive discourse among college students', in A. Livia and K. Hall, eds, *Queerly Phrased: Language, Gender, and Sexuality*, Oxford: Oxford University Press.

BAAL (2010) *Recommendations on Good Practice*. Online. Available HTTP: <http://www.baal.org.uk/about_goodpractice.htm>, accessed 1 June 2010.

Badran, M. and Cooke, M., eds, 1990 *Opening the Gates: A Century of Arab Feminist Writing*, London: Virago.

Baker, P. 2002 *Polari: The Lost Language of Gay Men*, London: Routledge.

Baker, P. 2004 *Public Discourses of Gay Men*, London: Routledge.

Baker, P. 2006 *Using Corpora in Discourse Analysis*, London: Continuum.

Baker, P. 2008a *Sexed Texts: Language, Gender and Sexuality*, London: Equinox.

Baker, P. 2008b '"Eligible" bachelors and "frustrated" spinsters: corpus linguistics, gender and language', in K. Harrington, L. Litosseliti, H. Sauntson and J. Sunderland, eds, *Gender and Language Research Methodologies*, Basingstoke: Palgrave, pp. 73–84.

Baker, P. 2010 *Corpus Linguistics and Sociolinguistics*, Edinburgh: Edinburgh University Press.

Bakir, M. 1986 'Sex differences in the approximation of Arabic: a case study', *Anthropological Linguistics* 28(1): 3–9.

Banyard, K. 2010 *The Equality Illusion: The Truth about Women and Men Today*, London: Faber.

Barrett, R. 1997 'The "homo-genius" speech community', in A. Livia and K. Hall, eds, *Queerly Phrased: Language, Gender, and Sexuality*, Oxford: Oxford University Press, pp. 181–202.

Barrett, R. 1999 'Indexing polyphonous identity in the speech of African American drag queens', in M. Bucholtz, A. Liang and L. Sutton, eds, *Reinventing Identities: The Gendered Self in Discourse*, Oxford: Oxford University Press, pp. 313–31.

Barrett, R. 2002 'Is queer theory important for sociolinguistic theory?', in K. Campbell-Kibler, R. Podesva, S. Roberts and A. Wong, eds, *Language and Sexuality: Contesting Meaning in Theory and Practice*, Stanford, CA: CSLI Publications, pp. 25–43.

Barrett, R. 2004 'As much as we use language: Lakoff's queer augury', in M. Bucholtz, ed., *Language and Women's Place: Text and Commentaries*, Oxford: Oxford University Press, pp. 296–302.

Basu, S. 2010 'Lads' mags: the great cover up', *Guardian*, 15 October. Online. Available HTTP: <http://www.guardian.co.uk/lifeandstyle/2010/oct/15/lads-magazines-feminist-protests>, accessed 16 October 2010.

Baxter, J. 2002 'A juggling act: a feminist post-structuralist analysis of girls' and boys' talk in the secondary classroom', *Gender & Education* 14(1): 5–19.

Baxter, J. 2003 *Positioning Gender in Discourse: A Feminist Methodology*, Basingstoke: Palgrave.

Baxter, J. 2006a 'Introduction', in J. Baxter, ed., *Speaking Out: The Female Voice in Public Contexts*, Basingstoke: Palgrave, pp. xiii–xviii.

Baxter, J. 2006b '"Do we have to agree with her?" How high school girls negotiate leadership in public contexts', in J. Baxter, ed., *Speaking Out: The Female Voice in Public Contexts*, Basingstoke: Palgrave, pp. 159–78.

Baxter, J., ed., 2006c *Speaking Out: The Female Voice in Public Contexts*, Basingstoke: Palgrave.

Baxter, J. 2010 *The Language of Leadership*, Basingstoke: Palgrave.

Baxter, J. and Wallace, K. 2009 'Outside in-group and out-group identities? Constructing male solidarity and female exclusion in UK builders' talk', *Discourse & Society* 20: 411–29.

Battistella, E. 2006 'Girly men and girly girls', *American Speech* 81(1): 100–10.

Bebout, L. 1995 'Asymmetries in male/female word pairs: a decade of change', *American Speech* 70(2): 163–85.

Bem, S. 1993 *The Lenses of Gender*, New Haven: Yale University Press.

Bennett, S. 2009 'A centenary of International Women's Day, UCU wallchart', *UCU Magazine*, March.

Benwell, B. 2005 '"Lucky this is anonymous!" Men's magazines and ethnographies of reading: a textual culture approach', *Discourse & Society* 16(2): 147–72.

Benwell, B., ed., 2006 *Masculinity and Men's Lifestyle Magazines*, Oxford: Blackwell.

Benwell, B. and Stokoe, E. 2006 *Discourse and Identity*, Edinburgh: Edinburgh University Press.

Bergvall, V., Bing, J. and Freed, A., eds, 1996 *Rethinking Language and Gender Research: Theory and Practice*, London: Longman.

Besnier, N. 2007 'Gender and interaction in a globalizing world: negotiating the gendered self in Tonga', in B. McElhinny, ed., *Words, Worlds, and Material Girls: Language, Gender, Globalisation*, Berlin and New York: Mouton de Gruyter, pp. 423–46.

Besnier, N. 2009 *Gossip and the Everyday Production of Politics*. Honolulu: University of Hawai'i Press.

Bhattacharyya, G. 2002 *Sexuality and Society*, London: Routledge.

Billig, M. 1999 'Whose terms? Whose ordinariness? Rhetoric and ideology in conversation analysis', *Discourse & Society* 10(4): 543–58.

Bing, J. and Bergvall, J. 1996 'The question of questions: beyond binary thinking', in V. Bergvall, J. Bing and A. Freed, eds, *Rethinking Language and Gender Research: Theory and Practice*, London: Longman, pp. 1–30.

Boone, J. 2010 'Afghan feminists fighting from under the burqa', *Guardian*, 30 April. Online. Available HTTP: <http://www.guardian.co.uk/world/2010/apr/30/afghanistan-women-feminists-burqa>, accessed 30 April 2010.

Borba, R. and Ostermann, A. C. 2007 'Do bodies matter? Travestis' embodiment of (trans) gender identity through the manipulation of the Portuguese grammatical gender system', *Gender and Language* 1(1): 131–47.

Bourdieu, P. 1991 *Language and Symbolic Power*, Cambridge: Polity Press.

Bradley, J. 1998 '"Yanyuwa": men speak one way, women speak another', in J. Coates, ed., *Language and Gender: A Reader*, Oxford: Blackwell, pp. 13–20.

Braun, F. 2001 'The communication of gender in Turkish', in M. Hellinger and H. Bußmann, eds, *Gender across Languages: The Linguistic Representation of Women and Men*, Amsterdam: John Benjamins, vol. 1, pp. 283–309.

Brown, P. 1980 'How and why women are more polite: some evidence from a Mayan community', in S. McConnell-Ginet, R. Borker and N. Furman, eds, *Women and Language in Literature in Society*, New York: Praeger, pp. 111–36.

Brown, P. and Levinson, S. 1987 *Politeness: Some Universals in Language Use*, Cambridge: Cambridge University Press.

Bucholtz, M. 1996 'Black feminist theory and African American women's linguistic practice', in V. Bergvall, J. Bing and A. Freed, eds, *Rethinking Language and Gender Research: Theory and Practice*, London: Longman, pp. 267–90.

Bucholtz, M. 1999a 'Bad examples: transgression and progress in language and gender studies', in M. Bucholtz, A. Liang and L. Sutton, eds, *Reinventing Identities: The Gendered Self in Discourse*, Oxford: Oxford University Press, pp. 3–20.

Bucholtz, M. 1999b 'Why be normal? Language and identity practices in a community of nerd girls', *Language in Society* 28(2): 203–25.

Bucholtz, M. 1999c 'You da man: narrating the racial other in the linguistic production of white masculinity', *Journal of Sociolinguistics* 3(4): 443–60.

Bucholtz, M., ed., 2004 *Language and Women's Place: Text and Commentaries*, Oxford: Oxford University Press.

Bucholtz, M. and Hall, K. 2005 'Theorising identity in language and gender research', *Language in Society* 33(4): 469–515.

Bucholtz, M., Liang, A. and Sutton L., eds, 1999 *Reinventing Identities: The Gendered Self in Discourse*, Oxford: Oxford University Press.

Butler, J. 1990 *Gender Trouble: Feminism and the Subversion of Identity*, London: Routledge.

Butler, J. 1993 *Bodies that Matter: On the Discursive Limits of 'Sex'*, London: Routledge.

Butler, J. 1997 *Excitable Speech: A Politics of the Performative*, London: Routledge.

Butler, J. 1999 *Gender Trouble: Feminism and the Subversion of Identity*, 2nd edn, New York: Routledge.

Butler, J. 2004 *Undoing Gender*, New York: Routledge.

Callaway, H. 1992 'Ethnography and experience: gender implications in fieldworks and texts', in Judith Okely and Helen Callaway, eds, *Anthropology and Autobiography*, New York: Routledge, pp. 60–85.

Cameron, D. 1985 *Feminism and Linguistic Theory*, Basingstoke: Palgrave.

Cameron, D. 1990 *The Feminist Critique of Language: A Reader*, 1st edn, London: Routledge.

Cameron, D. 1992 *Feminism and Linguistic Theory*, 2nd edn, Basingstoke: Palgrave.

Cameron, D. 1995 *Verbal Hygiene*, London: Routledge.

Cameron, D. 1996 'The language–gender interface: challenging co-optation', in V. Bergvall, J. Bing and A. Freed, eds, *Rethinking Language and Gender Research: Theory and Practice*, London: Longman, pp. 31–53.

Cameron, D. 1997 'Performing gender identity: young men's talk and the construction of heterosexual masculinity', in S. Johnson and U. Meinhof, eds, *Language and Masculinity*, Oxford: Blackwell, pp. 86–107.

Cameron, D. 1998a '"Is there any ketchup, Vera?": gender, power and pragmatics', *Discourse & Society* 9(4): 437–55.

Cameron, D. ed. 1998b *The Feminist Critique of Language: A Reader*, 2nd edn, London: Routledge.

Cameron, D. 2000 *Good to Talk? Living and Working in a Communication Culture*, London: Sage.

Cameron, D. 2003 'Gender and language ideologies', in J. Holmes and M. Meyerhoff, eds, *The Handbook of Language and Gender*, Oxford: Blackwell, pp. 447–67.

Cameron, D. 2005 'Language, gender and sexuality: current issues and new directions', *Applied Linguistics* 26(4): 482–502.

Cameron, D. 2006a *Language and Sexual Politics*, London: Routledge.

Cameron, D. 2006b 'Theorising the female voice in public contexts', in J. Baxter, ed., *Speaking Out: The Female Voice in Public Contexts*, Basingstoke: Palgrave, pp. 3–20.

Cameron, D. 2007a 'Unanswered questions and unquestioned assumptions in the study of language and gender: female verbal superiority', *Gender and Language* 1(1): 15–25.

Cameron, D. 2007b *The Myth of Mars and Venus*, Oxford: Oxford University Press.

Cameron, D. 2009 'Theoretical issues for the study of gender and spoken interaction', in P. Pichler and E. Eppler, eds, *Gender and Spoken Interaction*, Basingstoke: Palgrave, pp. 1–17.

Cameron, D., Frazer, E., Harvey, P., Rampton, B. and Richardson, K. 1992 *Researching Language: Issues of Power and Method*, London: Routledge.

Cameron, D. and Kulick, D. 2003 *Language and Sexuality*, Cambridge: Cambridge University Press.

Cameron, D. and Kulick, D. 2005 'Identity crisis?', *Language and Communication* 25: 107–25.

Cameron, D., McAlinden, F. and O'Leary, K. 1989 'Lakoff in context: the social and linguistic functions of tag questions', in J. Coates and D. Cameron, eds, *Women in their Speech Communities*, Harlow: Longman pp. 13–26.

Carroll, D. and Kowitz, J. 1994 'Using concordance techniques to study gender stereotyping in ELT textbooks', in J. Sunderland, ed., *Exploring Gender Questions and Implications for English Language Education*, Hemel Hempstead: Prentice Hall, pp. 73–83.

Case, S. S. 1995 'Gender, language and the professions: recognition of wide-verbal-repertoire speech', *Studies in the Linguistic Sciences* 25(2): 149–92.

Castaneda-Pena, H. A. 2008 'Interwoven and competing gendered discourses in a preschool EFL lesson', in K. Harrington, L. Litosseliti, J. Sunderland and H. Sauntson, eds, *Gender and Language Research Methodologies*, Basingstoke: Palgrave, pp. 256–69.

Castro, O. 2007 'Feminism, gender and translation', paper given to the Sheffield Hallam Linguistic Research Seminar.

Chambers, D., Tincknell, E. and van Loon, J. 2004 'Peer regulation of teenage sexual identities', *Gender and Education* 16(3): 397–415.

Chan, G. 1992 'Gender, roles and power in dyadic conversation', in K. Hall, M. Bucholtz and B. Moonwomon, eds, *Locating Power: Proceedings of the Second Berkeley Women and Language Conference*, Berkeley: Berkeley Women and Language Group, University of California, vol. 1, pp. 57–67.

Chan, M. 2010 'Chinese language and gender: online bibliography', Ohio State University. Online. Available HTTP: <http://people.cohums.ohio-state.edu/chan9/g-bib.htm>, accessed 10 June 2010.

Chandra, S. 2003 'Language, sexuality and desire: English ideology in West India, 1850–1940', unpublished PhD thesis, University of Pennsylvania.

Cheshire, J. 1998 'Linguistic variation and social function', in J. Coates, ed., *Language and Gender: A Reader*, Oxford: Blackwell, pp. 29–41.

Chirrey, D. 2007 'Women like us: mediating and contesting identity in lesbian advice literature', in H. Sauntson and S. Kyratzis, eds, *Language, Sexualities and Desires: Cross-Cultural Perspectives*, Basingstoke: Palgrave.

Christie, C. 2000 *Gender and Language: Towards a Feminist Pragmatics*, Edinburgh: Edinburgh University Press.

Coates, J. 1989 'Gossip revisited: language in all-female groups', in J. Coates and D. Cameron, eds, *Women in their Speech Communities*, Harlow: Longman, pp. 94–122.

Coates, J. 1996 *Women Talk*, Oxford: Blackwell.

Coates, J. 1997 'Competing discourses of femininity', in H. Kotthoff and R. Wodak, eds, *Communicating Gender in Context*, Amsterdam: John Benjamins, pp. 285–313.

Coates, J., ed., 1998 *Language and Gender: A Reader*, Oxford: Blackwell.

Coates, J. 1999 'Changing femininities: the talk of teenage girls', in M. Bucholtz, A. Liang and L. A. Sutton, eds, *Reinventing Identities: The Gendered Self in Discourse*, Oxford: Oxford University Press, pp. 123–44.

Coates, J. 2003 *Men Talk*, Oxford: Blackwell.

Coates, J. 2004 *Women, Men and Language*, 3rd edn, London: Longman.

Coates, J. and Cameron, D., eds, 1989 *Women in their Speech Communities*, Harlow: Longman.

Connell, R. 2005 *Masculinities*, 2nd edn, Cambridge: Polity Press.

Connell, R. and Messerschmidt, J. W. 2005 'Hegemonic masculinity: rethinking the concept', *Gender and Society* 19(6): 829–59.

Cooper, R. 1984 'The avoidance of androcentric generics', *International Journal of Social Language* 50: 5–20.

Coupland, J. and Gwyn, R., eds, 2003 *Discourse, the Body and Identity*, Basingstoke: Palgrave.

Crawford, M. 1995 *Talking Difference: On Gender and Language*, London: Sage.

Dako, K. 2002 'Student pidgin (SP): the language of the educated male elite', *IAS Research Review* n.s. 18(2): 53–62.

Day, D. 1998 'Being ascribed and resisting membership of an ethnic group', in C. Antaki and S. Widdicombe, eds, *Identities in Talk*, London: Sage, pp. 151–69.

Diamond, J. 1996 *Status and Power in Verbal Interaction: A Study of Discourse in a Close-Knit Social Network*, Amsterdam and Philadelphia: John Benjamins.

Dörnyei, Z. 2007 *Research Methods in Applied Linguistics*, Oxford: Oxford University Press.

Doyle, M. 1994 *The A–Z of Non-Sexist Language*, London: Women's Press.

Dröschel, Y. 2007 'Queering language: a love that dare not speak its name comes out of the closet', in H. Sauntson and S. Kyratzis, eds, *Language, Sexualities and Desires: A Cross-Cultural Perspective*, Basingstoke: Palgrave, pp. 66–82.

Dunant, S., ed., 1994 *The War of the Words: The Political Correctness Debate*, London: Virago.

Duranti, A. 1997 *Linguistic Anthropology*, Cambridge: Cambridge University Press.

Ebadi, S. 2008 'Women campaign in Iran', *Amnesty Magazine*, March.

Eckert, P. 1997 'Age as a sociolinguistic variable', in F. Coulmas, ed., *The Handbook of Sociolinguistics*, Oxford: Blackwell, pp. 151–67.

Eckert, P. 1998 'Gender and sociolinguistic variation', in J. Coates, ed., *Language and Gender: A Reader*, Oxford: Blackwell, pp. 64–76.

Eckert, P. 2000 *Linguistic Variation as Social Practice*, Oxford: Blackwell.

Eckert, P. 2009 'Ethnography and the study of variation', in N. Coupland and A. Jaworski, eds, *The New Sociolinguistics Reader*, Basingstoke: Palgrave, pp. 136–51.

Eckert, P. and McConnell-Ginet, S. 1992 'Think practically and look locally: language and gender as community-based practice', *Annual Review of Anthropology* 21: 461–90.

Eckert, P. and McConnell-Ginet, S. 1998 'Communities of practice: where language, gender and power all live', in J. Coates, ed., *Language and Gender: A Reader*, Oxford: Blackwell, pp. 484–94.

Eckert, P. and McConnell-Ginet, S. 1999 'New generalisations and explanations in language and gender research', *Language in Society* 28(2): 185–203.

Eckert, P. and McConnell-Ginet, S. 2003 *Language and Gender*, Cambridge: Cambridge University Press.

Eckert, P. and McConnell-Ginet, S. 2007 'Putting communities of practice in their place', *Gender and Language* 1(1): 27–38.

Edley, N. and Wetherell, M. 1997 'Jockeying for position: the construction of masculine identities', *Discourse & Society* 8(2): 203–17.

Edley, N. and Wetherell, M. 2008 'Discursive psychology and the study of gender: a contested space', in K. Harrington, L. Litosseliti, H. Sauntson and J. Sunderland, eds, *Gender and Language Research Methodologies*, Basingstoke: Palgrave, pp. 161–73.

Edwards, D. 1998 'The relevant thing about her: social identity categories in use', in C. Antaki and S. Widdicombe, eds, *Identities in Talk*, London: Sage, pp. 15–33.

Edwards, V. and Katbamna 1989 'Female speech events in cultural context: the wedding songs of British Gujarati women', in J. Coates and D. Cameron, eds, *Women in their Speech Communities*, Harlow: Longman, pp. 158–76.

Eelen, G. 2001 *A Critique of Politeness Theories*, Manchester: St. Jerome Publishing.

Ehrlich, S. 2001 *Representing Rape: Language and Sexual Consent*, London and New York: Routledge.

Ehrlich, S. 2003 'Coercing gender: language in sexual assault adjudication processes', in J. Holmes and M. Meyerhoff, eds, *The Handbook of Language and Gender*, Oxford: Blackwell, pp. 645–70.

Equal Opportunities Commission 2006 *Sex and Power Index*, London: Equal Opportunities Commission UK.

Equality and Human Rights Commission 2008 *Sex and Power 2008*, London: Equality and Human Rights Commission.

Fairclough, N. 1989 *Language and Power*, Harlow: Longman.

Fairclough, N. 1992 *Discourse and Social Change*, Cambridge: Polity Press.

Fairclough, N. 1995 *Critical Discourse Analysis: The Critical Study of Language*, Harlow: Longman

Fairclough, N. 2001 *Language and Power*, 2nd edn, New York: Longman.

Fairclough, N. 2003 *Analysing Discourse*, London: Routledge.

Faludi, S. 2008 *The Terror Dream: Fear and Fantasy in Post-9/11 America*, New York: Scribe Publications.

Fan, C. 1996 'Language, gender and Chinese culture', *International Journal of Politics, Culture and Society* 10(1): 95–114.

Fishman, P. 1980 'Conversational insecurity', in H. Giles, P. Robinson and P. Smith, eds, *Language: Social Psychological Perspectives*, Oxford: Pergamon, pp. 127–32.

Foucault, M. 1972 *The Archaeology of Knowledge*, London: Routledge.

Foucault, M. 1978 *History of Sexuality*, vol. 1, Harmondsworth: Penguin Books.

Foucault, M. 1981 'The order of discourse', in R. Young, ed., *Untying the Text: A Post-Structuralist Reader*, Boston: Routledge and Kegan Paul, pp. 48–78.

Foucault, M. 1991 'Governmentality', in G. Burchell, C. Gordon and P. Miller, eds, *The Foucault Effect: Studies in Governmentality*, Chicago: University of Chicago Press, pp. 87–104.

Frank, F. and Treichler, P. 1989 *Language, Gender and Professional Writing*, New York: MLA.

Frankenberg, R. 1993 *White Women, Race Matters: The Social Construction of Whiteness*, London: Routledge.

Freed, A. 1996 'Language and gender research in an experimental setting', in V. Bergvall, J. Bing and A. Freed, eds, *Rethinking Language and Gender Research: Theory and Practice*, London: Longman, pp. 54–76.

Freed, A. 1999 'Communities of practice and pregnant women: is there a connection?', *Language in Society* 28(2): 257–71.

Freed, A. 2003 'Epilogue: reflections on language and gender research', in J. Holmes and M. Meyerhoff, eds, *The Handbook of Language and Gender*, Oxford: Blackwell, pp. 699–721.

Friedan, B. 1963/2010 *The Feminine Mystique*, Harmondsworth: Penguin Books.

Fuss, D. 1989 *Essentially Speaking: Feminism, Nature and Difference*, London: Routledge.

Gal, S. 1979 *Language Shifts*, New York: Academic Press.

Gal, S. 1995 'Language and gender: an anthropological review', in K. Hall and M. Bucholtz, eds, *Gender Articulated: Language and the Socially Constructed Self*, London: Routledge, pp. 169–82.

Gal, S. 1998 'Peasant men can't get wives: language change and sex roles in a bilingual community', in J. Coates, ed., *Language and Gender: A Reader*, Oxford: Blackwell, pp. 147–63.

Galasinski, D. 2004 *Men and the Language of Emotions*, Basingstoke: Palgrave.

Gaudio, R. 2007 'Out on video: gender, language and new public spheres in Islamic northern Nigeria', in B. McElhinny, ed., *Words, Worlds, and Material Girls: Language, Gender, Globalisation*, Berlin and New York: Mouton de Gruyter, pp. 237–86.

Gill, R. 2007 *Gender and the Media*, London: Polity.

Givhan, R. 2007 'Hilary Clinton's tentative dip into new neckline territory', *Washington Post Online*, 20 July. Online. Available: <http://www.washingtonpost.com/wpdyn/content/article/2007/07/19/AR2007071902668.html>, accessed 8 August 2009.

Goodwin, C. and Duranti, A. 1992 'Rethinking context: an introduction', in A. Duranti, and C. Goodwin, eds, *Rethinking Context: Language as an Interactive Phenomenon*, Cambridge: Cambridge University Press.

Goodwin, M. H. 1998 'Games of stance: conflict and footing in hopscotch', in S. Hoyle and C. Adger, eds, *Kids Play: Strategic Language Use in Later Childhood*, Oxford: Oxford University Press, pp. 22–46.

Goodwin, M. H. 2006 *The Hidden Life of Girls: Games of Stance, Status and Exclusion*, Oxford: Blackwell.

Gray, J. 1992 *Men Are from Mars, Women Are from Venus*, New York: HarperCollins.

Gray, J. 2002 *Mars and Venus in the Workplace*, New York: HarperCollins.

Greater Manchester Police 2001a *Mind Our Language*. Online. Available: <www.gmp.police.uk/language>.

Greater Manchester Police 2001b *Reporting a Hate Crime*. Online. Available: <www.gmp.police.uk/working-with/pages>.

Green, J. and Bloome, D. 1997 'Ethnography and ethnographers of and in education: a situated perspective', in J. Flood, S. Heath and D. Lapp, eds, *A Handbook of Research on Teaching Literacy through the Communicative and Visual Arts*, New York: Macmillan, pp. 181–202.

Hachimi, A. 2001 'Shifting sands: language and gender in Moroccan Arabic', in M. Hellinger and H. Bußmann, eds, *Gender across Languages: The Linguistic Representation of Women and Men*, Amsterdam and Philadelphia: John Benjamins, vol. 1, pp. 27–51.

Haeri, N. 1994 'A linguistic innovation of women in Cairo', *Language Variation and Change* 6: 87–112.

Halberstam, J. 1998 *Female Masculinity*, London: Routledge.

Hall, K. 2003 'Exceptional speakers: Contested and problematized gender identities', in J. Holmes and M. Meyerhoff, eds, *The Handbook of Language and Gender*, Oxford: Blackwell, pp. 352–80.

Hall, K. 2005 'Intertextual sexuality: Parodies of class, identity and desire in Liminal Delhi', *Journal of Linguistic Anthropology* 15(1): 125–44.

Hall, K., Bucholtz, M. and Moonwomon, B., eds, 1992 *Locating Power: Proceedings of the Second Berkeley Women and Language Conference*, vol. 1, Berkeley: Berkeley Women and Language Group, University of California.

Hammersley, M. and Atkinson, P. 1995 *Ethnography: Principles in Practice*, 2nd edn, London: Routledge.

Handford, M. and Gee, J., eds, 2011 *The Handbook of Discourse Analysis*. London: Routledge.

Hanong Thetela, P. 2002 'Sex discourses and gender constructions in Southern Sotho: a case study of police interviews of rape/sexual assault victims', *Southern African Linguistics and Applied Language Studies* 20(3): 177–89.

Harrington, K. 2008 'Perpetuating difference? Corpus linguistics and the gendering of reported dialogue', in K. Harrington, L. Litosseliti, H. Sauntson and J. Sunderland, eds, *Gender and Language Research Methodologies*, Basingstoke: Palgrave, pp. 85–102.

Harrington, K., Litosseliti, L., Sauntson, H. and Sunderland, J., eds, 2008 *Gender and Language Research Methodologies*, Basingstoke: Palgrave.

Hayes, J. 1981 'Gayspeak', in J. W. Cheseboro, ed., *Gayspeak: Gay Male and Lesbian Communication*, New York: Pilgrim Press, pp. 43–57.

Hellinger, M. 1998 'Gender across languages: international perspectives on language variation and change', in S. Wertheim, A. Bailey and M. Corston-Oliver, eds, *Engendering Communication: Proceedings of the Fifth Berkeley Women and Language Conference*, Berkeley: Berkeley Women and Language Group, University of California, pp. 211–20.

Hellinger, M. 2001 'English – gender in a global language', in M. Hellinger and H. Bußmann, eds, *Gender across Languages: The Linguistic Representation of Women and Men*, Amsterdam and Philadelphia: John Benjamins, vol. 1, pp. 105–13.

Hellinger, M. and Bußmann, H., eds, 2001 *Gender across Languages: The Linguistic Representation of Women and Men*, vol. 1, Amsterdam and Philadelphia: John Benjamins.

Hellinger, M. and Bußmann, H., eds, 2002 *Gender across Languages: The Linguistic Representation of Women and Men*, vol. 2, Amsterdam and Philadelphia: John Benjamins.

Hellinger, M. and Bußmann, H., eds, 2003 *Gender across Languages: The Linguistic Representation of Women and Men*, vol. 3, Amsterdam and Philadelphia: John Benjamins.

Hellinger, M. and Pauwels, A. 2007 'Language and sexism', in M. Hellinger and A. Pauwels, eds, *Handbook of Language and Communication: Diversity and Change*, Berlin and New York: Mouton de Gruyter, pp. 651–81.

Henley, N. 1995 'Ethnicity and gender issues in language', in H. Landrine, ed., *Bringing Cultural Diversity to Feminist Psychology*, Washington, DC: American Psychological Association, pp. 361–96.

Herring, S. 2003 'Gender and power in online communication', in J. Holmes and M. Meyerhoff, eds, *The Handbook of Language and Gender*, Oxford: Blackwell, pp. 202–28.

Hertz, R., ed., 1997 *Reflexivity and Voice*, London: Sage.

Hester, S. and Francis, D. 1994 'Doing data: the local organization of a sociological interview', *British Journal of Sociology* 45(4): 675–96.

Hirsi Ali, A. 2007 *Infidel: My Life*, London: Free Press.

Hobby, E. 1988 *Virtue of Necessity*, London: Virago.

Holmes, J. 1995 *Women, Men and Politeness*, London: Longman.

Holmes, J. 2000 'Women at work: analysing women's talk in New Zealand', *Australian Review of Applied Linguistics* 22(2): 1–17.

Holmes, J. 2001 'A corpus-based view of gender in New Zealand English', in M. Hellinger and H. Bußmann, eds, *Gender across Languages: The Linguistic Representation of Women and Men*, Amsterdam and Philadelphia: John Benjamins, vol. 1, pp. 115–36.

Holmes, J. 2005 'Power and discourse at work: is gender relevant?', in M. Lazar, ed., *Feminist Critical Discourse Analysis*, Basingstoke: Palgrave, pp. 31–60.

Holmes, J. 2006 *Gendered Talk at Work*, Oxford: Blackwell.

Holmes, J. 2007 'Social constructionism, postmodernism and feminist sociolinguistics', *Gender and Language* 1(1): 51–78.

Holmes, J. and Marra, M. 2004 'Relational practice in the workplace: women's talk or gendered discourse?', *Language in Society* 33: 377–98.

Holmes, J. and Meyerhoff, M. 1999 'The community of practice: theories and methodologies in language and gender research', *Language in Society* 28(2): 173–85.

Holmes, J. and Meyerhoff, M. 2003a 'Different voices, different views: an introduction to current research in language and gender', in J. Holmes and M. Meyerhoff, eds, *The Handbook of Language and Gender*, Oxford: Blackwell, pp. 1–17.

Holmes, J. and Meyerhoff, M., eds, 2003b *The Handbook of Language and Gender*, Oxford: Blackwell.

Holmes, J. and S. Schnurr 2005 'Politeness, humor and gender in the workplace: negotiating norms and identifying contestation', *Journal of Politeness Research: Language, Behaviour, Culture* 1(1): 121–49.

Holmes, J. and Schnurr, S. 2006 'Doing femininity at work: more than just relational practice', *Journal of Sociolinguistics* 10(1): 31–51.

Holmes, J. and R. Sigley 2001 'What's a word like *girl* doing in a place like this? Occupational labels, sexist usages and corpus research', in A. Smith and P. Peters, eds, *New Frontiers of Corpus Linguistics*, Amsterdam: Rodopi, pp. 247–63.

Holmes, J. and Stubbe, M. 2003 '"Feminine" workplaces: stereotype and reality', in J. Holmes and M. Meyerhoff, eds, *The Handbook of Language and Gender*, Oxford: Blackwell, pp. 573–600.

Holstein, J. and Gubrium, J. 1995 *The Active Interview*, London: Sage.

Hong, W. 1997 'Gender differences in Chinese request patterns', *Journal of Chinese Linguistics* 25(2): 193–210.

hooks, b. 1989 *Talking Back: Thinking Feminist – Thinking Black*, London: Sheba Feminist Publishers.

hooks, b. 1990 *Feminism is for Everybody: Passionate Politics*, London: South End Press.

Hultgren, A. K. 2008 'Reconstructing the sex dichotomy in language and gender research: call centre workers and "women's language"', in K. Harrison, L. Litosseliti, H. Sauntson and J. Sunderland, eds, *Gender and Language Research Methodologies*, Basingstoke: Palgrave, pp. 29–42.

Hunston, S. 2002 *Corpora in Applied Linguistics*, Cambridge: Cambridge University Press.

Ide, S. 2005 'How and why honorifics can signify dignity and elegance: the indexicality and reflexivity of linguistic rituals', in R. Lakoff and S. Ide, eds, *Broadening the Horizon of Linguistic Politeness*, Amsterdam and Philadelphia: John Benjamins, pp. 45–64.

Inoue, M. 2004 'Gender, language and modernity: towards an effective history of "Japanese women's language"', in S. Okamoto and J. Shibamoto Smith, eds, *Japanese Language, Gender and Ideology: Cultural Models and Real People*, Oxford and New York: Oxford University Press, pp. 57–75.

Inoue, M. 2006 *Vicarious Language: Gender and Linguistic Modernity in Japan*, Berkeley and Los Angeles: University of California Press.

Iyer, R. 2009 'Entrepreneurial identities and the problematic of subjectivity in media-mediated discourses', *Discourse & Society* 20: 241–64.

James, D. 1996 'Women, men and prestige speech forms: a critical review', in V. Bergvall, J. Bing and A. Freed, eds, *Rethinking Language and Gender Research: Theory and Practice*, London: Longman, pp. 98–125.

Jaworski, A. 2003 'Talking bodies: representations of norm and deviance in the BBC *Naked* programme', in J. Coupland and R. Gwyn, eds, *Discourse, the Body and Identity*, Basingstoke: Palgrave, pp. 151–76.

Jaworski, A. and Coupland, J. 2005 'Othering in gossip: "you go out you have a laugh and you can pull yeah okay but like …"', *Language in Society* 34: 667–94.

Jespersen, O. 1922 *Language: Its Nature, Development and Origin*, London: Allen & Unwin.

Johnson, N. 2006 *An Examination of the Concrete Ceiling: Perspectives of Ten African American Women Managers and Leaders*, Boca Raton, FL: Dissertation.Com.

Johnson, S. 1997 'Theorizing language and masculinity: a feminist perspective', in S. Johnson and U. H. Meinhof, eds, *Language and Masculinity*, Oxford: Blackwell, pp. 47–64.

Johnson, S., Culpeper, J. and Suhr, S. 2003 'From "politically correct councillors" to "Blairite nonsense": discourse of "political correctness" in three British newspapers', *Discourse & Society* 14(1): 29–47.

Johnson, S. and Meinhof, U. H., eds, 1997 *Language and Masculinity*, Oxford: Blackwell.

Johnson, S. and Suhr, S. 2003 'From "political correctness" to "politische Korrektheit": discourses of "PC" in the German newspaper Die Welt', *Discourse & Society* 14(1): 49–69.

Jones, D. 2000 'Gender trouble in the workplace: "language and gender" meets "feminist organisational communication"', in J. Holmes, ed., *Gendered Speech in Social Context: Perspectives from Gown to Town*, Wellington, NZ: Victoria University Press, pp. 192–210.

Jones, L. 2009 'The construction of identity in a lesbian community of practice: a sociocultural linguistics approach', unpublished PhD thesis, University of Sheffield.

Jones, L. forthcoming *Dyke/Girl: Language and Identities in a Lesbian Group*, Basingstoke: Palgrave.

Joyce, P., ed., 1995 *Class*, Oxford: Oxford University Press.

Jule, A. 2003 *Gender, Participation and Silence in the Classroom: Sh-shushing the Girls*, Basingstoke: Palgrave.

Jule, A., ed., 2005 *Gender and the Language of Religion*, Basingstoke: Palgrave.

Jule, A. 2007 *Language and Religious Identity: Women in Discourse*, Basingstoke: Palgrave.

Jule, A. 2008 *A Beginner's Guide to Language and Gender*, Clevedon: Multilingual Matters.

Jule, A. and Pedersen, B. 2006 *Being Feminist, Having Faith: Essays from Academia*, New York: Palgrave.

Kamada, L. 2008 'Discursive "embodied" identities of "half" girls in Japan: a multi-perspectival approach', in K. Harrington, L. Litosseliti, H. Sauntson and J. Sunderland, eds, *Gender and Language Research Methodologies*, Basingstoke: Palgrave, pp. 174–92.

Keating, E. 1998 'A woman's role in constructing status hierarchies: using honorific language in Pohnpei, Micronesia', *International Journal of the Sociology of Language* 129(1): 103–16.

Keenan, E. 1974 'Norm-makers, norm-breakers: uses of speech by men and women in a Malagasy community', in R. Bauman and J. Sherzer, eds, *Ethnography of Communication*, Cambridge: Cambridge University Press.

Kendall, S. 2003 'Creating gender demeanors of authority at work and at home', in J. Holmes and M. Meyerhoff, eds, *The Handbook of Language and Gender*, Oxford: Blackwell, pp. 600–23.

Kendall, S. and Tannen, D. 1997 'Gender and language in the workplace', in R. Wodak, ed., *Gender and Discourse*, London: Sage, pp. 81–106.

Kerswill, P. 2007 'Social class', in C. Llamas, L. Mullany and P. Stockwell, eds, *The Routledge Companion to Sociolinguistics*, London: Routledge, pp. 51–61.

Kielkiewicz-Janowiak, A. and Pawelczyk, J. 2009 'Socio-cultural conditioning of the sex/ prestige pattern: the local Polish context', in J. de Bres, J. Holmes and M. Marra, eds, *Proceedings of the 5th Biennial International Gender and Language Association Conference IGALA5*, Wellington, NZ: Victoria University of Wellington, pp. 453–64.

Kiesling, S. 2003 'Prestige, cultural models, and other ways of thinking about underlying norms and gender', in J. Holmes and M. Meyerhoff, eds, *The Handbook of Language and Gender*, Oxford: Blackwell, pp. 509–27.

Kinsey, A., Pomeroy, B. and Martin, C. 1948 *Sexual Behavior in the Human Male*, Philadelphia: W. B. Saunders.

Kitzinger, C. 2000 'Doing feminist conversation analysis', *Feminism and Psychology* 10: 163–93.

Kitzinger, C. 2008 'Conversation analysis: technical matters for gender research', in K. Harrington, L. Litosseliti, H. Sauntson and J. Sunderland, eds, *Gender and Language Research Methodologies*, Basingstoke: Palgrave, pp. 119–38.

Kitzinger, C. and Thomas, A. 1995 'Sexual harassment: a discursive approach', in S. Wilkinson and C. Kitzinger, eds, *Feminism and Discourse*, London: Sage, pp. 32–49.

Koller, V. 2004 *Metaphor and Gender in Business Media Discourse: A Critical Cognitive Study*, Basingstoke: Palgrave.

Kramarae, C. and Treichler, P. 1985 *A Feminist Dictionary*, London: Pandora.

Kristof, N. and Wudunn, S. 2010 *Half the Sky: How to Change the World*, London: Virago.

Kuiper, K. 1998 'Sporting formulae in New Zealand English: two models of male solidarity', in J. Coates, ed., *Language and Gender: A Reader*, Oxford: Blackwell, pp. 285–94.

Kulick, D. 2000 'Gay and lesbian language', paper presented at the International Gender and Language Association Conference, Stanford University, California, May.

Labov, W. 1966 *The Social Stratification of English in New York City*, Washington, DC: CAL.

Labov, W. 1972 *Language in the Inner City: Studies in the Black English Vernacular*, Philadelphia: University of Pennsylvania Press.

Labov, W. 1981 *Field Methods Used by the Project on Linguistic Change and Variation*, Sociolinguistics Working Paper 81, Austin, TX: South Western Educational Development Laboratory.

Lakay 2008 'Comment, Lakay says', 7 February 2008, in 'Language and Sexism', Feminist Law Professors. Online. Available HTTP: <http://feministlawprofs.law.sc.edu/?p=2966>.

Lakoff, R. 1975 *Language and Woman's Place*, New York: Harper and Row.

Lakoff, R. 2003 'Language, gender and politics: putting "women" and "power" in the same sentence', in J. Holmes and M. Meyerhoff, eds, *The Handbook of Language and Gender*, Oxford: Blackwell, pp. 161–78.

Langford, W. 1997 '"Bunnikins, I love you snugly in your warren": voices from subterranean cultures of love', in K. Harvey and C. Shalom, eds, *Language and Desire: Encoding Sex, Romance and Intimacy*, London: Routledge, pp. 170–85.

Lazar, M. 2005a 'Politicizing gender in discourse: feminist critical discourse analysis as political perspective and praxis', in M. Lazar, ed., *Feminist Critical Discourse Analysis: Gender, Power and Ideology in Discourse*, Basingstoke: Palgrave, pp. 1–30.

Lazar, M., ed., 2005b *Feminist Critical Discourse Analysis: Gender, Power and Ideology in Discourse*, Basingstoke: Palgrave.

Lazar, M. 2006 '"Discover the power of femininity!" Analyzing global "power femininity" in local advertising', *Feminist Media Studies* 6(4): 505–17.

Lazar, M. 2009 'Entitled to consume: postfeminist femininity and a culture of post-critique', *Discourse and Communication* 3(4): 371–400.

Leap, W. 1995 *Beyond the Lavender Lexicon: Authenticity, Imagination and Appropriation in Lesbian and Gay Languages*, Amsterdam: Gordon and Breach.

Leap, W. 1997 'Performative affect in three gay English texts', in A. Livia and K. Hall, eds, *Queerly Phrased: Language, Gender, and Sexuality*, Oxford: Oxford University Press, pp. 310–34.

Leap, W. 2008 'Queering gay men's English', in K. Harrington, L. Litosseliti, H. Sauntson and J. Sunderland, eds, *Gender and Language Research Methodologies*, Basingstoke: Palgrave, pp. 283–96.

Levy, A. 2005 *Female Chauvinist Pigs: Women and the Rise of Raunch Culture*, New York and London: Free Press.

Lewis, R. and Mills, S. 2003 *Feminist Postcolonial Theory: A Reader*, Edinburgh: Edinburgh University Press.

Liladhar, J. 2000 'Making and remaking femininities', unpublished PhD thesis, Sheffield Hallam University, Sheffield.

Liming, Z. 1998 'Nushu: Chinese women's characters', *International Journal of the Sociology of Language* 129(1): 127–38.

Litosseliti, L. 2003 *Using Focus Groups in Research*, London: Continuum.

Litosseliti, L. 2006a *Gender and Language: Theory and Practice*, London: Hodder Arnold.

Litosseliti, L. 2006b 'Constructing gender in public arguments: the female voice as emotional voice', in J. Baxter, ed., *Speaking Out: The Female Voice in Public Contexts*, Basingstoke: Palgrave, pp. 40–58.

Litosseliti, L. and Sunderland, J., eds, 2002 *Gender Identity and Discourse Analysis*, Amsterdam: John Benjamins.

Livia, A. 2003 '"One man in two is a woman": linguistic approaches to gender in literary texts', in J. Holmes and M. Meyerhoff, eds, *The Handbook of Language and Gender*, Oxford: Blackwell, pp. 142–59.

Livia, A. and Hall, K. 1997a '"It's a girl": bringing performativity back to linguistics', in A. Livia and K. Hall, eds, *Queerly Phrased: Language, Gender, and Sexuality*, Oxford: Oxford University Press, pp. 3–21.

Livia, A. and Hall, K., eds, 1997b *Queerly Phrased: Language, Gender, and Sexuality*, Oxford: Oxford University Press.

Lloyd, K. and Madden, M. 2009 'A limp response to women's erotica', *Guardian*, 13 August. Online. Available HTTP: <http://www.guardian.co.uk/commentisfree/2009/aug/13/women-erotica-sex-objects-magazine>, accessed 30 August 2009.

LPFMG 2010 The London Pro-Feminist Men's Group, <http://londonprofeminist-mensgroup.blogspot.com/>, accessed 31 July 2010.

Lovering, K. 1995 'The bleeding body: adolescents talk about menstruation', in S. Wilkinson and C. Kitzinger, eds, *Feminism and Discourse*, London: Sage, pp. 10–32.

Lunsing, W. and Maree, C. 2004 'Shifting speakers: negotiating reference in relation to sexuality and gender', in S. Okamoto and J. Shibamoto Smith, eds, *Japanese Language, Gender, and Ideology: Cultural Models and Real People*, Oxford and New York: Oxford University Press, pp. 92–109.

Lupton, D. 1994 *Medicine as Culture: Illness, Disease and the Body in Western Societies*, London: Sage.

McElhinny, B. 1997 'Ideologies of private and public language in sociolinguistics', in R. Wodak, ed., *Gender and Discourse*, London: Sage, pp. 106–39.

McElhinny, B. 1998 '"I don't smile much anymore": affect, gender and the discourse of Pittsburgh police officers', in J. Coates, ed., *Language and Gender: A Reader*, Oxford: Blackwell, pp. 309–27.

McElhinny, B. 2003 'Theorizing gender in sociolinguistics and linguistic anthropology', in J. Holmes and M. Meyerhoff, eds, *The Handbook of Language and Gender*, Oxford: Blackwell, pp. 21–42.

McElhinny, B. 2007a 'Introduction: language, gender and economies in global transitions: provocative and provoking questions about how gender is articulated', in B. McElhinny, ed., *Words, Worlds, and Material Girls: Language, Gender, Globalization*, Berlin and New York: Mouton de Gruyter, pp. 1–38.

McElhinny, B., ed., 2007b *Words, Worlds, and Material Girls: Language, Gender, Globalization*, Berlin and New York: Mouton de Gruyter.

McElhinny, B. and Mills, S. 2007 'Launching studies of *Gender and Language* in the early 21st century', *Gender and Language* 1(1): 1–13.

McLoughlin, L. 2008 'The construction of female sexuality in the "sex special": transgression and containment in magazines' information on sexuality for girls?', *Gender and Language* 2(2): 171–95.

McRae, S. 2009 'It's a blokes' thing: gender, occupational roles and talk in the workplace', in P. Pichler and E. Eppler, eds, *Gender and Spoken Interaction*, Basingstoke: Palgrave, pp. 186–210.

McRobbie, A. 2007 'Postfeminism and popular culture: Bridget Jones and the new gender regime', in Y. Tasker and D. Negra, eds, *Interrogating Post-Feminism: Gender and the Politics of Popular Culture*, Durham, NC: Duke University Press, pp. 27–39.

McRobbie, A. 2009 *The Aftermath of Feminism: Gender, Culture and Social Change*, London: Sage.

Manke, M. 1997 *Classroom Power Relations: Understanding Student–Teacher Interaction*, Mahwah, NJ and London: Lawrence Erlbaum Associates.

Marra, M., Schnurr, S. and Holmes, J. 2006 'Effective leadership in New Zealand workplaces', in J. Baxter, ed., *Speaking Out: The Female Voice in Public Contexts*, Basingstoke: Palgrave, pp. 240–60.

Matsumoto, Y. 2004 'The new (and improved?) language and place of women in Japan', in M. Bucholtz, A. Liang and L. Sutton, eds, *Reinventing Identities: The Gendered Self in Discourse*, Oxford: Oxford University Press, pp. 244–59.

Maynard, M. and Purvis, J.1995 *(Hetero)sexual Politics*, London: Taylor and Francis.

Messner, M. A. and Sabo, D. F., eds, 1990 *Sport, Men and the Gender Order: Critical Feminist Perspectives*, Champaign, IL: Human Kinetics Books.

Meyerhoff, M. 1996 'Dealing with gender identity as a sociolinguistic variable', in V. Bergvall, J. Bing and A. Freed, eds, *Rethinking Language and Gender Research: Theory and Practice*, London: Longman, pp. 202–27.

Meyerhoff, M. 2002 'Communities of practice', in J. K. Chambers, P. Trudgill and N. Schilling-Estes, eds, *The Handbook of Language Variation and Change*, Oxford: Blackwell, pp. 526–48.

Meyerhoff, M. 2007 *Introducing Sociolinguistics*, London: Routledge.

Miller, C. and Swift, K. 1982/1989 *The Handbook of Non-Sexist Writing*, London: Women's Press.

Miller, E. 1995 'Inside the switchboard of desire', in W. Leap, ed., *Beyond the Lavender Lexicon: Authenticity, Imagination and Appropriation in Lesbian and Gay Languages*, Amsterdam: Gordon and Breach, pp. 30–42.

Miller, J. and Glassner, B. 1997 'The "inside" and the "outside": finding realities in interviews', in D. Silverman, ed., *Qualitative Research: Theory, Method and Practice*, London: Sage, pp. 99–112.

Miller, L. 2004 'You are doing *burikko*! Censoring/scrutinising artificers of cute femininity in Japanese', in S. Okamoto and J. Shibamoto Smith, eds, *Japanese Language, Gender, and Ideology: Cultural Models and Real People*, Oxford and New York: Oxford University Press, pp.148–65.

Mills, J. 1989 *Womanwords*, Harlow: Longman.

Mills, S. 1995 *Feminist Stylistics*, London: Routledge.

Mills, S. 1999 'Discourse competence: or how to theorise strong women speakers', in C. Hendricks and K. Oliver, eds, *Language and Liberation: Feminism, Philosophy, and Language*, Albany, NY: SUNY Press, pp. 81–99.

Mills, S. 2003a *Gender and Politeness*, Cambridge: Cambridge University Press.

Mills, S. 2003b 'Caught between sexism, anti-sexism and political correctness: feminist women's negotiations with naming practices', *Discourse & Society* 14(1): 87–110.

Mills, S. 2004 *Discourse*, London: Routledge; 1st edn 1997.

Mills, S. 2006 'Gender and performance anxiety at academic conferences', in J. Baxter, ed., *Speaking Out: The Female Voice in Public Contexts*, Basingstoke: Palgrave, pp. 61–80.

Mills, S. 2008 *Language and Sexism*, Cambridge: Cambridge University Press.

Milroy, L. 1987 *Observing and Analysing Natural Language*, London: Sage.

Minh-ha, T. 1989 *Woman, Native, Other: Writing Postcoloniality and Feminism*, Bloomington: Indiana University Press.

Miskimmin, S. 2007 'When aboriginal equals "at risk": the impact of institutional discourse on Aboriginal Head Start families', in B. McElhinny, ed., *Words, Worlds, and Material Girls: Language, Gender, Globalization*, Berlin and New York: Mouton de Gruyter, pp. 107–28.

Miyazaki, A. 2004 'Japanese junior high school girls' and boys' first-person pronoun use and their social world', in S. Okamoto, and J. Shibamoto Smith, eds, *Japanese Language, Gender and Ideology: Cultural Models and Real People*, Oxford and New York: Oxford University Press, pp. 256–74.

Mohanty, C. 1984 'Under Western eyes: feminist scholarship and colonial discourse', *Boundary* 2(3): 333–58.

Mojumdar, A. 2009 'Afghan women's election turnout likely to be low', *Women's E-News. Org*, 20 August. Online. Available HTTP: <http://www.womensenews.org/article.cfm/dyn/aid/4114/context/archive>, accessed 21 August 2009.

Mooneeram, R. and Mullany, L. 2011 'World Englishes, globalisation and gender discourses: representations of the global female citizen in mainland China advertising', paper to be presented at AILA, Beijing, Beijing Foreign Studies University, August 23–28.

Morgan, M. 2004 '"I'm every woman": black women's (dis)placement in women's language study', in M. Bucholtz, ed., *Language and Women's Place: Text and Commentaries*, Oxford: Oxford University Press, pp. 252–9.

Morgan, M. 2007 'When and where we enter: social context and desire in women's discourse', *Gender and Language* 1(1): 119–29.

Morrish, E. 1997 'Falling short of God's ideal: public discourse about lesbians and gays', in A. Livia and K. Hall, eds, *Queerly Phrased: Language, Gender, and Sexuality*, Oxford: Oxford University Press, pp. 335–49.

Morrish, E. and Sauntson, H. 2007 *New Perspectives on Language and Sexual Identity*, Basingstoke: Palgrave.

Mullany, L. 2004 '"Become the man that women desire": gender identity and dominant discourses in email advertising language', *Language and Literature* 13: 291–305.

Mullany, L. 2007 *Gendered Discourse in the Professional Workplace*, Basingstoke: Palgrave.

Mullany, L. 2008 'Negotiating methodologies: making language and gender relevant in the professional workplace', in K. Harrington, L. Litosseliti, H. Sauntson and J. Sunderland, eds, *Gender and Language Research Methodologies*, Basingstoke: Palgrave, pp. 43–55.

Mullany, L. 2010a 'Im/politeness, rapport management and workplace culture: truckers performing masculinities on Canadian ice-roads', in F. Bargiela-Chiappini and D. Kadar, eds, *Politeness across Cultures*, Basingstoke: Palgrave, pp. 61–84.

Mullany, L. 2010b 'Gendered identities in the professional workplace: negotiating the glass ceiling', in C. Llamas and D. Watt, eds, *Language and Identities*, Edinburgh: Edinburgh University Press, pp. 179–91.

Mullany, L. 2010c 'Gender and interpersonal pragmatics', in S. L. Graham and M. Locher, eds, *The Handbook of Interpersonal Pragmatics*, Berlin: Mouton de Gruyter, pp. 225–50.

Mullany, L. 2011 'Gender, discourse and professional communication', in M. Handford and J. Gee, eds, *The Routledge Handbook of Discourse Analysis*, Abingdon: Routledge.

Mullany, L. forthcoming *The Sociolinguistics of Gender in Public Life*, Basingstoke: Palgrave.

Murphy, B. 2010a '"You're not supposed to be wearing tight jeans with that scarf": examining discourse, identity and young Muslim women in UK society', paper presented at BAAL Gender and Language Special Interest Group, Lancaster University, 30 March.

Murphy, B. 2010b *Corpus and Sociolinguistics: Investigating Age and Gender in Female Talk*, Amsterdam: John Benjamins.

Nair, R. B. 2002 *Lying on the Postcolonial Couch: The Idea of Indifference*, Minneapolis: University of Minnesota Press.

Nayak, A. and Kehily, M. J. 2008 *Gender, Youth and Culture: Young Masculinities and Femininities*, Basingstoke: Palgrave.

Negra, D. 2009 'Time crisis and the postfeminist heterosexual economy', in S. Griffin, ed., *Hetero: Queering Representations of Straightness*, Albany, NY: SUNY Press, pp. 173–90.

Nguyen, B. 2007 'Gender, multilingualism and the American war in Vietnam', in B. McElhinny, ed., *Words, Worlds, and Material Girls: Language, Gender, Globalization*, Berlin and New York: Mouton de Gruyter, pp. 349–67.

Nichols, P. 1998 'Black women in the rural South: conservative and innovative', in J. Coates, ed., *Language and Gender: A Reader*, Oxford: Blackwell, pp. 55–63.

Nwoye, O. 1998 'Linguistic gender differences in Igbo', *International Journal of the Sociology of Language* 129(1): 87–102.

Oakley, A. 1975 *The Housewife*, Harmondsworth: Penguin Books.

Oakley, A. 1984 *The Sociology of Housework*, Harmondsworth: Penguin Books.

O'Barr, W. and Atkins, B. 1980 '"Women's language" or "powerless language"?', in S. McConnell-Ginet, R. Borker and N. Furman, eds, *Women and Language in Literature and Society*, New York: Praeger, pp. 93–110.

Ochs, E. 1992 'Indexing gender', in A. Duranti and C. Goodwin, eds, *Rethinking Context: Language as an Interactive Phenomenon*, Cambridge: Cambridge University Press, pp. 335–59.

Ochs, E. and Taylor, C. 1992 'Mothers' role in the everyday reconstruction of "father knows best"', in K. Hall, M. Bucholtz and B. Moonwomon, eds, *Locating Power: Proceedings of the Second Berkeley Women and Language Conference*, Berkeley: Berkeley Women and Language Group, University of California, vol. 1, pp. 447–63.

O'Hara, M. 2010 'The pursuit of flexibility', *Guardian*, 6 March, pp. 1–2.

Okamoto, S. and Shibamoto Smith, J. 2004a 'Introduction', in S. Okamoto and J. Shibamoto Smith, eds, *Japanese Language, Gender, and Ideology: Cultural Models and Real People*, Oxford and New York: Oxford University Press, pp. 3–20.

Okamoto, S. and Shibamoto Smith, J., eds, 2004b *Japanese Language, Gender, and Ideology: Cultural Models and Real People*, Oxford and New York: Oxford University Press.

Page, R. 2005 *Literary and Linguistic Approaches to Feminist Narratology*, Basingstoke: Palgrave.

Pauwels, A. 1998 *Women Changing Language*, London: Longman.

Pauwels, A. 2001 'Spreading the feminist word: the case of the new courtesy title Ms in Australian English', in M. Hellinger and H. Bußmann, eds, *Gender across Languages: The Linguistic Representation of Women and Men*, Amsterdam and Philadelphia: John Benjamins, vol. 1, pp. 137–51.

Pauwels, A. 2003 'Linguistic sexism and feminist linguistic activism', in J. Holmes and M. Meyerhoff, eds, *The Handbook of Language and Gender*, Oxford: Blackwell, pp. 550–70.

Pearce, M. 2009 'Kera tone and voicing interaction', *Lingua* 119: 846–64.

Philips, S. 2003 'The power of gender ideologies in discourse', in J. Holmes and M. Meyerhoff, eds, *The Handbook of Language and Gender*, Oxford: Blackwell, pp. 252–76.

Pichler, P. 2008 'Gender, ethnicity and religion in spontaneous talk and ethnographic-style interviews: balancing perspectives of researcher and researched', in K. Harrington, L. Litosseliti, H. Sauntson and J. Sunderland, eds, *Gender and Language Research Methodologies*, Basingstoke: Palgrave, pp. 56–70.

Pichler, P. 2009 *Talking Young Femininities*, Basingstoke: Palgrave.

Pichler, P. and Eppler, E., eds, 2009 *Gender and Spoken Interaction*, Basingstoke: Palgrave.

Potter, J. 1996 *Representing Reality: Discourse, Rhetoric and Social Construction*, London: Sage

Preece, S. 2009 '"A group of lads, innit": performances of laddish masculinity in British higher education', in P. Pichler and E. Eppler, eds, *Gender and Spoken Interaction*, Basingstoke: Palgrave, pp. 115–38.

Pujolar, J. 2007 'African women in Catalan language courses: struggles over class, gender and ethnicity in advanced liberalism', in B. McElhinny, ed., *Words, Worlds, and Material Girls: Language, Gender, Globalization*, Berlin and New York: Mouton de Gruyter, pp. 305–47.

Queen, R. 1997 '"I don't speak Spritch": locating lesbian language', in A. Livia and K. Hall, eds, *Queerly Phrased: Language, Gender, and Sexuality*, Oxford: Oxford University Press, pp. 233–42.

Queen, R. 2004 '"I am a woman hear me roar": the importance of linguistic stereotype for lesbian linguistic identity performances', in M. Bucholtz, ed., *Language and Women's Place: Text and Commentaries*, Oxford: Oxford University Press, pp. 289–95.

Ramazanoglu, C. 1993 'Love and the politics of heterosexuality', in S. Wilkinson and C. Kitzinger, eds, *Heterosexuality*, London: Sage, pp. 59–67

Raven, C. 2010 'Strike a pose', *Guardian*, 6 March, pp. 2–4.

Redfern, C. and Aune, K. 2010 *Reclaiming the F Word: The New Feminist Movement*, London: Zed Books.

Romaine, S. 2001 'A corpus-based view of gender in British and American English', in M. Hellinger and H. Bußmann, eds, *Gender across Languages: The Linguistic Representation of Women and Men*, Amsterdam and Philadelphia: John Benjamins, vol. 1, pp. 154–75.

Romaine, S. 2003 'Variation in language and gender', in J. Holmes and M. Meyerhoff, eds, *The Handbook of Language and Gender*, Oxford: Blackwell, pp. 98–118.

Romaniuk, T. 2009 '"I'm your girl": revisiting sexism and naming practices in the public sphere', in J. de Bres, J. Holmes and M. Marra, eds, *Proceedings of the 5th Biennial International Gender and Language Association Conference IGALA5*, Wellington, NZ: Victoria University of Wellington, pp. 167–78.

Rowbotham, S. 1973 *Woman's Consciousness, Man's World*, London: Pelican Books.

Rowbotham, S. 1977 *Hidden from History: 300 Years of Women's Oppression*, London: Pluto.

Rubin, G. 1984 'Thinking sex: notes for a radical theory of the politics of sexuality', in C. Vance, ed., *Pleasure and Danger: Exploring Female Sexuality*, London: Pandora, pp. 267–319.

Sadiqi, F. 2003 *Women, Men and Language in Morocco*, Leiden and Boston: Brill.

Sadiqi, F. 2010 'Women's rights in North Africa'. Online. Available HTTP: <http://freedomhouse.org>.

Sadiqi, F. and Ennaji, M. 2010 *Women in the Middle East and North Africa*, New York: Routledge.

Sandoval, C. 1991 'US Third World feminism: the theory and method of oppositional consciousness in the postmodern world', *Genders* 10 (Spring): 1–24.

Sauntson, H. 2008 'The contribution of Queer Theory to gender and language research', in K. Harrington, L. Litosseliti, H. Sauntson and J. Sunderland, eds, *Gender and Language Research Methodologies*, Basingstoke: Palgrave, pp. 271–82.

Sauntson, H. and Kyratzis, S., eds, 2007 *Language, Sexualities and Desires: Cross-Cultural Perspectives*, Basingstoke: Palgrave.

Schegloff, E. 1992 'In another context', in A. Duranti and C. Goodwin, eds, *Rethinking Context: Language as an Interactive Phenomenon*, Cambridge: Cambridge University Press, pp. 191–28.

Schegloff, E. 1997 'Whose text? Whose context?', *Discourse & Society* 8(2): 165–85.

Schegloff, E. 2000 'Overlapping talk and the organisation of turn-taking for conversation', *Language in Society* 29: 1–63.

Schegloff, E. 2001 'Accounts of conduct in interaction: interruptions, overlap and turn-taking', in J. Turner, ed., *Handbook of Sociological Theory*, London: Kluwer Academic.

Schegloff, E. 2007 'A tutorial on membership categorization', *Journal of Pragmatics* 39: 462–92.

Schnurr, S. 2009 *Leadership Discourse at Work: Interactions of Gender and Workplace Culture*, Basingstoke: Palgrave.

Schultz, M. 1990 'The semantic derogation of women', in D. Cameron, ed., *The Feminist Critique of Language: A Reader*, 1st edn, London: Routledge, pp. 134–48.

Schwarz, J. 2003 'Quantifying non-sexist usage: the case of Ms', in J. Sunderland, ed., 2006, *Language and Gender: An Advanced Resource Book*, London: Routledge, pp. 142–8.

Scott, M. 1999. WordSmith Tools, version 3, Oxford: Oxford University Press.

Seidler, V. J. 1991 *Recreating Sexual Politics: Men, Feminism and Politics*, London: Routledge.

Shalom, C. 1997 'That great supermarket of desire: attributes of the desired other in personal ads', in K. Harvey and C. Shalom, eds, *Language and Desire: Encoding Sex, Romance and Intimacy*, London: Routledge.

Shaw, S. 2002 'Language and gender in the House of Commons', unpublished PhD thesis, University of London.

Shaw, S. 2006 'Governed by the rules? The female voice in parliamentary debates', in J. Baxter, ed., *Speaking Out: The Female Voice in Public Contexts*, Basingstoke: Palgrave, pp. 81–102.

Shepherd, J. and Learner, S. 2010 'Lessons on gay history cut homophobic bullying in north London school', *Guardian*, 26 October. Online. Available HTTP: <http://www.guardian.co.uk/education/2010/oct/26/gay-history-lessons-bullying-schools?INTCMP=SRCH>, accessed 27 October 2010.

Sidnell, J. 2003 'Constructing and managing male exclusivity in talk-in-interaction', in J. Holmes and M. Meyerhoff, eds, *The Handbook of Language and Gender*, Oxford: Blackwell, pp. 327–45.

Sigley, R. and J. Holmes, 2002 'Looking at girls in corpora of English', *Journal of English Linguistics* 30(2): 138–57.

Silverman, D. 2000 *Doing Qualitative Research: A Practical Guide*, London: Sage.

Skeggs, B. 1997 *Formations of Class and Gender: Becoming Respectable*, London: Sage.

Skeggs, B 2004 *Class, Self and Culture*, London: Routledge.

Spencer-Oatey, H., ed., 2000 *Culturally Speaking: Managing Rapport through Talk across Cultures*, London: Continuum.

Spender, D. 1980 *Man Made Language*, London: Routledge.

Sperber, D. and Wilson, D. 1996 *Relevance: Communication and Cognition*, 2nd edn, Oxford: Blackwell.

Spivak, G. 1990 *The Post-Colonial Critic: Interviews, Strategies, Dialogues*, ed. S. Harasym, London: Routledge.

Stewart, A. 1998 *The Ethnographer's Method*, London: Sage.

Stokoe, E. 2008 'Categories, actions and sequences: formulating gender in talk-in-interaction', in K. Harrington, L. Litosseliti, H. Sauntson and J. Sunderland, eds, *Gender and Language Research Methodologies*, Basingstoke: Palgrave, pp. 139–57.

Stokoe, E. and Smithson, J. 2001 'Making gender relevant: conversation analysis and gender categories in interaction', *Discourse & Society* 12(2): 217–44.

Stone, A. 2004 'On the genealogy of women: a defence of anti-essentialism', in S. Gillis, G. Howie and R. Munford, eds, *Third Wave Feminism: A Critical Exploration*, Basingstoke: Palgrave Macmillan, pp. 85–96.

Subhuti 1994 *Sangharakshita: A New Voice in the Buddhist Tradition*, Birmingham: Windhorse Publications.

Sunaoshi, Y. 2004 'Farm women's professional discourse in Ibaraki', in S. Okamoto and J. Shibamoto Smith, eds, *Japanese Language, Gender, and Ideology: Cultural Models and Real People*, Oxford and New York: Oxford University Press, pp. 184–205.

Sunderland, J. 1995 '"We're boys miss!": finding gendered identities and looking for gendering of identities in the foreign language classroom', in S. Mills, ed., *Language and Gender: Interdisciplinary Perspectives*, Harlow: Longman, pp. 160–79.

Sunderland, J. 2000 'New understandings of gender and language classroom research: texts, teacher talk and student talk', *Language Teaching Research* 4(2): 149–73.

Sunderland, J. 2004 *Gendered Discourses*, Basingstoke: Palgrave.

Sunderland, J. ed., 2006 *Language and Gender: An Advanced Resource Book*, London: Routledge.

Sunderland, J. 2007 'Contradictions in gendered discourses: feminist readings of sexist jokes?', *Gender and Language* 1(2): 207–28.

Sunderland, J. 2009 'Language and gender in African contexts', in *Proceedings of the BAAL 2009 Conference*, Edinburgh: University of Edinburgh, pp. 127–9.

Sunderland, J. and Litosseliti, L. 2008 'Current research methodologies in gender and language study: key issues', in K. Harrington, L. Litosseliti, H. Sauntson and J. Sunderland, eds, *Gender and Language Research Methodologies*, Basingstoke: Palgrave, pp. 1–18.

Swann, J. 1998 'Talk control: an illustration from the classroom of problems in analysing male dominance of conversation', in J. Coates, ed., *Language and Gender: A Reader*, Oxford: Blackwell, pp. 185–96.

Swann, J. 2002 'Yes, but is it gender?', in L. Litosseliti and J. Sunderland, eds, *Gender Identity and Discourse Analysis*, Amsterdam: John Benjamins, pp. 43–67.

Swann, J. 2009 'Doing gender against the odds: a sociolinguistic analysis of educational discourse', in P. Pichler and E. Eppler, eds, *Gender and Spoken Interaction*, Basingstoke: Palgrave, pp. 18–41.

Swann, J. and Maybin, J. 2008 'Sociolinguistic and ethnographic approaches to language and gender', in K. Harrison, L. Litosseliti, H. Sauntson and J. Sunderland, eds, *Gender and Language Research Methodologies*, Basingstoke: Palgrave, pp. 21–42.

Sznycer, K. 2010 'Strategies of powerful self-presentation in the discourse of female tennis players', *Discourse & Society* 21(4): 458–79.

Talbot, M. 1995 'A synthetic sisterhood: false friends in a teenage magazine', in K. Hall and M. Bucholtz, eds, *Gender Articulated: Language and the Socially Constructed Self*, New York: Routledge. pp. 143–65.

Talbot, M. 1998/2010 *Language and Gender: An Introduction*, Cambridge: Polity Press.

Talbot, M. 2003 'Gender stereotypes: reproduction and challenge', in J. Holmes and M. Meyerhoff, eds, *The Handbook of Language and Gender*, Oxford: Blackwell pp. 468–86.

Talbot, M. 2007 'Political correctness and freedom of speech', in M. Hellinger and A. Pauwels, eds, *Handbook of Language and Communication: Diversity and Change*, Berlin and New York: Mouton de Gruyter, pp. 751–64.

Tannen, D. 1984 *Conversational Style: Analysing Talk among Friends*, Norwood, NJ: Ablex.

Tannen, D. 1989 *Talking Voices: Repetition, Dialogue and Imagery in Conversational Discourse*, Cambridge: Cambridge University Press.

Tannen, D. 1991 *You Just Don't Understand: Women and Men in Conversation*, London: Virago.

Tannen, D. 2003 'Gender and family interaction', in J. Holmes and M. Meyerhoff, eds, *The Handbook of Language and Gender*, Oxford: Blackwell, pp. 179–201.

Tannen, D., Kendall, S. and Gordon, C. 2007 *Family Talk*, New York: Oxford University Press.

Tashakkori, A. and Teddlie, C. 1998 *Mixed Methodology: Combining Qualitative and Quantitative Approaches*, London: Sage.

Tasker, Y. and Negra, D. 2007 *Interrogating Post-Feminism: Gender and the Politics of Public Culture*, London: Duke University Press.

Thomas, B. 1989 'Differences of sex and sects: linguistic variation and social networks in a Welsh mining village', in J. Coates and D. Cameron, eds, *Women in their Speech Communities*, Harlow: Longman, pp. 51–60.

Thornborrow, J. 2002 *Power Talk: Language and Interaction in Institutional Discourse*, Harlow: Longman.

Tobin, Y. 2001 'Gender switch in modern Hebrew', in M. Hellinger and H. Bußmann, eds, *Gender across Languages: The Linguistic Representation of Women and Men*, Amsterdam and Philadelphia: John Benjamins, vol. 1, pp. 177–98.

Toolan, M. 1996 *Total Speech: An Integrational Linguistic Approach to Language*, Durham, NC: Duke University Press.

Trabelsi, M. (forthcoming) 'A corpus linguistics/CDA analysis of the representation of Muslim women in the media', unpublished PhD thesis, Sheffield Hallam University, Sheffield.

Traynor, I. 2010 'Pledge to cut EU gender pay gap after 15 years without progress', *Guardian*, 5 March. Online. Available HTTP: <http://www.guardian.co.uk/world/2010/mar/05/europe-gender-pay-gap?INTCMP=SRCH>, accessed 12 March 2010.

Trechter, S. 1999 'Contextualising the exotic few: gender dichotomies in Lakhota', in M. Bucholtz, A. Liang and L. Sutton, eds, *Reinventing Identities: The Gendered Self in Discourse*, Oxford: Oxford University Press, pp. 101–22.

Trechter, S. 2003 'The Marked man: language, gender and ethnicity', in J. Holmes and M. Meyerhoff, eds, *The Language and Gender Handbook*, Oxford: Blackwell, pp. 478–501.

Trechter, S. 2004 'Contradictions of the indigenous Americas: feminist challenges to and from the field', in M. Bucholtz, ed., *Language and Women's Place: Text and Commentaries*, Oxford: Oxford University Press, pp. 269–76.

Troemel-Ploetz, S. 1998 'Selling the apolitical', in J. Coates, ed., *Language and Gender: A Reader*, Oxford: Blackwell, pp. 446–58.

Troutman, D. 2006 '"They say that it's a man's world, but you can't prove that by me": African American comediennes' construction of voice in a public sphere', in J. Baxter, ed., *Speaking Out: The Female Voice in Public Contexts*, Basingstoke: Palgrave, pp. 61–80.

Trudgill, P. 1974 *The Social Differentiation of English in Norwich*, Cambridge: Cambridge University Press.

Tyler, I. 2008 'Chav mum, chav scum', *Feminist Media Studies* 8(1): 17–34.

Valenti, J. 2007 *Full Frontal Feminism: A Young Woman's Guide to Why Feminism Matters*, Berkeley, CA: Seal Press.

Valenti, J. 2008 *He's a Stud, She's a Slut and 49 Other Double Standards Every Woman Should Know*, Berkeley, CA: Seal Press.

van Dijk, T. 1994 'Editorial: academic nationalism', *Discourse & Society* 5(3): 275–6.

van Dijk, T. 1995 'Elite discourse and the reproduction of racism', in R. Whillock and D. Slayden, eds, *Hate Speech*, London: Sage, pp. 1–27.

van Dijk, T. 2001 'Critical discourse studies', in D. Schiffrin, D. Tannen and H. Hamilton, eds, *The Handbook of Discourse Analysis*, Oxford: Blackwell, pp. 352–71.

Vetterling-Braggin, M. 1981 *Sexist Language*, New York: Littlefield Adams.

Vicinus, M. 1980 *The Widening Sphere: Changing Roles of Victorian Women*, London: Methuen.

Wahlin, W. 2007 'Women in the workplace', *J@pan.Inc* 73 (September/October). Online. Available HTTP: <http://www.japaninc.com/mgz_sep-oct_2007_issue_women-in-the-workplace>.

Walsh, C. 2001 *Gender and Discourse: Language and Power in Politics, the Church and Organisations*, Harlow: Pearson Education.

Walsh, C. 2006 'Gender and the genre of the political broadcast interview', in J. Baxter, ed., *Speaking Out: The Female Voice in Public Contexts*, Basingstoke: Palgrave, pp. 121–38.

Walter, N. 1999 *The New Feminism*, London: Virago.

Walter, N. 2010 *Living Dolls: The Return of Sexism*, London: Virago.

Walters, K. 1991 'Women, men and linguistic variation in the Arab world', in B. Comrie and M. Eid, eds, *Perspectives on Arabic Linguistics*, Amsterdam: John Benjamins, vol. 3, pp. 199–229.

Wareing, S. 1994 'And then he kissed her: the reclamation of female characters to submissive roles in contemporary fiction', in K. Wales, ed., *Feminist Linguistics in Literary Criticism*, Woodbridge: Boydell and Brewer.

Wetherell, M. 1998 'Positioning and interpretative repertoires: conversation analysis and post-structuralism in dialogue', *Discourse & Society* 9(3): 387–412.

Wetherell, M. and Edley, N. 1999 'Negotiating hegemonic masculinity: imaginary positions and psycho-discursive practices', *Feminism and Psychology* 26: 59–71.

Wetherell, M. and Potter, J. 1992 *Mapping the Language of Racism: Discourse and the Legitimisation of Exploitation*, Hemel Hempstead: Harvester Wheatsheaf.

Whelehan, I. 1995 *Modern Feminist Thought: From Second Wave to 'Post-Feminism'*, Edinburgh: Edinburgh University Press.

Whelehan, I. 2000 *Overloaded: Popular Culture and the Future of Feminism*, London: Women's Press.

Wilkinson, S. and Kitzinger, C., eds, 1993 *Heterosexuality: A Feminism and Psychology Reader*, London: Sage.

Williamson, J. 1986 *Consuming Passions: The Dynamics of Popular Culture*, London: Marion Boyars.

Wodak, R., ed., 1997 *Gender and Discourse*, London: Sage.

Wodak, R. 1998 *Disorders of Discourse*, Harlow: Longman.

Wodak, R. 2003 'Multiple identities: the roles of female parliamentarians in the EU Parliament', in J. Holmes and M. Meyerhoff, eds, *The Handbook of Language and Gender*, Oxford: Blackwell, pp. 671–98.

Wodak, R. and Benke, G. 1997 'Gender as a sociolinguistic variable: new perspectives on variation studies', in F. Coulmas, ed., *Handbook of Sociolinguistics*, Oxford: Blackwell, pp. 127–50.

Wodak, R. and Meyer, M., eds, 2001 *Methods of Critical Discourse Analysis*, London: Sage.

Wolfram, W. 1993 'Ethical considerations in language awareness programs', *Issues in Applied Linguistics* 4: 225–55.

Women and Work Commission 2006 *Shaping a Fairer Future*, London: Women and Work Commission.

Wong, A. 2008 'The trouble with *Tongzhi*: the politics of labeling among gay and lesbian Hongkongers', *Pragmatics* 18(2): 277–301.

Wright, D. 2007 'Disability discourse and women's writing', unpublished MPhil thesis, Sheffield Hallam University, Sheffield.

Wright, S. and Hay, J. 2000 'Fred and Wilma: a phonological conspiracy', paper presented at the International Gender and Language Association Conference, Stanford University, California, May.

Yang, J. 2007a '"Re-employment stars": language, gender and neoliberal restructuring in China', in B. McElhinny, ed., *Words, Worlds, and Material Girls: Language, Gender, Globalization*, Berlin and New York: Mouton de Gruyter, pp. 77–105.

Yang, J. 2007b 'Zuiqian "deficient mouth": discourse, gender and domestic violence in urban China', *Gender and Language* 1(1): 107–18.

Yoshida, M. and Sakurai, C. 2005 'Japanese honorifics as a marker of sociocultural identity: a view from a non-Western perspective', in L. Lakoff and S. Ide, eds, *Broadening the Horizon of Linguistic Politeness*, Amsterdam: John Benjamins, pp. 197–216.

Yukawa, S. and Saito, M. 2004 'Cultural ideologies in Japanese language and gender studies', in S. Okamoto and J. Shibamoto Smith, eds, *Japanese Language, Gender and Ideology: Cultural Models and Real People*, Oxford and New York: Oxford University Press, pp. 23–37.

Zhang, Q. 2007 'Cosmopolitanism and linguistic capital in China: language, gender and the transition to a globalized market economy in Beijing', in B. McElhinny, ed., *Words, Worlds, and Material Girls: Language, Gender, Globalization*, Berlin and New York: Mouton de Gruyter, pp. 403–22.

Zimman, L. and Hall, K. 2010 'Language, embodiment and the third sex', in C. Llamas and D. Watt, eds, *Language and Identities*, Edinburgh: Edinburgh University Press, pp. 166–78.

Zimmerman, D. and West, C. 1975 'Sex-roles, interruptions and silences in conversation', in B. Thorne, K. Kramarae and N. Henley, eds, *Language, Gender and Society*, Rowley: Newbury House, pp. 89–101.

Zwicky, A. 1997 'Two lavender issues for linguists', in A. Livia and K. Hall, eds, *Queerly Phrased: Gender, Language, and Sexuality*, Oxford: Oxford University Press, pp. 21–35.

Index